RAMBLERS
SCRAMBLERS
&TWINERS

RAMBLERS SCRAMBLERS & TWINERS

High-performance Climbing Plants
& Wall Shrubs

MICHAEL JEFFERSON-BROWN

David & Charles

Note: Throughout the book the time of year is given as a season to make the reference applicable to readers all over the world. In the northern hemisphere the seasons may be translated into months as follows:

Early winter - December	*Early summer - June*
Midwinter - January	*Midsummer - July*
Late winter - February	*Late summer - August*
Early spring - March	*Early autumn - September*
Mid-spring - April	*Mid-autumn - October*
Late spring - May	*Late autumn - November*

Page 1: A wooden arch in a beech hedge, surrounded by honeysuckle.
Pages 2-3: With its abundant and fragrant, deep pink flowers, rose 'Zéphirine Drouhin' is a perfect partner for the deep, rich red blooms of clematis 'Niobe'.
Pages 4-5: A lovely example of clematis 'Twilight' climbs through railings at the Old Rectory in Northamptonshire.

A DAVID & CHARLES BOOK

First published in the UK in 1999

Copyright © Michael Jefferson-Brown 1999
Layout Copyright © David & Charles 1999

Michael Jefferson-Brown has asserted his right to be identified as the author of this work in accordance with the Copyright, Designs and Patents Act, 1988.

A catalogue record for this book is available from the British Library.

ISBN 0 7153 0942 0

Book design by Ian Muggeridge
Line illustrations by Coral Mula
Photographs supplied mainly by Clive Nichols
Garden Pictures (see page 256)

Printed in Hong Kong by Hong Kong Graphic and Printing Limited
for David & Charles
Brunel House, Newton Abbot, Devon

CONTENTS

INTRODUCTION

The main aim of this book is to look at how much more can be made of our gardens if we think not laterally but vertically. The space above and around our heads is often not fully exploited, and this is most obvious when we view the outside walls of our home, our garden fences and other structures. Here is a whole dimension waiting to be used.

There are perhaps two categories of gardeners: those who have very small gardens where there does not seem to be enough space to grow more than a token plant or two, and those who have more reasonably sized plots where there does not seem to be room for one more plant! Hopefully, this book will suggest new departures for both categories. It is certain that there can never be too much help given to those who are buying, or have bought, one of the new houses with the sort of garden that would have been scornfully described as 'pocket handkerchief-size' only a few years ago. In Britain it seems that developers are only concerned with how many dwellings they can erect per acre; the so called 'landscaping' of the gardens of these houses prior to selling is usually an exercise in the art of minimalism. Although not so critical in the USA and countries such as Australia and New Zealand, more and more urban development is resulting in very restricted gardening space.

Plants in pots, including sweet peas and a hydrangea, surround a wall fountain in this London roof garden.

The challenge, therefore, is to make more of less, and let us be optimistic and aim to make much more of the restricted space. It is a true challenge, but one that presents very real opportunities – unique and too often ignored opportunities.

This book is full of practical suggestions and guidance to help maximize gardening possibilities by looking upwards. Every gardener will have different ideas and visions, every garden will have its own specifications and limitations. You are lord of your estate and you can pick and choose from these suggestions, rejecting some and adapting others. This is a 'pick and mix' guide, a very practical one, not a purple prose travelogue around the garden.

Throughout the book, I have tried to access the merits of each plant and give priority to the most worthy. Among the criteria that gets a plant special mention is year-round appeal, which means giving due consideration to habit and foliage as well as to flowers, and hardiness. The book has three parts. First the planning and planting of the garden is considered. Next the sites – walls, fences and so on – are looked at, together with ways in which they can be exploited. The third part gives a review of some of the large number of plants that can be used in the venture: self-clinging climbers, twiners, ramblers, shrubs that benefit from the support and protection of walls, plants that grow well at wall bases and, finally annuals and some of the less hardy plants and the role they have to play.

Parthenocissus
quinquefolia *at its
wall-dressing best.*

Part One
PLANNING &
PLANTING

Opportunities & Planning
Challenges

Space, Illusion & Adding Plants

Walls, Fences & Hedges

Pergolas, Screens, Arbours &
Gazebos

Support Considerations

Planting & Cultivation

Climates & Microclimates

*This wooden rose pergola with its brick base is
smothered with the generous blooms of the roses 'Aloha',
'Sanders' White Rambler' and 'Compassion'.*

OPPORTUNITIES & PLANNING CHALLENGES

With a little care and forethought, even the most unpromising site can be transformed into a haven. Indeed, many an awkward garden has stimulated inspired inventiveness resulting in a real triumph.

We garden for a variety of reasons. Sometimes because, like climbing Everest, it is there. Perhaps we dodge outside because we are happier in the fresh air than inside doing housework or other domestic duties. Maybe we are primarily concerned with having a safe play area for our children. A few of us may view the ground as an opportunity to grow wholesome organic food. Some may work outside as an aid to being more healthy.

However, once we have started on the garden, certain common aims begin to emerge: most of us find that contact with living plants is a therapy that helps keep us sane and balanced in our increasingly busy and technological world; most of us want to create a living environment that gives us pleasure, perhaps a place primarily of peace but without excluding some excitement, and full of the interest and beauty of a wide range of different plants.

A pleasing garden gives lasting satisfaction but it can also help to improve the value of the property to which it is attached. The house and garden can be made to combine in happy unity, some more than others. This can be taken even further: very few houses are not improved by the addition of plants that clothe all or part of the walls and some very, or not so very, ugly out-buildings can be transformed by living cover into structures of real beauty.

A keen gardener never has enough space, even in a large garden. Despite this there are many times that such a gardener will buy a plant on impulse and, on bringing it home, will have to take a walk all around the garden to try to find a space for it. This gardener–garden space requirement is even more problematic for the owner of a newly-built house who usually has only a meagre number of square metres. The newer the house, the more heavily the ratio of plot-size to wall and fence space veers in favour of the latter. Yet the gardening opportunities afforded by such items are often totally overlooked. With a bit of ingenuity and discrimination, the owner of a crowded garden, and the gardener with very limited space, can make better use of all the room available. This may mean adopting a changed attitude to plants and artifacts. For example, if space is short a piece of sculpture can be used as a focal point, a carefully chosen design will also direct the eye upwards to where there is space, and, finally, there is now additional room for yet another plant – one that is happy embracing the sculpture.

THOUGHTS ON PLANNING

We all have different needs and will place different emphasis on different aspects of garden design. However, there are certain things that all gardens should have in common, and we need to bear this firmly in mind as planning and choice of plants goes ahead. Gardens should be accessible at all times and in all weathers, barring two metres of snow. They should be attractive to view for the twelve months of the year. A garden should be a pleasure, not a treadmill. It should provide just that amount of purposeful activity as is pleasurable without causing an overload or fear of impending return to jungle conditions. Of course, you can choose to make

In this small garden, raised beds make good use of the space available with climbers and tumbling plants. An interesting mix of evergreens, including santolina, conifers, lavender and ivy, will avoid any winter dreariness.

it a labour-intensive unit, or you can veer towards designing for labour-saving as far as possible: groundcover stops weeds, thick gravel obviates the need for grass cutting, trees and shrubs look after themselves.

A CHANGING SCENE

No design should be considered static: the garden will change over the years. Plants grow, we get older. Children grow and have different requirements of the outdoor space. What was once their sporting arena becomes the parents' area for exercising their gardening arts; there is space for resting and for social occasions. Increasing age may limit the energies available for garden work, but may also give more time to enjoy the outside. The garden may end up as an almost labour-free zone, a pleasurable haven like that of a ninety-year-old friend of ours, described by her as her 'geriatric unit'.

Garden planning should take into account special interests – horticultural or otherwise. Domestic pets and children need to be considered. Wildlife interests focusing on birds, or the type of animal life to be found in a small pond, can dictate some of the shape of the garden or the emphasis of parts of it.

Gardeners are also often inveterate collectors; sometimes eclectic and amassing all sorts of plants, sometimes specializing in particular types. A genus will capture interest for some seasons before another begins to eclipse it. It is always surprising the quantity of different plants that can be cramped into a small space. This can be done with proper intent, knowing that the more plants there are, the more difficult it is for weeds to appear. Many plants grow well in associations. Some detail of these will come later.

No hard and fast rules are going to be laid down in this book about the planning of the vertical garden. Certain things will be suggested, but even some of the most apparently obvious pieces of received wisdom can be turned on their heads: the gardener is the boss. However, it helps to take note of Nature's ways and to learn from the experience of others, and some

CONSIDERATIONS

* Garden users. Everyone has different demands of the garden space; children and pets are part of the equation and the more mature citizen will want safe access and gardening activities within their capabilities. How can they all be accommodated?

* New structures. What can be added that will really improve a three-dimensional garden?

* Other permanent features. How can the patio and pathways play a part?

* Soil type and health. What regime will improve the soil's nutritional value and its physical structure?

The ever-popular aubrieta is useful in many difficult sites, provided they are sunny. Here it cascades down a wall that could otherwise look quite cold and bleak. A mixture of different colours – lavenders, pinks, mauves and purples – could make it even more splendid.

disasters may be averted by a little forethought.

It is obviously a mistake to try to grow forest trees in a tiny space; pampas grass looks out of place in a pocket-handkerchief plot. It is necessary to plan to scale, but a lot can be done by intelligent surgery. Many shrubs and even herbaceous plants can be kept healthy within very confined bounds. If they are to be cut back, pruning shrubs should be done as a two-pronged treatment, pruning above ground and root trimming below, so that the plant's metabolism is kept in balance.

A year slips by quickly. As we fashion our gardens and note the changing seasons, we shall be well rewarded by planting some of the less obvious plants and by ensuring that there is plenty of winter interest, and if this seems to appear as a prominent sub-plot to the vertical garden, so be it.

Considerations

EXPLOITING THE THIRD DIMENSION

All too often it is only the horizontal area that is considered when gardens are designed; drawn up plans are simply ground plans. Ways of using the air space are particularly vital in a small garden, and we must take our eyes upwards if we want to create a truly exciting environment that is also a haven of peace and a place of relaxation and recreation. No opportunity should be left unconsidered: this means attention must be paid to carving out designs in the air, to screening or disguising fences, sheds and other erections. All sorts of plants will help to join earth to sky so that wherever we look there is variety, a living 3-D jigsaw of plant life and artifacts.

Walls, of the house or elsewhere, can be attractive in themselves, but will look even more pleasing with the contrast of living foliage and flower in juxtaposition. Care must be taken that the choice of plant does, in fact, complement the wall: some colours do not enhance, and are not enhanced by, red bricks; on the other hand the harshness of yellow bricks or the very newness of brickwork can be softened

considerably by the green of foliage and by flower colours.

Planning for planting on walls must also take into account that the house has to be cared for; painting and other maintenance needs to be undertaken periodically.

It is possible to plan in advance so that you can always get behind climbers or other shrubs that are growing up walls by providing supports that are fastened to the walls in such a way as to be detachable without lessening their efficiency. This is dealt with fully in Support Considerations pp.70-77. Self-clinging climbers, such as ivy, are inappropriate for certain types of walls, but do not take too much notice of the prophets

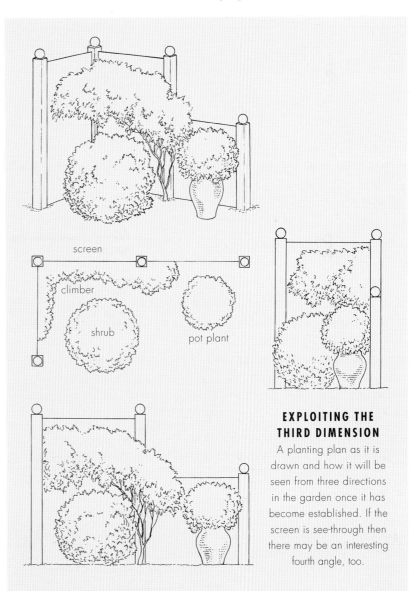

screen

climber

shrub

pot plant

EXPLOITING THE THIRD DIMENSION

A planting plan as it is drawn and how it will be seen from three directions in the garden once it has become established. If the screen is see-through then there may be an interesting fourth angle, too.

MICROCLIMATES

One of the major factors that makes gardening around walls so exciting are those special microclimates that enable the use of a whole range of plants that would otherwise either be impossible to grow in the open or, as they struggled to survive there, would never reveal their full flowering potential.

Microclimates are not hot news. Gardeners have valued such positions from the earliest of times; fruit, herbs and vegetables have been given favoured-site-status in gardens from Roman times onwards. In Britain, the stately homes of the past had their walled gardens to ensure fruit and vegetables all the year round. Gardeners learnt from practice how to provide delicacies for their betters.

What is manifestly clear is that walls help provide warmth not available elsewhere. They cushion the effect of many extreme fluctuations. Not only do they trap warmth and husband it like storage heaters to mitigate the cold of the nights, but they also provide support for those plants with less backbone than others: the climbers, scramblers and twiners of this world, as well as some shrubs that take a few seasons to build up a strong skeleton to support themselves. They also temper the wind so providing extra protection against the weather.

Fences, other structures and hedges all play a similar role to that of walls. But unless they are fashioned of brick or stone they will not retain heat efficiently and their influence in this way will be less.

Shade is another consideration that can make certain walls and nooks of particular value for some less extrovert plants (by 'extrovert' I mean strong growing plants often luxuriating in a sunny spot). Shade can be an important factor in modern gardens, whose smaller size means that the house and the fences, walls or hedges around the property will be shading a much higher proportion of the ground for greater stretches of time than is the case in larger gardens, though even in these, the walls will cast their fair share of shade.

Fortunately there are plenty of plants that are very happy with such sun-rationed sites. In our garden we have a narrow border some 23m (76ft) long, alongside the shaded west wall of the house. The border is home to a collection of ferns; the walls are mainly given over to a number of brightly variegated ivies – it is not the least successful part of the freehold. The ferns look wonderful through the growing months, and they hold well through the winter. Many forms that would be deciduous in more exposed spots, remain evergreen in this sheltered site.

Warmth, shelter and shade are three aspects of interest to those gardening beside walls; the fourth one is moisture, or the relative lack of it. The soil at the base of a wall can be wet, especially in wetter areas or with walls that face rain-bearing winds, where the rain beats against the wall and runs down to add its contribution to that falling naturally on the soil. However, this is the minority case: usually the rootrun at the base of a wall is drier than in the open. As well as acting as a shelter from the rain for some areas of soil, the wall, and the drainage around the foundations, can have a dramatic drying effect.

More details on microclimates can be found on pp.104-109.

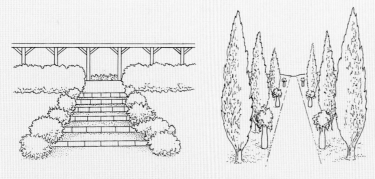

HORIZONTAL VERSUS VERTICAL

Horizontal elements are restful, whereas verticals produce more exciting effects.

of doom who try to suggest that they destroy mortar or make walls damp. Almost invariably a cover of foliage, such as that provided by closely clinging plants, will keep walls drier and warmer than otherwise.

Pergolas and Strong Lines

Pergolas and similar structures with upright lines can be an important feature. The heavier the uprights the more impact they may make. Any feeling of over-massive strength can be mitigated by plant growth (for example, plenty of clambering roses and clematis). The strong vertical lines of the posts can be emphasized and balanced by creating a clean horizontal plane with a paved pathway.

Relaxation versus Stimulation

There are things that impinge on our consciousness in ways that are not immediately obvious. For example, a scene in a painting heavily dominated by horizontal lines and masses induces a sense of calm whereas one with the verticals massively in the ascendent engenders more of a feeling of excitement. The same feelings occur in the garden: peace needs to be balanced by stimulation. So in a mainly horizontal landscape, careful positioning of, say, a group of fastigiate trees, reaching narrowly for the sky, will create the necessary contrast.

PRIVACY, INTIMACY AND MAGIC

One of the most pleasing features of many gardens is their sense of privacy. This is likely to be underlined by any emphasis on vertical planting, which will help enclose the space. The house itself, partially clothed in plants, will no longer be the undressed and exposed structure that it was before. Pergolas, pots, plant-covered

DAMP COURSES

When gardening beside walls make sure you know the whereabouts of your damp course. Damp rises up walls from the ground and is prevented from getting too far and causing damage by a layer of water-impermeable material around the base of the house at a few centimetres above soil level. This damp course level is easily recognizable: in old houses it is often a layer of slate, while in newer houses the position of the impermeable layer is normally indicated by a wider than normal layer of mortar. Any garden engineering project must make sure that altered soil levels remain below the damp course level; care should also be taken that air bricks, which allow the movement of air below wooden floors, are not obstructed. Plants, water butts and any new structures must leave them clear and able to do their job efficiently.

Fastigiate cypresses at La Casella in France produce a dramatic, uplifting vista. In cooler spots hardy conifers can be used to engineer a similar effect (see p.30).

fences and the upward reach of trees and climbing plants all add to the feeling of a hidden and intimate place.

THE OUTSIDE ROOM

Talk and writing about garden design in Britain and elsewhere for the past decade or so has laid greater and greater emphasis on viewing part or the whole of the garden as an outside room or rooms. It is no wonder that this is so. We British envy the outdoor living of our more southerly neighbours on the European Continent, and many of us find ourselves short of space in our relatively small houses so we need the extra room outside to enable us to spend our leisure time more enjoyably. A run of warmer summers and milder winters has made global warming seem a real likelihood and has encouraged us to pave areas by the house and furnish them with chairs, tables, barbecues and all the necessities of alfresco living. Shade may be provided through something as simple as an adjustable umbrella or it could come from a more permanent structure such as a full-scale or partial pergola with extra shade and beauty added by the climbing plants.

From inside the house there are various views of the garden; designs for the garden should take account of these important vistas. However, when sitting outside on the patio, the viewpoint is very different. Now we are only conscious of the house in relation to the garden. To one side is the permanent, comparatively unaltering structure of the dwelling, to the other is the daily-changing seasonal drama of the garden. The garden can be considered as a piece of theatre that is exciting in its various scene changes through the year or, perhaps, dare we admit, a rather boring set-piece. The patio is a mid-zone, a transitional area betwixt house and garden, or perhaps more vitally, an almost independent entity, one that has its own distinct character while still linking the house to the garden.

Whatever the form of the patio, when we are on it we are conscious of the house walls and of the space around and above us. If a structure, several structures, or a selection of artifacts are used to define the area then the feeling of an outside room, or even of a completely separate entity, will become even more marked. Look at the house walls: they are begging for plants at their base and climbing up at least part of their height. Consider lower walls framing the patio: they could be constructed with hollow centres for planting into; they will certainly encourage us to look for plant drapery. In addition, posts, pergolas or trellis-embellished screens are desirable residences for any number of the plants mentioned in later chapters.

This patio environment, as well as the house walls, means that there is a always going to be a contrast between living plant and inanimate brick, stone or wood, a dichotomy that can have a certain resonance, the one emphasizing the character of the other, with the plant life softening the less flexible lines and mass of the inanimate part of the duet.

Elements

PATHWAYS

Whatever planning is done in our heads, sooner or later we must get down to the practical details of the infrastructure. It is bound to rain and on occasion the ground is unpleasant to walk upon, so good paths are needed for gardeners, wheelbarrows, children and children's toys. The pathways must make sense in leading into the garden scene and adding pleasantly to its whole, while allowing for quick access to greenhouses, garden sheds, summerhouses, washing lines, children's play areas and the dustbin.

Paths carve up the plot and, even without being stepped on, can take our eyes for walks. They may meander or they may be rigidly formal. They need to be reliable in use and attractive within the garden design as a whole. This means that the materials from which they are made and the methods by which they are built, including allowing for drainage, need to chosen and undertaken with care. And don't forget the less mobile, who will need paths to be level so that they can be certain of being sure-footed.

STEPS AND LEVELS

Playing around with the levels of the garden surrounds can create all sorts of spatial illusions. Steps, for example, attract the eye and can look good in themselves, even if they only mark a change of level of a few centimetres. Even these small dimensions can be made to be exaggerated by the eye and work equally well going down or rising.

A lower level, in the form of a modest sunken garden, will have a big effect on the feeling of cubic space of the whole of your outdoor

The importance of the steps, leading to the pergola, is underlined by the pair of stone griffins in this garden at Trewithen in Devon.

PATHS

A curving path meandering into the garden draws the eye forward even within a confined space.

Terraces with steps lead the eye forward and upward. At La Casella in France this has been achieved to great effect but in a restrained manner. The greens play the major role with the shaped bushes creating focal points and the eye ends up being sent skywards by the fastigiate conifers.

area. This impression of extra space will be hugely enhanced by a pool.

Climbing two or three shallow steps to borders or other areas that have been somewhat raised above the general level of the garden will, again, make the plot fill out and become more intriguing. Such small changes of level can be made much more of by planting low-growing shrubs and plants by the side of the steps; these will bring the eye higher, will enhance the impact of the steps and tend to exaggerate their vertical dimensions.

WATER

If water is included as part of the plan, it will certainly add a new dimension. A small sheet of water expands space outside in the same way that a large mirror will do the trick inside.

It is a temptation to add the magic sound of moving water. Water seems synonymous with life, and moving water especially so. Lucky are those who have a natural supply to play with – a stream, waterfalls or a gentle cascade. Most of us have to arrange the water and if it is to move anywhere this is by courtesy of the electricity board and payment of their charges. A small fountain may be a possibility, or you can reject the mini-Versailles plan and choose instead to

At Wakehurst the little pool creates a real focal point, making a visual well, with the surrounding pathway and carpet lawn, and acting as a very obvious horizontal contrast to the walls of hedges and the brick wall. The figure in the middle of the little pool helps to catch the eye and direct it both up and down.

FRONT OF HOUSE

For the front of the house choose shrubs and plants that are well behaved all round the year – or at least most of the time. Aim for a balance of evergreens and deciduous plants. Avoid things such as the twisted willow, *Salix babylonica* var. *pekinensis* 'Tortuosa', which looks good but sheds pieces of twig seemingly each day. Together with other deciduous kinds, it can be dropping leaves for many weeks through the autumn and winter – better to have deciduous things that get undressed quickly. Also, avoid items, such as *Forsythia* 'Lynwood', which are brilliant for a few weeks in spring and then nondescript for the rest of the year.

Evergreen shrubs of tidy demeanour or those lending themselves to simple topiary effect are useful. Flowering evergreen camellias can be grown in large tubs if the natural soil is not lime-free. They are best out of the early morning sun. Hydrangeas, although deciduous, can be fresh in leaf and are in splendid bloom for several months, but they should not be placed in very frosty spots or in soils that can dry out badly.

have a bubbling spring of water falling over stones or other surfaces.

If you do not fancy the idea of a pond on the ground, look at the wall where all other activity is taking place. It is quite a straightforward task to arrange a fall of water from some spot on it, either as an apparently natural phenomenon, or as a carefully designed, formal artifact. There are lots of prefabricated 'spouts' at larger garden centres, some not without merit. Or, if you prefer something more original, consider sculptors and other artisans or artists in the community, who could produce something interesting and successful, not necessarily at an exorbitant price. Students at art schools may welcome the chance to put their skills into practice with a well conceived and imaginative design. It is worth exploring the possibilities. Wherever you get your water feature from, think about its long-term appeal before you purchase. You should be totally convinced that it is going to look right, that you will not tire of it, and that it is not going to stick out like sore thumb against the rest of the garden.

Whole Themes

FORMAL THOUGHTS

The formality of a Georgian-type house can be enhanced by creating a platform of paving around it and erecting neat angular pergolas, walls, posts and steps. With such houses, the addition of shrubs and plants that are taken upwards in a controlled and carefully groomed manner is quite correct. Although all of a piece, a unity, the living components will soften some of the geometrical strictness of the house and surrounding structures. If not overdone, it is even possible to use such informal things as climbing or rambling roses. They will not necessarily clash with the formal style, but perhaps just provide a contrast. However, rustic pergolas or rough-hewn supports can tend to look somewhat inappropriate.

A smallish house of formal aspect can have the formality underlined by careful planning of the part of the garden that is near the house. Or, being of a modest size, the house could, if the spirit moved one, be almost enveloped in plants to give a totally different effect. To an extent, this is dependent not only on one's own inclinations, but the appearance of the surrounding properties, if they are close by. To be glaringly different to all the other dwellings on an estate with houses closely built may look incongruous, cause comment and maybe even friction. Be careful with those leylandiis!

Formality can be taken into the garden, and will suit gardeners with a predisposition towards the heavily-groomed and ordered look (see also Topiary p.38).

It may be that formality has to be observed, in which case the plants introduced can be rather regimental, perhaps well-shaped, unfussy shrubs such as box, Portuguese laurel, bay or privet. Some of the less obvious *Euonymus* or *Olearia* forms will also stand sentry duty. But I cannot think of any house that would not be improved by some living garden features. Even those buildings that are almost without any space for gardens proper, will be enhanced by plants growing in containers. Houses with no garden at all can be clothed by one or more creeping plants – deciduous ones such as the Virginia creeper or its relatives, evergreen ones such as ivies. In a corner, where two walls meet in a cosy, embracing right-angle, such a plant as the evergreen, winter-flowering *Clematis armandii* could be given its considerable head.

The other obvious adjunct of the formal building is hedgework. Well-cared-for hedges, both those reaching to about head height, or the type of small mini-hedges of box that enclose knot gardens, can add a lot to the overall appearance and give it extra prestige. (See p.48 for hedge plant suggestions.)

THE URBAN JUNGLE

In towns and cities the small gardens normally surrounded by masonary and concrete may be treated in such a way as to provide an oasis among the uncompromising buildings – a green and leafy secluded place, apparently a thousand miles from traffic jams and the bustle of modern urban life. The leafier it becomes below, around and above, the more the aspect approaches the feel of the jungle, such a wonderful and healthy contrast to the surrounds, which are very effectively masked. Even a quite small space can be made into a little paradise with all the encircling buildings hidden. To obtain this effect may mean using lots of climbing and hanging plants up walls and supports such as pergolas, with the result that only a limited amount of direct sunlight gets through, but, with care, some part of the sky can be allowed as part of the total picture. Happily the range of plants that can be grown in shade or partial shade is probably greater than those that demand wall-to-wall sunshine (see pp.120-135).

For such a 'hanging garden of Babylon' it will be fortunate if one's interest is in those plants that climb and are happy with shade around their feet. The old adage 'heads in the sun and feet in the shade', that is trotted out as cultural advice for clematis, may be put into effect – if one is careful about other tall items. The aim is to make double or treble use of any one spot so that, if there is light enough for a climbing or scrambling rose, it will be introduced to a neighbouring clematis and perhaps an annual climber, too.

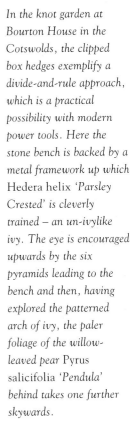

TREES WITH INTERESTING BARK

Many of the not-too-big acers have particularly attractive barks as do many eucalyptus and cherries. Some to consider are:

Acer griseum with rich brown, flaking bark
Arbutus menziesii and others
Betula (silver birches)
Eucalyptus pauciflora subsp. *niphophila* and others
Prunus serrula
Salix tortuosa for its twisted form

In the knot garden at Bourton House in the Cotswolds, the clipped box hedges exemplify a divide-and-rule approach, which is a practical possibility with modern power tools. Here the stone bench is backed by a metal framework up which Hedera helix *'Parsley Crested' is cleverly trained – an un-ivylike ivy. The eye is encouraged upwards by the six pyramids leading to the bench and then, having explored the patterned arch of ivy, the paler foliage of the willow-leaved pear* Pyrus salicifolia *'Pendula' behind takes one further skywards.*

SPACE, ILLUSION & ADDING PLANTS

Be prepared to experiment. Space can be made to seem vastly more than its actual dimensions. In many gardens, convincing suggestion goes more than half way to winning the battle.

Confront your garden and conjure up a vision of how it could be transformed by making more use of the air space. With a bare new site you will probably be able to look from the living room straight across in all directions to the fences that border the plot, and beyond these, to other houses and buildings. In such circumstances we can hardly wait to block out the ridigity of the fences and much of the buildings so that we can claim some privacy to enjoy our own garden. The first step is to avoid laying your garden out like a fruiterer's window with all on instant display. Screening is the beginning of the solution, but to truly exploit our domain we need to direct our gaze upwards, to draw the sky down and make it a vital part of the picture.

One of the most important things to consider is the way the eyes can be deceived about the size and form of the garden. With a very small garden, make the dominant lines, or dare we glorify them by calling them vistas, run diagonally across the length to gain an extra few

SCREENS IN A GARDEN
Partial screens punctuate a narrow garden.

metres. Contemplate adding some punctuating barriers, draped with plants, so the eye moves from the house window or the patio and is brought up short, accentuating the garden's possibilities. Careful placement of other features at this point might make the eye journey to another screen further afield or it may be encouraged to leap over the screen to a higher focal point. Introduce curves and corners to explore. Make sure there is a suggestion of more space, more plantings, more paths and more interest hidden behind these. There may well be something there, or it could all be an illusion to camouflage the compost heap, it does not matter; what is important is the psychological satisfaction of this slight sense of mystery.

Creating an illusion of space can be a major part of much garden design, and is not the most difficult of things to achieve. Partial screens, archways, plants or doorways can all suggest a further extension of the garden. The illusion can be created simply by hanging a door in front of a solid wall or by using mirrors, especially small ones – their angled reflections can confuse even the most knowing eye.

False perspectives are very effective. A path or a lawn that gets a little narrower away from the point of vantage adds greatly to the apparent length. Even a border can be used to produce this deception. False perspectives can be particularly convincing when produced with a pergola that leads away into the distance: just a few centimetres' narrowing of the arches will make the walkway seem much longer, especially if the solid path beneath is similarly narrowed.

By the introduction of such strong vertical design elements, we are trying to deceive the

This garden contains much in a relatively small space, and there is the hint of more behind corners. The fig tree and the arch carry the rambling rose 'Bobby James', which is capable of going 10m (30ft) high.

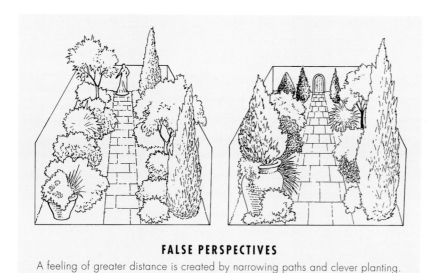

FALSE PERSPECTIVES

A feeling of greater distance is created by narrowing paths and clever planting.

eye. However much space there is, we are suggesting more: we are trying to encourage the questing eye to go journeying forward around this corner or that. That is one side of the task. The other is the need to mask obvious intrusions: fences, walls, garden sheds, compost heaps, dustbin areas and neighbouring buildings may need screening or disguising or, at the least, softening in their visual impact. Just draping a fence with a large-leaved ivy, such as *Hedera colchica* 'Dentata Variegata', or a similar climber, can eradicate the stark artificiality of a boundary, with its abrupt sense of restricted space, replacing it with a suggestion of further plant growth behind.

PLANTS TO COVER SHEDS, FENCES, AWKWARD SPOTS

Aucuba japonica
Clematis armandii
Clematis cirrhosa
Clematis montana
Fallopia aubertii
Fallopia baldschuanica
Hedera (ivies) in variety
Hydrangea petiolaris
Jasminum nudiflorum and
other jasmines
Lonicera (honeysuckles)
in variety
Rosa 'New Dawn'
Rosa 'Rambling Rector'
Rosa 'Bobby James'
and others

A gateway is a natural focal point. Here, the brick pillars help to dramatize the garden entrance, but the archway makes the effect more exciting and very special at this season with clematis 'Perle d'Azur' in full bloom.

Colour can play a part in space and illusion. Yellows, oranges and reds tend to walk towards you and shout, paler colours are much more introvert, and blues are positively retiring. Any large mass of blue, be it from serried columns of delphiniums, or the clouded forms of ceanothus species or hybrids, will help to give added depth to the overall picture.

The Plants

Garden designers seem to be falling over themselves these days to introduce more and more painted woodwork and other artifacts to garden design. While not absolutely against these fashion statements, I feel happier in a garden where the plants are very much the prime design factors, the inanimate artifacts and other structures playing a secondary supporting role to aid or enhance the plants. There is room for plants from the bases of walls or pergolas all the way up to the gutters over the bedrooms, each area having a 'me first' list of plants waiting to be tried.

As they are right by the house, the plants will come in for especially close scrutiny; those that are dullish out of flower need to be avoided for such positions. We also want plants with good manners. Deciduous ones that do their undressing over many weeks or months, causing the maximum of work tidying up, are not among

At Lower Severalls in Somerset impressive stone pillars point heavenwards, the vertical impact underscored by the rails of the gate. The gateway invites further exploration while the reliable stand-bys lining the path (including hardy geraniums and Alchemilla mollis) provide interest, too.

BUYER BEWARE

Be careful of all shrubs and trees offered as 'multi-personalities', with two or three cultivars grafted on one stock plant. They are very rarely successful; the usual result is a lopsided specimen with unbalanced flower displays. Multi-cultivar rose bushes are sometimes offered and are usually a disaster. Multi-cultivar hydrangeas usually turn out to be several different small plants sharing one pot. 'Family' trees of several kinds of apples, plums or other fruits may be just slightly more successful, but eventually one type tends to dominate. Better by far to grow the separate kinds on their own roots. If space-saving is the aim this is best done by using dwarfing rootstocks and/or training them as cordons or similarly disciplined shapes.

the first choices, unless they have other spectacular qualities. If possible plants should be exciting as they come on stage, hold our eye while in full growth and then die away with decent discretion, if not with a final fling of autumn pageantry.

A FLIGHT OF IMAGINATION

The main concern of this book is with climbing and high-reaching plants, but thought must also be given to the plants around our feet. The patio is a natural starting point. In the cracks of the paving stones consider creeping thymes. Mark

A quiet corner with impressive stone walls, brick pathways and rustic fencing, all set off by the upward-reaching growth – a multi-faceted contrast of the vertical with the horizontal.

the boundaries of the patio by a low wall planted with hanging plants such as aubrieta, clumps of dianthus or a rounded bush of *Genista lydia*. Behind the patio/house, near the backdoor, position bushes of sage and bay, handily close to the kitchen.

Imagine the base of the house wall planted with *Cotoneaster horizontalis*, working its layered, fish-bone patterns up the vertical support. It is usually still berried well into the winter and, during this important time, the wall-ripened stems of *Chaenomeles* can be busy with vibrant bloom for months. Above this are the wall-supported dark green stems of the winter jasmine and then some climbing or rambling roses, wrapped around with clematis. By stages, gentle or abrupt, the picture travels upwards. On the walls by the bedroom windows and the gutters are the curtaining effects of Virginia creepers and, perhaps, the gnarled grey stems of wisteria, with its delicate green pinnate leaves and fantastic hanging swags of blossom.

Venturing out from the house walls, the wisteria reaches over our heads as it swathes the pergola, or perhaps it can be persuaded to give over the task to vines such as the huge-leaved *Vitis coignetiae*, the neat dark-leaved *Vitis vinifera* var. *purpurea*, with its tight dark bunches of fruit, or a more utilitarian cultivar that will provide grapes for wine-making, such as V. 'Muller-Thurgau', 'Madeleine Angevine' or 'Siegerrebe'. Those not wishing to contemplate trampling grapes in the bath may forgo these more useful fruits and choose 'Brant' instead for the sake of its particularly good autumn foliage colouring – not that the others are without their appeal in this respect.

CONSIDERATIONS FOR PLANT CHOICE

By building a living environment we create a changeable atmosphere that alters with the season and also the time of day, as if by magic. Such a place will have its delights increased by sights and sounds, such as leaves rustling or water moving, and also by scents. All these aspects will need to be considered carefully during the process of choosing the right plants.

The different conditions found in different parts of the plot also need to be remembered: shade, cool corners and the extraordinarily warm spots offered by walls that face the sun. The choice in these sites can be radically different from the plants traditionally grown in the open areas of a garden. In particular there can be many more unusual plants from other parts of the world that will flourish in the shelter of the wall or fence. For example, in cool climates a wall that faces the sun may accommodate tender plants from hotter climates.

All gardeners are concerned to get the maximum possible effect at all times of the year and in as many sites as possible. More and more this requires a careful look at the available space and trying to contrive ways of making more of it. This can mean working out combinations of plants that will play a relay race through the year with one handing over the baton to another as the months pass: the same yard that is a bulbous bonanza in spring, then becomes a burgeoning mass of shrubby blossom that in its

turn gives way to the reaching branches of a rambling rose which itself is supporting the twining stems of a late-flowering clematis. This way double or treble rent can be had from the same patch of soil: we are into sure profit.

Give a hundred people similar plots and the same collection of plants to make a garden and there will be a hundred different results. In a vertical garden there are a variety of locales for the plants. Most obviously a wall facing the sun will experience conditions totally dissimilar to those of a shaded wall. Plants growing up posts or pergolas will face more weather than those sheltering by the wall. To use a version of a well-known cliché: square plants are needed to fit into square holes.

Much more can be made of many plants by grouping them so that neighbours highlight each other's qualities. Foliage colour is the most obvious factor but others, such as leaf texture, shape and size, can be equally important. When deciding what to plant where, it is common to have the flowering and fruiting qualities at the forefront of the consideration. The sort of

Ornamental trellis work adorned by sweet peas and runner beans. The growth is vertical, but the thinking is lateral! Gourds and climbing vegetables and ornamentals would also make good use of these decorative features, which are sold in garden centres as 'obelisks'.

mistake that has the flowering effort of one plant at total odds with its neighbour is something to be avoided, although I think it is a rare occurrence in reality; nature seems to have a way of reconciling apparently warring colours or characters, and two plants are not necessarily going to be at the height of their flowering endeavour at exactly the same time.

TREES

First to be considered for a vertical garden are the players of the larger, more important roles: the trees and stronger climbers may be chosen and installed. In this a sensible balance of deciduous and evergreen kinds needs to be maintained.

In restricted spaces, as well as elsewhere, the claims of fastigiate trees have to be admitted. If space allows, *Juniperus communis* 'Hibernica' or a slim-line *Chamaecyparis*, such as 'Green Pillar', can be effective as a single specimen or grouped. *C. lawsoniana* 'Columnaris' or 'Golden Spire' might also be tried. The Irish yew, *Taxus baccata* 'Fastigiata', is a character that will add plenty of atmosphere as it makes its way slowly up to an eventual height of 10m (30ft) while spreading no further than half of this. The glowing gold-variegated form, *T. baccata* 'Fastigiata Aurea' is even slower growing, and only reaches two-thirds the height. These trees will make a good job of adding vertical interest but will be best at a little distance from house walls or fences.

Corsetted variations of large species make possible the inclusion of trees that in their type form would be hopelessly oversized. It should be remembered, however, that these can still reach a considerable height and, though narrow when young, will produce a certain amount of middle-age spread. The tulip tree, *Liriodendron tulipifera*, can make a very tall tree (30m/100ft) – it would be impossible in a modestly-sized garden – but *L. tulipifera* 'Fastigiatum' makes a reasonably tight column and starts flowering early in its life. It would make a fine specimen tree to point to the heavens. When it eventually gets too big

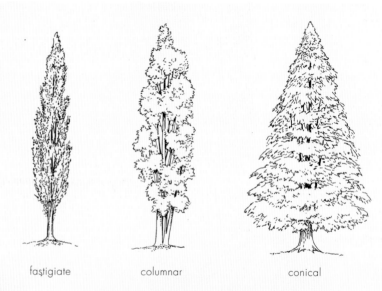

fastigiate   columnar   conical

FASTIGIATE AND OTHER UPRIGHT TREES

Trees that have slim-line forms include:
Aralia chinensis 'Pyramidalis'
Betula pendula 'Fastigiata' (birch)
Buxus sempervirens 'Pyramidalis' (box)
Carpinus betulus 'Fastigiata' (hornbeam)
Chamaecyparis lawsoniana 'Grayswood Pillar' and 'Green Pillar' (cypress)
Crataegus monogyna 'Stricta' (hawthorn)
Fagus sylvatica 'Fastigiata' (beech)

Juniperus communis 'Hibernica' and *J. scopulorum* 'Skyrocket' (juniper)
Liriodendron tulipifera 'Fastigiata' (tulip tree)
Populus alba 'Raket', *P.* 'Balsam Spire' and *P. nigra* var. *italica* (poplar)
Prunus 'Amanogawa' and *P.* 'Spire' (flowering cherry)
Robinia pseudoacacia 'Pyramidalis' (false acacia)
Taxus baccata 'Fastigiata' and *T. baccata* 'Aurea' (yew)

Left: the fastigiate tulip tree, Liriodendron tulipifera 'Fastigiata', makes a large specimen but is far more manageable than the standard spreading one.

Right: rose 'Fritz Nobis' in a duet with purple-leaved Berberis thunbergii 'Atropurpurea'. This pair is planted in The Old Rectory, Farnborough, the former home of poet laureat Sir John Betjeman.

TREES OF MODEST SIZE

Arbutus x andrachnoides (strawberry tree)
Betula ermanii (birch)
Catalpa bignonioides 'Aurea' (golden Indian bean tree)
Cercis siliquastrum (Judas tree)
Cornus mas (Cornelian cherry)
Crataegus laevigata 'Paul's Scarlet' (scarlet hawthorn) and *C. x lavallei* 'Carrierei'
Eucalyptus nicholii (narrow-leaved black peppermint) and *E. pauciflora* subsp. *niphophila* (snow gum)
Laburnum x watereri 'Vossii'
Magnolia in variety
Malus floribunda and other ornamental apples
Prunus x subhirtella 'Autumnalis' and others
Pyrus salicifolia 'Pendula' (weeping willow-leaved pear)
Sorbus vilmorinii and others

(its mature height is about 20m/70ft), let those who inherit your garden decide what to do.

Notwithstanding those mentioned above in their straitened forms, forest trees are only really acceptable where there are the acres to allow their development without horrible butchery. Most gardens are happier with modestly sized trees and, of these, there is a wide range. Ornamental apples, pears and cherries are all likely candidates. Once established and a reasonable size they can be host to one or more climbing plants such as clematis or vines.

LARGE CREEPERS

For the walls it is a temptation to plant fast-growing climbers that will fill the space quickly. This may be exactly what is wanted, especially on less inviting shaded walls or ones that are on the borderline of ugliness. However, even in these cases, it is wise to stop to think of the year-round effect. *Parthenocissus quinquefolia* (Virginia creeper), or one of its relatives, will soon cover a wall, will look handsome through the growing months and positively breathtaking when in full autumn colour, but – and this is not a small 'but' – the plant is rather late into leaf and is among the first to lose its foliage. For about half the year it is devoid of leaves, reduced to a tracery of clinging branches. If you can view things objectively, this state is not without some beauty: it is a matter of adjusting your attitude of mind – if you cannot, better to consider the ivies and other evergreens, which are open for business every day of the year.

Climbing Companions

By growing two or three plants in close association it is possible to have different seasons of
flower and fruit or, at the very least, an interesting combination at certain times. In winter the
yellow-flowered winter jasmine (*Jasminum nudiflorum*) can be splayed across the orange-fruited
Cotoneaster horizontalis or one of its relatives,
or in front of a wall cover of variegated ivy.
Climbing or rambling roses of modern breeding
can have extended flowering seasons; older
favourites are still thought worth growing,
despite their more limited periods of bloom. As
always, any roses will be enhanced by the reaching twisting stems of clematis. Their growth
embraces that of the roses and makes better use
of space with a mix of flower types and colours.
The roses have more permanent branch structures than the many clematis cultivars that are
typically severely pruned before growth starts in
spring. Choose your clematis variety carefully if
you want to be able to tidy it away each year:
some clematis do not want such severe treatment.

Strong clematis, that only require minimal
pruning, such as the *C. montana* cultivars, will
clamber up all sorts of support, veteran fruit
trees or tall conifers almost scraping the sky.
Twining *Celastris orbiculatus* will cling on to any
shrub or tree and has lots of inconspicuous green
flowers in summer, followed by little narrow
fruits that start green, become black in autumn
and then split open to reveal their very conspicuous golden insides with polished scarlet seeds
that stay stuck in their cases for weeks.

The vigorous climbing hydrangea, *H. petiolaris*, makes a dense cover over any wall, including the cooler shady ones. In front may be
placed evergreen shrubs such as the dark *Garrya
elliptica* or a camellia with its polished and glittering rich green foliage.

Annuals, such as the bright nasturtiums,
their relative the Canary creeper (*Tropaeolum
peregrinum*), black-eyed Susan (*Thunbergia alata*),

SPACE, ILLUSION & ADDING PLANTS

sweet peas (*Lathyrus*) and morning glory (*Ipomoea tricolor* 'Heavenly Blue'), can be allowed to scramble up hedges and shrubs, perhaps running through more permanent climbers on trellis work and mixing with the summer and autumn displays – also filling in gaps while the more long-term employees get established and fill out their allotted space.

Effects for Different Seasons

The gardens of real enthusiasts are interesting at all times of the year; those of the less dedicated or thoughtful can be slightly depressing as soon as the first real frosts arrive and they will remain so until the easy magic of spring bulbs and shrubs brings all to life again. There follow some suggestions for ensuring all-year colour in the vertical garden.

Left: delphiniums and the rose 'Madame Knorr' ('Comte de Chambord') with complementary plants at Ashtree Cottage in Wiltshire. The pergola is almost lost in the summer celebrations.

Rose 'Elizabeth of Glamis' is an established favourite seen here in a happy on-going relationship with Clematis 'Huldine'.

WINTER

Winter is the longest season and certainly feels it; anything that can be done to alleviate the threat of gloom and despondency needs to be tackled energetically. I feel sure that all garden design should start by envisaging the various effects possible for the winter. Infrastructure, artifacts and plants need to make the most of these months; the other seasons almost look after themselves, or seem to. Winter is a time when the hard landscaping in the garden pays the greatest dividends – paths, pergolas, walls, screens, rock beds, summer houses and other constructions all play a major part. Areas of paving and gravel will be important. Items such as bird baths and tables, sundials and garden benches act as focal points; pieces of sculpture obviously perform the same important function of punctuating the space and so too may simple, large blocks of rock.

Erica carnea 'King George' with taller E. arborea var. alpina, which blooms from the end of winter into spring, blessing the nose with a honey scent.

How the choice of plants for winter interest is made depends on many factors and there is at least one that is not immediately obvious. Most visits to garden centres are made during the more clement seasons and, thus, it is only natural that most plants that are bought are those that look attractive during those months. We know we are doing it, but it just cannot be resisted – we are likely to choose first those plants that have flowers or promising buds on them. This means that the winter-flowerers tend to be at the back of the queue and it is my contention that these are the very plants that we really ought to be giving special priority. A single flowering shrub in the middle of winter is surely worth half a forest of bloom in mid-summer.

Evergreen and deciduous trees, shrubs and climbers highlight each other at this time of the year. Some evergreens are more lively in colour through the cold weather. For example *Elaeagnus pungens* 'Maculata' and the variegated *Euonymus fortunei* cultivars become more richly toned, variegated ivies are painted in more exaggerated shades and some take on pink, purple or reddish hues.

Winter-flowering heathers are great value. For example, the honey-scented *E. arborea* var. *alpina* (pictured left) moves upwards to a height of 2m (6ft) and is complemented by some *E. carnea* varieties in front of it.

Bankers for the winter are such as the winter flowering cherry, *Prunus × subhirtella* var. *autumnalis*, witch hazels, winter jasmine (*Jasminum nudiflorum*), viburnums, mahonias, *Garrya*

elliptica and wintersweet (see margin list). On warmer walls the hybrid quinces (*Chaenomeles* cultivars) can be in bloom from leaf-fall until they are again fully leaved in spring. The end of winter will not be here before *Forsythia suspensa* winks opens its first sprinkle of primrose flowers or *Corylopsis spicata* and *C. pauciflora* have unfurled their classy catkins.

SPRING

Spring is an easy time to paint bold strokes of colour. Everywhere there is forsythia, above are the pinks clouds of almonds (*Prunus dulcis*) and the breaking buds of a thousand trees and shrubs. The early magnolias succeed again in up-staging all else with their exotic bloom, while we mutter prayers to try to assuage the coming of any frosts.

Clematis armandii, its evergreen overcoat huddled around its twisted stems, bridges winter and spring with long-lasting displays of cream-

Far left: Garrya elliptica 'James Roof' decorates itself well before the Christmas festivities begin and is still en fête well into the New Year. It is usually grown as a reliable wall shrub.

SCENTED WINTER PLANTS

It is a happy fact that winter-flowering plants are very often ones blessed with a pleasing scent. Of many that might be considered for special winter duty, the following are some that *must* be given priority:

Abeliophyllum distichum with its early fragrant blossom; *Iris unguicularis* forms for the base of the wall; shrubby *Lonicera fragrantissima*; the evergreen climbing *Clematis armandii*; and shrubs such as *Chimonanthus praecox* (wintersweet); *Hamamelis* (witch hazel); *Mahonia japonica* or the hybrids 'Charity', 'Winter Sun' and 'Lionel Fortesque'; and *Viburnum farreri* and *Viburnum* x *bodnantense* varieties such as 'Dawn', 'Charles Lamont' or 'Deben'.

Left: The classy catkins of Corylopsis spicata *festoon the bare twigs at the end of winter and beginning of spring.*

Right: Abeliophyllum distichum, *a restrained relative of the forsythia, makes an attractive picture towards the end of winter.*

white blossom. Not so long after the last of these has faded, the leafless *C. montana*, in its various splendid manifestations, amazes again with galaxies quite without number. The walls and pergolas come alive, but not all climbers are out of bed; the vines are late to start into growth and even the Virginia creeper and its relatives may be a bit tardy about getting to work. With a Virginia creeper that embraces two walls it is interesting to see those branches on the warmer one unfurling leaves significantly earlier than those on the cooler one even break bud, a clear demonstration of the immediate microclimate effect (see p.16).

Late spring is the time for many ornamental apples to crowd their stems with white, pink, and red blossom. Much the same period is open season for many of the cherries. *Prunus* 'Amanogawa' with its columnar form pointing to the sky is pale pink; *P.* 'Spire' is a narrow cone when young, but, with middle-age, spreading occurs and it opens to a vase shape, though still erect. This plant, full of pale pink flowers, probably beats 'Amanogawa' into bloom. Wisterias, especially ancient ones, may be expected to take their time arousing themselves; the first flower buds will begin to lengthen before spring is at an end and may open in warm spots.

SUMMER

Spring recedes and now it is time for the wisterias to come into their own. The vines at last come into fresh leafy growth, full of promise. The lilacs that opened late spring are still with us and casting their scent abroad. Ceanothus cultivars, trained up walls and elsewhere, are moving into bloom in a range of blue shades, with an occasional white. Ivies that have had their 'short back and sides' haircut in the early spring are now fully clothed in shining new gear. And, of course, it is roses, roses and roses all the way; the taller ones are to be seen on the walls, pergolas or rustic screens, in hedgerows and tied to posts, the lower forms in beds, on the patio or in a formal rose garden. Here, too, are the large-flowered clematis cultivars as well as some of the interesting small-flowered species.

The patio, the house and almost any place where it is practical may be exploding with colour from a range of hanging baskets and other containers. Even tiny town gardens and houses with no really defined garden can become an oasis of life and colour. Morning glory (*Ipomoea purpurea* and *I. tricolor*) has now twined its way upwards and suddenly opens its huge purple blue trumpets, their silent blasts bringing down any walls of scepticism about annuals in the garden scene.

AUTUMN

There are several things that signal autumn: leaf fall is the obvious one but with the drier summers of recent times we find leaves falling earlier, or at least substantial scatters of browned foliage lie below trees before the real autumn is here. I begin to say goodbye to summer as, at the foot of warm walls, groups of *Nerine bowdenii* and *Amaryllis belladonna* suddenly shoot up, naked of leaf, and open their fresh florescent-pink blossoms. The fruiting shrubs and trees take on more and more dominant roles as the deciduous plants begin to undress. Pyracanthas on walls, up supports or used as hedges are loaded with fruit in golds, oranges and reds. The decorative crab-apple *Malus* 'Golden Hornet' reaches for the sky as strongly as through the other seasons but is now heavily burdened with bright fruit. Cotoneasters compete to see which can get the most fruit per metre of stem. Autumn foliage all around is a blaze of carnival colours.

On the walls, the Virginia creeper (*Parthenocissus quinquefolia*) and others in the genus almost blind the onlooker with the vividness of their display. For a few weeks it is difficult to think of anything that can match this brilliance. *Vitis coignetiae* has at least as many wonderful colours, but its foliage texture is rougher, it glows rather than glitters, but what a glow – you can almost warm your hands by it! The *Parthenocissus* climbers have the good manners, once the party is over, to drop their leaves and

HERBS

Close to the house is a likely place to find herbs, so the temptation to crush a stalk of mint, sage or thyme can be indulged; the occasional leaf of lavender or rosemary will be sacrificed to please the senses. Many of our culinary herbs are from Mediterranean lands and are happy to have a relatively warm, dryish spot in the lee of the house walls or by the patio. Mints are an exception; they enjoy moister ground.

Basic herbs

Chives *Allium schoenoprasum*
Dill *Anethum graveolens*
Coriander *Coriandrum sativum*
Fennel *Foeniculum vulgare*
Mint *Mentha spicata*
Marjoram *Origanum vulgare*
Parsley *Petroselinum crispum*
Sage *Salvia officinalis*
Thyme *Thymus vulgaris*

leaf stalks within a short period of time to be taken to the compost heap in one go, not like the provocative wisterias with their long-drawn-out striptease.

And then it is winter again with the evergreen gaining ascendency in the picture, especially the tall reaching columnar kinds such as the yew, *Taxus baccata* 'Fastigiata', the junipers, J. 'Skyrocket', *J. communis* 'Fastigiata', the narrower *Chamaecyparis lawsoniana* cultivars such as 'Green Pillar, C. *lawsoniana* 'Erecta', C. *lawsoniana* 'Grayswood Pillar', or C. *lawsoniana* 'Columnaris' forms.

Thoughts on Pruning

Where plants are planted very thickly, some help may be needed to allow each its fair share of a place in the sun! This can mean some pruning, with some things a repeated resort to the secateurs, but with many, light finger-pruning will suffice – just nipping off any new growths threatening to reach into another's space.

Perfectly hardy plants, that do not need the microclimate of a wall in order to survive (see p.16), can benefit from being given wall or fence space and, in such sites, will be encouraged to grow much higher and be somewhat different in character. They are likely to be less leafy and more floriferous. Obviously plants on fences and walls lend themselves to grooming with secateurs, shears or powered trimmer.

Shaping wall plants can affect the general appearance of walls and other structures. A few plants made into relatively narrow columns will give an illusion of added height. Conversely, allowing plants to make broad sweeps of growth will have the opposite effect, especially if they are not allowed above the height of the ceiling

A peep into one of the many compartments in the garden of The Anchorage, West Wickham, Kent. This is hedged and full of herbs such as Symphytum × uplandicum, Phlomis fruticosa, lavender, chives and golden marjoram.

of the ground floor. On cool shady sites, panels of coloured ivies kept within defined bounds can be very effective as design aids. To keep them bright and fresh the older foliage can be trimmed off at the end of the winter; in no time at all the panels will be renovated with sparkling new foliage.

There are a number of scrambling plants that are equally at home at attention against a wall or fence as they are serving as ground-covering shrubs in procumbent mode. Many euonymus forms, especially of the *E. fortunei* persuasion, can be easily induced to reach upward and spread themselves over walls, often reaching the gutters above the bedrooms. The ones with decorative variegated foliage particularly repay attention and can be made sparkling fresh by a light trim at the end of winter, shearing off some of the older leaves to allow a reclothing in new.

TOPIARY AND OTHER FORMS OF DISCIPLINE

Pruning regimes can lead to the ancient art of topiary, well established in Roman times and in some form or another exercised by most gardeners. The hedge is a form of topiary, so too is the close clipping of wall shrubs, such as pyracantha and ceanothus, to make very well-defined shapes. The formality of this type of work can be used to great effect near the house, especially if it is one that is Georgian or Georgian-inspired, and built on geometrical lines. The low hedges of box or similar plants used for knot gardens can look comfortable near many buildings, not only the Elizabethan ones we tend to associate them with.

Those trees of a fastigiate habit mentioned above, especially the conifer cultivars, look as if nature has taken a hand in the topiary game. These will probably need no help to maintain their chaste slender shapes, apart from the removal of a misplaced twig once in a while. In venerable old age when their sinews may weaken and the upward branches tend to fall away from the strictly vertical, a discrete loop or two of garden wire will keep them together

without anyone noticing. It makes life easier if we can fully exploit these natural sculptured forms that take our eyes upward and bring the sky firmly into the picture. In mild areas it could be possible to echo the effects that are so admired in places like the south of France where the slender conifers reach for the sky.

Topiary can become a quite major hobby, or it can be restricted to the tailoring of one or two pieces whose obvious manipulated forms contrasts effectively with the natural shapes of surrounding plants. In the abstract or made into animal shapes, it can create focal points, halting the eye on its horizontal journey and perhaps moving it upwards. Within a very informal setting an odd, mimicked character can add to the atmosphere – perhaps even giving it a surreal aura.

PLANTS FOR PRUNING

Very prunable wall plants include *Actinidia kolomikta*, for attractive foliage colours through the growing season, ivies (*Hedera*), quinces (*Chaenomeles*), winter jasmine (*Jasminum nudiflorum*) and *Forsythia suspensa*, with some support for its main stems. Pyracanthas are valuable for their long-lasting berries and a good flowering display with evergreen cover, and ceanothus for their dark evergreen foliage and usually blue flowers. *Euonymus fortunei* in its evergreen, variegated cultivars repays pruning as do fruit trees such as apples, pears, peaches and figs.

PLANTS USEFUL FOR TOPIARY

Box (*Buxus sempervirens*) and yew (*Taxus baccata*) are the best pair to use for forming the more intricate shapes, such as peacocks or the leader of the opposition at the dispatch box. Yew is particularly good in the open garden. Box and bay (*Laurus nobilis*) are excellent in a large container.

Box is historically the pre-eminent topiary plant, most often used in its 'Suffruticosa' form. It is slow to start from very small plants, but has the benefit that once grown and groomed into shape it is not so rampant as to make it difficult to maintain.

Lonicera nitida, the dark, small, oval-leaved relative of the honeysuckle, puts on centimetres very quickly and is useful for making a quick interior hedge or perhaps a strong geometrical shape, but it is too strong a grower to recommend for some more adventurous shapes – despite what might be indicated by such plants offered in garden centres. If it is used for rather intricate shapes, it will certainly need the extra support from wire.

Large-scale geometrical shapes such as globes and pyramids can be successfully achieved with bold plants such as holly (*Ilex* species and cultivars) and less likely ones such as hornbeam (*Carpinus betulus*) and beech (*Fagus sylvatica*).

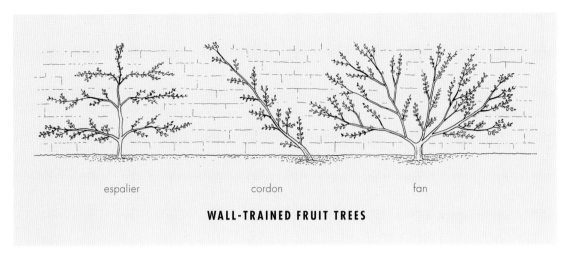

espalier   cordon   fan

WALL-TRAINED FRUIT TREES

At Levens Hall in Cumbria there are hedges and forms of some considerable antiquity, and very impressive they look, but effective shapes are possible to achieve within a short timescale. Nor do you need a lot of room. Even plants such as yew, which are generally thought of as slow growing, can make an impressive statement after only a few seasons, and a very reasonable feature in ivy can be made within one growing season.

FRUIT AND FRUIT TREES

One can be surprised by the fruiting effects of plants grown in the shelter of walls or fences. The passion flowers (*Passiflora*), mainly grown for their extraordinary flowers, can be quite bewitching after a warm summer when they festoon themselves with large, long orange and golden fruits. Those of *Akebia quinata* are purplish, while *Celastris orbiculatus* freely decorates its branches with fruits that start green, then turn black, and then split to reveal their yellow inner surfaces that back the brilliant, long-lasting, glittering scarlet seeds. In such conditions some of the tender plants will fruit before they fall prey to the bad weather. *Billardiera longiflora* (see p.244) can produce a good crop of fruits in purple-blue or other colours.

Sun-blessed walls have long been the valued domain of growers of fruit trees who teach their plants the discipline of cordon or espalier. Most gardeners would grant that such parade-ground exactness is not without considerable beauty.

Apples, pears and peaches are happy in their attractive blossoming and are again pleasing in fruit. The fig too is a handsome fellow with its large bumbling-fingered leaves. Some of these wall-bound performers give reasonable or even brilliant autumn colour, and their bare winter branches can be admired, especially after completion of a session with the secateurs.

The purists and those whose first interest is in producing top-class fruit will keep their wall-trained fruit trees away from the embraces of climbing plants, but in more relaxed, liberal regimes the fruiting branches may be entwined with climbers and scramblers to give, hopefully, a cornucopian Garden-of-Eden expression to the whole. Who will pick the first apple?

Solemnity is not an essential in garden design. This clever topiary is part of the delightful landscaped gardens to be found at the National Trust property Knighthayes in Devon.

WALLS, FENCES & HEDGES

How often does the frame make the picture? Garden walls, fences and hedges can perform a similar benign function and hugely increase the impact of the plants within their embrace.

Planting plans close to the house will depend in part on the walls or other structures up which the plants will grow. Those that do not look all that wonderful will be all the better for extensive growing cover, whereas those finished with wooden boards will need regular maintenance, so any added plant growth should be detachable. The choice to exploit house walls as a gardening area is one that is made after deciding whether they, and the house, will be physically improved – or at least not damaged – by the plants. Often it is vaguely thought that plants that climb and cling to the wall can damage it. Usually the facts of the matter are not really properly evaluated. If plants are given proper support where needed (see pp.70-77), there should be no damage at all to the walls. In almost every case the addition of plants will enhance the various properties of the walls; plants will keep walls drier and will provide extra insulation, which is especially welcome in the winter.

Aesthetic considerations may weigh as heavy as practical ones. The frisson that can be engendered from a well-conceived contrast between a living plant and an inanimate structure is to be welcomed – one enhances the quality of the other. I have already touched on Georgian properties and the formal design of many modern brick-built houses, suggesting that they may require a rather structured approach to planting (see p.22). The larger the wall plant, the more this formality may be deemed necessary, and it can be pruned and trimmed to its allotted space. Stone walls usually form a pleasing comparatively informal background and support for plants. Houses in the Cotswolds are characterized by their warm honey-coloured stone. In that part of Britain, house walls and those surrounding the gardens are usually generously festooned with climbers and other plants. The same principle can be applied to most other stone types.

There may be other buildings needing plant camouflage. Garden buildings can look rather utilitarian and will be more pleasing with a complete cover of climbers. The mile-a-minute plant, Russian vine, *Fallopia baldschuanica*, leads in the rampant stakes. This easy, rapid grower may invite the scorn of expert gardeners, but it does not do to be snobbish – this is a useful species that will succeed in poor conditions.

The climber Campsis × tagliabuana 'Madame Galen' with variegated yuccas and high-rise algaves in a corner of the 'secret garden' at Osler Road, Hedington, Oxford. The garden specializes in plants for dry soils and has a Mediterranean feel.

Below: here the mile-a-minute plant, Fallopia baldschuanica, also known as Russian vine, has covered a ruinous wall in company with morning glory (Ipomoea).

Wisteria floribunda 'Multijuga' overhangs the doorway of a sixteenth-century tithe barn in the garden of Bourton House, Bourton-on-the-Hill in the Cotswolds.

Greenhouses need all the light they can get; however, if they have solid bases these could be covered with ivies, cotoneasters, *Euonymus fortunei* or other climbers or scramblers that will help to keep the structure dry, and warmer in winter and cooler in summer.

Walls that surround the garden and mark its boundaries provide a surface that is ideal for plants. A brick or stone wall can be pleasing in itself and even more so if its colour and texture match the house and help to underline the sense of unity. In areas where there is a plentiful supply of suitable stone, such walls can be contemplated, but elsewhere their cost may be prohibitive. A dry stone wall is a practical proposition if it is only made to a height of 90-120cm (3-4ft). It must have sure foundations, the side profile should narrow towards the top and each layer of stones should be arranged to bridge the joins of those of the previous course.

MAINTENANCE CONSIDERATIONS

Old timbered Elizabethan houses look as if they should have intimate connection with the plants. However, having had such a house as a home, I know that all parts of their exterior walls need to be readily accessible to keep them in order. This did not stop us planting up the walls – we were simply very selective in what we used so that all the beams could be inspected at any time. (Adding supports to allow for easy maintenance is fully dealt with on pp.70-77.)

Modern brickwork bound by cement will support all sorts of plants. We are limited only by our own inclinations. There is no fear of climbers weakening the mortar, which is how the argument ran when old-fashioned lime mortar was more common. Even then, the reasoning may have been specious – ivy pulled off such walls might have brought away some mortar but if it was left in place, it would have been doing a double job of keeping the walls dry and prolonging their life.

SOME THOUGHTS ON COLOUR

The more adventurous use of colour is one of the hallmarks of modern garden design, especially of smaller gardens and those dominated by buildings. Thanks to modern technology, fences, walls and other structures can be painted almost any shade, even vibrant oranges and reds, and the colour can be altered almost at will. There is still a place in gardens for natural woods and traditional woodstains but these are joined by a wider selection of colours that can fulfil different requirements.

A raised bed made behind a low stone wall at La Casella in France. Plants include the scrambling little daisy Erigeron karvinskianus, Convolvulus cneorum and there are olives in the background.

IN PRAISE OF IVY

Ivy is the plant that bears the brunt of the, mostly unfounded, criticism. I am a believer in ivies. There is a huge variety, some 400 different kinds being offered for sale at present. Part of our present house is a small former stable block with very undistinguished walls: a series of ivies is currently answering the problem of how to disguise them. Here is a shortlist of good cultivars; more details are given on pp.143-146.

Favourite ivies

Hedera canariensis 'Gloire de Marengo' has large, broad, bluntly triangular leaves which are basically dark with some grey areas and cream variegation. Takes on purplish tinges in winter.

Hedera helix 'Luzii' is much used as a house plant but with us looks effective outside, its light green cover enlivened by yellowish mottling.

Hedera helix 'Sagittifolia' is the name now almost universally used for an ivy with small, dark, deeply divided leaves, which are bird clawed and very pointed. (The original is arrow-shaped and much less lobed.)

Hedera helix 'Sagittifolia Variegata' is an excellent plant with typical deeply indented lobes and much silvery-cream-edged variegation.

Hedera helix 'Glacier' has wide grey-green leaves with silvery patches and cream edges.

Hedera helix 'Fluffy Ruffles' has dark leaves so goffered at the edges that the lobes are lost, they look rounded. This is a character with such a distinctive line in tailoring that it looks almost unlike an ivy – but it is nevertheless interesting and effective in the garden.

Colours are very much a matter of personal choice, but there are generally accepted guidelines. Rich dark greens, blues, mauves and other cool colours are viable foils for a variety of plants, while reds, oranges and very rich yellows are less easy to handle. For example, masses of pink roses usually look more pleasing against grey or similarly coloured stone walls than they will displayed against the yellows or the orange-reds of brickwork. The same applies to red

COLOUR THERAPY

When choosing colours for the garden, it should be remembered that the more vivid shades produce a lively environment, but they can be very obtrusive, particularly to those who regard a garden first and foremost as a growing creation. The extrovert oranges, reds and rich golds reach forward and may tend to wear less well over the seasons than the cooler recessive blues, greens and greys.

Below: bright-flowered nasturtiums start to race up a painted fence, providing a really colourful background to the children's swings in this garden. One need not be afraid of colour.

flowers. The exuberance and massed quantity of blossom produced by such climbers as the pink forms of *Clematis montana* can often negate the usual overwhelming effect of the orange-red background. Foliage, in all its green hues, looks well against any wall, particularly richer-coloured ones. White blossom will look effective in combination with most wall colours but will obviously be less flattered by those that are white or pale cream. Orange-red walls show off pale colours well and can enhance yellows and some pastel shades. Rich bottle greens, full blues, purples and mauves enhance the look of shrubs and other plants. Mauves and blues handsomely emphasize the colours of a collection of silvery- or grey-leaved plants. A yellow or golden area brings sunshine into darkness.

WALL-MOUNTED SCULPTURES

Walls can be enlivened by hanging baskets, pots or pieces of sculpture on them. Such items will take the eye upwards and create a focal point. A rather dull piece of wall near our house is made decorative with a flat-sided hanging earthenware pot which looks reasonable empty

Above: a touch of surrealism is created here with a lively fish sculpture mounted on a wall and surrounded by the magnificent foliage of the extrovert vine, Vitis coignetiae.

and a lot more pleasant with a hanging geranium or ivy in it.

A popular item for a wall fixture is a lion head's in stone with the facility to allow water to fall from its mouth. There are variations on this theme, one of which may be just the thing to enliven a dull corner or add extra interest near the patio.

With little difficulty there can also be the sound of water falling on to a bowl of boulders: the water is simply recycled whenever a small electric pump is started. One can forgo the water and just have a stone motif such as the fish shown opposite.

Fences

There are places where a solid wall of bricks or stone surrounding the garden is appropriate and attractive. Alternatively the boundary could be marked by constructing pillars every 1.5-1.8m (5-6ft) and filling the space in between with panels of wooden trellis, palings or even a solid fence of overlapping boards.

Fences made from chain-link mark the boundary and effectively keep out animals, but are not the last word in the aesthetic stakes. When employed between pillars and framed by

An urn or earthenware artifact can be used as a focal point without necessarily being planted up. This large-scale terracotta pot justifies its place alone and offers a good contrast to the lively foliage and flowers of the flowerbed. The eye is taken up from the ferns, hostas and London pride to the container, counterbalancing the standard wisteria.

wood or brick, they look quite different and can be used to allow air and light through where this might be an advantage. Chain mesh is also useful when it acts as a support for a selection of climbers so that the eventual appearance is that of a hedge. Not far from my home *Hedera colchica* 'Dentata Variegata' has been used to make such a 'hedge'. It looks handsome all round the year but the variegation seems to take on a richer golden through the winter. Some cotoneasters, especially *C. sternianus* can be very effective against a fence. This species can be trained tightly and will look good with its rich green foliage, very pleasing with creamy flowers and quite splendid for months with copious crops of long-lasting orange-red berries. *Euonymus fortunei* can be pressed up fences to give evergreen cover. The vigorous *Clematis montana* forms, though deciduous, are worth considering as they can look wonderful in bloom.

If the fences are to act as a windbreak, it is rather more sensible to use palings at fixed intervals to moderate the wind's strength than to have heavyweight constructions of abutted or overlapping board, or woven lapwood. Solid fences effectively form huge sails. To withstand major wind strengths, they will need ample upright supports, that are very well secured. Metal post supports driven 45-75cm (18-30in) into the ground will go a long way to help the fence resist the wind, but must themselves be formidably strong, too.

The upright lines of a picket fence contrast with the draped growth of clematis 'Victoria' at Eastgrove Cottage in Worcestershire. This one-acre garden/nursery is very intensively planted and specializes in hardy perennials.

Often such fences are the earliest defence made by the gardener to protect the plants in his or her care. Their importance lessens as the years pass, and shrubs and other structures augment their work in providing shelter.

Railings

Railings are undervalued in garden schemes. In Britain most of our Victorian railings were lost to the manufacture of armaments during the Second World War. The Victorians energetically exploited the Industrial Revolution and used railings of various kinds, especially ornate cast-iron ones, to reinforce privacy and status in the burgeoning towns and cities. They have not regained their former position, partly because they are not cheap. This is a pity. They can be very effective in the garden, either as a boundary or as an interior feature, especially if they are used in dramatic or subtle juxtaposition with

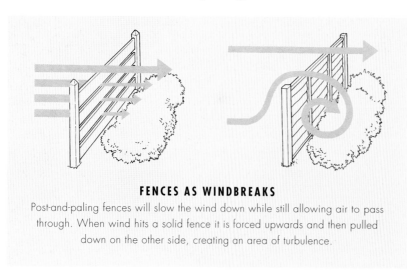

FENCES AS WINDBREAKS

Post-and-paling fences will slow the wind down while still allowing air to pass through. When wind hits a solid fence it is forced upwards and then pulled down on the other side, creating an area of turbulence.

suitable plants. For example, their rigid upright lines can be used as an attractive contrast to plants, such as *Cotoneaster horizontalis*, that make a play for the other dimension. Another, perhaps more sophisticated, idea is to combine them for colour, such as with the silvery-blue foliage of rue (*Ruta graveolens*). The variety 'Jackman's Blue' has an especially vivid colour to contrast with dark-painted railings.

Various clematis will wind happily around railings and festoon their whole length. The interplay of natural with artificially wrought lines is something that definitely pleases the eye and is an opportunity too often missed. The twining and curling tendrils of plants of this genus are particularly appropriate around railings with curved tops. Early in the year, *C. montana* or *C. alpina* could be chosen to do the honours, followed by some of the larger-flowered hybrids such as 'Twilight' which later will come into their own.

ADDING HEIGHT TO A FENCE

It may be that a fence is perfectly sound but is not quite high enough to do the job required of it: the extra height may be necessary to block out an unsightly view, to provide extra shelter for your plants or to further your plan of growing things upwards and enclosing the plot with luxuriant growth and blossom.

Adding extra height, particularly to solid fencing, could be a problem in that it will make the fence even more vulnerable to any stormy weather. Instead the desired effect can be obtained by using attractive trellis work.

Trellis is available in prefabricated lengths, usually straightforward rectangles, in various widths, such as 1.8m (6ft) by 30cm (1ft), 60cm (2ft), or 90cm (3ft) wide. Alternatively, there are concave or convex pieces, again usually about 1.8m (6ft) long and about 40cm (16in) at their widest point.

With the latter types there is the choice of having a series of rising arches, undulating waves or, if you combine both types, a regular switchback.

Trellis performs the blocking out function perfectly adequately – not only will it support plant growth, but it will also allow some of the wind through, so is less of a hazard than solid fencing.

Below: the rigidity and strong lines of the iron railings creates a support and a pleasing contrast to the tangled growth of the popular and attractive Clematis macropetala.

Hedges

Hedges have various functions. Boundary hedges not only mark the site but look good, give shelter and stop animal intrusion. Interior hedges are more important for their decorative appeal and to make partial screens but they can also help with shelter. Modern power tools make hedge management so much easier that even within the garden taller ones become more practical; they can do well as a boundary, too, provided they are not threatening a neighbour's air space.

There are some disadvantages to extensive hedges. They take time and effort to keep in shape – those that grow fast need a significant number of cuts each year. Tall hedges cast a lot of shade and the rootruns can extend into the important topsoil inside the garden for several feet beyond the outreach of the hedge, making it impossible to grow other plants nearby. The worst root invaders are privet, leylandii and yew; less dominant kinds are box, holly and roses. Some root restriction is possible by regular slicing into the soil 15-30cm (6-12in) from the outreach of the hedge and to a depth of a spade, one spit. More effective and, eventually, less time consuming is to open a trench at least 38cm (15in) deep along the garden side of the hedge – again 15-30cm (6-12in) from the hedge's upper outreach. Line the side of the trench with strong, root-resistant material, such as heavy grade polythene sheeting, and then back fill. This may help to curb the more exuberant growth of hedge plants and allow you to plant other things quite close, making use of the hedge as a backcloth.

In rural areas some hedges may be part of former farm hedgerows. If these are a mix of species, it is impossible to force them into the immaculate uniform suburban hedge, but it might be a mistake to uproot them. You may have a rich inheritance – hawthorn, dogwood, blackthorn, hazel, field maple, goat willow, spindleberry, dog rose, honeysuckle, old man's

beard and wild privet can support a wildlife city of birds, small mammals and a legion of insects. Clambering hedgerow plants like bryony and ditchside ones like meadowsweet, milkmaids, primroses, bluebells, bedstraws and even nettles should be allowed space for their own sake and for the insect life they encourage. In such a mixed hedge it is possible to allow selected plants, such as ash, field maple, hazel and holly, to grow into mature trees, if space allows. Elder can look attractive but is an extensive seeder and may be more nuisance than it is worth. Into such a mixed hedge of native species could be allowed a few attractive foreigners such as the tough rose, *R. rugosa*, with its large single flowers and huge bulbous hips.

CHOOSING HEDGE PLANTS

Before choosing what plants you want to make your hedge, think of what you need from the hedge – consider the ultimate height and width you desire, how strong you need it to be, how much work you are prepared to do to keep it tidy and the required appearance through the different seasons of the year. Along with the latter goes the decision about whether you want a uniform 'wall-like' hedge or would prefer a mixture of plants. Obviously evergreens will maintain better shelter through the full twelve months but regularly clipped beech and hornbeam retain their dead leaves in rusty brown shades through the winter and so will provide some protection and in a sense are not fully deciduous.

Hollies make first-class hedges and can be taken to any height that is sensible. The basic dark green cultivars make a wonderful background for large herbaceous plants and shrubs; those that are variegated may serve to provide additional highlights. Yew is magnificent with its matt-green, needle leaves, and is wonderful for precisely shaped hedges or for topiary effects; it should be borne in mind, however, that its foliage and berries are toxic to humans and animals. *Viburnum tinus* can be used to make a dense, dark, smart hedge and is a mass of blossom through the long winter months.

All pyracanthas are top-value in the garden. They are great on walls and fine for hedges as well as for use as free-standing shrubs. They provide good evergreen cover, several weeks of abundant creamy-white blossom in spring and at the end of the summer are hung with innumerable bunches of bright berries, gold, orange or red, that can persist until spring.

COLOURFUL HEDGES

Bright foliage hedges can be grown from the following:

Fagus sylvatica Atropurpurea Group (copper beech), deciduous but retains dead rusty foliage.

Ilex aquifolium 'Argentea Marginata' or other brightly variegated cultivar.

Berberis thunbergii 'Atropurpurea' or similar cultivar, maroon, deciduous.

Elaeagnus pungens 'Maculata', heavily variegated in gold, evergreen.

Elaeagnus x ebbingei 'Limelight', evergreen leaves with yellow centres.

Taxus baccata 'Elegantissima' (golden yew).

x Cupressocyparis 'Castlewellan', lime-yellow leylandii.

There are other highly decorative hedge plants. Pyracantha can be very effective and carries huge crops of highly coloured berries from autumn until spring – just the months when extra colour is especially needed. Escallonia makes a very dense hedge and grows quickly. Its highly polished green is enlivened by an annual crop of flowers if the hedge is not cut severely until the second half of the summer. Eleagnus forms can be very effective, especially the *E. × ebbingei* types such as 'Gilt Edge', with dark green leaves edged gold, and 'The Hague', with strong leaves, silvery in youth and dark with age. Copper beech can be very effective in the right place where its dark colour will not be too dominant.

HEDGE PROFILES

Some hedging plants tend to make naturally wide hedges – *Viburnum tinus* is an example – but most can be kept to a slim outline. The ideal is to produce a triangular profile. The lowest branches then get their fair share of light which helps to keep foliar cover right down to the ground. The top can be trimmed lightly to give a few centimetres of flat surface, which will be easier to keep level along the whole length than if it were pointed. Don't make the top too wide or the edges too upright: a broad flat top and vertical sides may end with the hedge gaping open, something that can be disastrously

exaggerated after a snowstorm, when heavy loads of snow can force branches outwards.

Even the much-abused leylandii can be kept to a slope-sided neat profile if the top-growth is frequently trimmed, the roots are curbed and the whole is not overfed. Such hedges are easy to manage up to head height; they become progressively more work as they grow over 1.8m (6ft). We have interior hedges of *Lonicera nitida* at just under this height. In this comparatively sheltered position, they are easily maintained by frequent trimming but would be almost impossible in a site with more direct wind. In tempest-tossed spots, hedges of this type of lax plant will have to be kept lower.

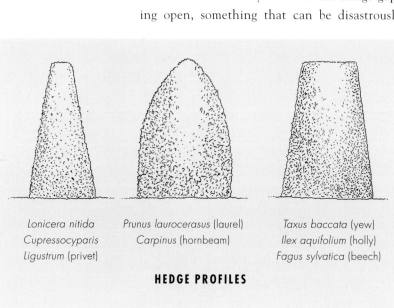

| *Lonicera nitida*
Cupressocyparis
Ligustrum (privet) | *Prunus laurocerasus* (laurel)
Carpinus (hornbeam) | *Taxus baccata* (yew)
Ilex aquifolium (holly)
Fagus sylvatica (beech) |

HEDGE PROFILES

Trimmings can be collected easily using a garden tidy or sheet of plastic stretched below the hedge before starting to cut. Soft trimmings of hedges like lonicera, privet or even beech can be rotted down in the compost heap. Holly, barbed berberis or thicker pieces of debris are best burnt or taken to the municipal reclamation centre.

PLANTS TO GROW UP HEDGES

Growing climbers up and into hedges may be successful if the hedge plants are relatively slow growing and do not need frequent trimming, and if the climbing plants get into top gear quickly. A repeated success in our garden is the perennial relative of the nasturtium, *Tropaeolum tuberosum*, which reaches 2-3m (6-10ft) from a tuberous rootstock. Its flame-coloured blossom lights up the dark mass of a yew hedge from summer into late autumn, before dying back with the frosts. Its relative *T. peregrinum* (Canary creeper) is also a perennial but is usually best treated as an annual in more bracing climates. There are plenty of other annual climbers that can be cheap, easy to raise, rapid in growth and spectacular in bloom – see p.241.

Fedges

Where you desire neither a fence or a hedge, a 'fedge' is a very useful compromise. A fedge is able to perform the function of both fence and hedge without demanding the space of the latter above ground or below. Fedges can be a chain-link fence or a system of wires supporting climbers that will form a complete foliage cover of plants growing over trellis. In this sort of situation the evergreens are very effective. Consider the ivies; some of the large-leaved types are the most satisfying. Try *Hedera colchica* (rich green), *H. colchica* 'Dentata Variegata' (bold golden variegation) or *H.* 'Sulphur Heart' (cream and gold patches towards the centre of the leaves).

A different effect results from planting tight-growing shrubs such as *Cotoneaster horizontalis* so that they are supported by wires, trellis, palings or railings. *C. horizontalis* is often semi-evergreen and will hold heavy crops of orange-red berries well into the winter. Even if all the leaves are dropped, the network of branches is so dense that it makes good cover.

A serious gentleman on a column overlooks orange-gold Tropaeolum tuberosum *growing through conifers in this cool corner.*

Sweet peas growing up a screen of trellis in my garden. Cutting away the old flowers can make a remarkable difference to the crop of flowers produced and the length of the season – it can be extended by weeks or even months.

PERGOLAS, SCREENS, ARBOURS & GAZEBOS

Prepare to think three-dimensional. Garden structures are invaluable in their contribution to the overall effect as well as providing support and shelter for innumerable plants.

Pergolas

The traditional role of a pergola is to be a sheltered walkway, giving some shade from the sun. Little wonder that they are popular in warm climes, but they have also long had their place in countries like Britain where the shade aspect is less vital. Pergolas make use of air space and give vertical and overhead support for plants. Used carefully, they can change our perspective dramatically. They can be a major feature of the garden, perhaps linking one part of it with another, or they may be run along the side of the house with one end of the rafters supported by a runner fixed to the house wall.

On a personal level, a pergola helps to create a sense of privacy. For example, a pergola-like structure can be used to enclose and cover part, or the whole of the patio. They are also the ideal support for some of the most attractive climbers, which can then be seen 'in the round'. *Vitis coignetiae*, with its wonderful bold foliage patterns of large, textured leaves, is an ideal candidate for growing on a pergola for this very reason. Fruiting vines can also look good and produce excellent crops. A rose walkway is a possibility, in season a tunnel of bloom and scent. Clematis or other climbers could be added to lengthen the period of floral interest. Pergolas can also give partial shelter for plants other than those decorating the structure. These could include one of the lace-cap hydrangeas, such as the white *H. macrophylla* 'Veitchii' or the spreading *H. serrata* 'Bluebird'.

The exotic-looking lantern tree, *Crinodendron hookerianum* would be worth considering. A classy evergeen, it has gorgeous red blossom for weeks through late spring well into summer.

TYPES OF PERGOLA

Like many other garden structures, pergola designs range from the modest, which might be a simple rustic length made of larch poles, or similar natural materials, to the super-sophisticated, which can be a serious building with brick pillars and major runners and rafters.

Most often the construction is something between these extremes, neither a somewhat whimsical lightweight erection, nor a permanent architectural one, suggesting Greek or Roman colonnades. The most easy to handle and usually most successful material for the domestic pergola is machined wood. Machined wood pergolas also seem to be the most appropriate for small or medium-sized gardens. To give a more permanent appearance, the columns can have brick or stone bases which really need not add a jot to the physical strength of the whole but give visual weight.

An alternative to wood is metal. Pergolas in metal usually consist of a series of linked arches. The narrower specification possible in a metal pergola will give it a lighter feel and may thus direct more attention to the climbing plants. For a more imposing structure, stone or possibly blocks of prefabricated or reinforced concrete, can be used. The concrete columns can be rounded and can be painted an appropriate colour to produce the effect of a colonnade.

READY-MADE UNITS

Nowadays, prefabricated wooden units are produced in a variety of shapes and sizes so that almost any combination can be made up to create exactly what is needed – a screen, an arbour, or even more involved items such as pergolas or gazebos. Some of these units also use trellis. Branded wooden prefabricated units are quality controlled and good value. However, if you have a good local wood yard or an independent woodworking firm you may find that they can provide pieces that are almost as good at a much cheaper price. It is worth shopping around.

The brilliant autumn colours of the ornamental grape, Vitis coignetiae, set fire to the columns of the pergola walk at Pyrford Court in Surrey.

PLANNING

The best place for a pergola is in the full sunshine. In such a position a wide range of plants can be encouraged to clothe the whole structure, the more insatiable sun-lovers on the sunny sides with those less demanding of sun on the shady sides. Pergolas can be successful in semi-shaded spots as well; wherever one is positioned it will add interest to the scene.

Most pergolas will lead in a straight line from one part of the garden to another, or from the house to a point in the garden. False perspective was mentioned on p.24. It is used to give the illusion of distance and can be particularly dramatic with a pergola. Two things can be done to create this feeling of added distance. Firstly, the width of the pergola pathway can be narrowed as it goes towards the point furthest from the normal viewing spot. Secondly, the upright supports can be brought slightly closer to each other along the length of the pergola. Even reducing the gaps between the uprights progressively by as little as 6cm (2in) will help to enhance the illusion.

A full right-angle turn to give an L-shaped pathway and pergola is a variation on the straight theme and is very effective; three sides or a complete square or rectangle are other possibilities given a large enough garden. A pergola following a gently curved pathway is a design that may suit some sites; it will tease the eye and encourage the desire to explore the bend. The ultimate of this would be a complete circle.

In very small plots a complete pergola may be too grandiose and would take up too much space. In this case a pathway with a series of linked uprights at the back on one side of it might be a solution. Short rafters can be fixed to overhang equidistantly or even be cantilevered.

THE STRUCTURE

Wood for pergolas should be substantial rather than very light. All timber should be thoroughly treated with preservative: prefabricated pieces should be already treated, it is part of what you pay for. Recommended calibres for each section are: uprights 10 × 10cm (4 × 4in), crossbeams (runners) 10 × 6cm (4 × 2in) and rafters 10 × 6cm (4 × 2in).

Heights and widths should be chosen to be appropriate to the site. Usual heights of uprights are in the 2.1-2.7m (7-9ft) range, and they are best erected about 1.8m (6ft) apart. The width

Left: this pergola is almost lost in the embrace of the roses 'Minnehaha' and 'Aloha' and the clematis 'Royal Velours', accompanied by Campanula latifolia.

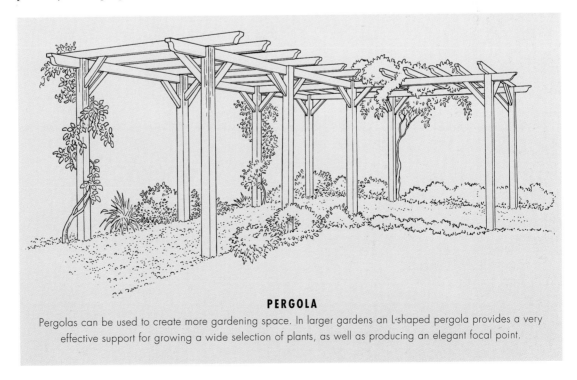

PERGOLA

Pergolas can be used to create more gardening space. In larger gardens an L-shaped pergola provides a very effective support for growing a wide selection of plants, as well as producing an elegant focal point.

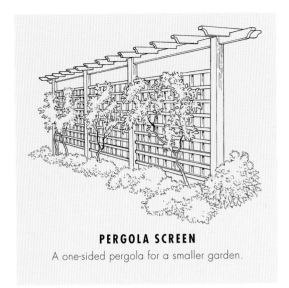

PERGOLA SCREEN
A one-sided pergola for a smaller garden.

of the walkway could be around 1.8m (6ft), but possibly more; the rafters will need to be 60cm (2ft) longer than the width (so 2.4m/8ft long) to allow an overhang each side of around 25cm (10in) – less looks mean.

The uprights can be secured in position with concrete or purpose-made metal post-supports, or a combination of the two. Metal post-supports come in two basic designs and are readily available at garden centres and larger do-it-yourself stores. They make the correct alignment of the whole installation somewhat easier and render everything very secure. The first type is basically an open metal box fixed on to a long four-flanged point for driving deep into the ground. The second is a similar open metal box but this is set on a square metal base drilled with holes to take bolts. The whole thing is intended to be attached to hard surfaces by means of these anchoring bolts.

Pointed metal supports are available in two spike sizes – 60cm (2ft) and 75cm (30in) long. For pergolas with 10 × 10cm (4 × 4in) posts, choose the longer ones. The shorter ones will only suffice for posts up to 1.2m (4ft) high.

Prepare the site of the pergola by setting pegs into the ground at the position of each of the spikes. Check each peg with its neighbours using a spirit-level to ensure that all are at the same height. The spikes should be lowered into holes deep enough to take half their length and

Left: a brick pathway underlines this bold pergola which makes good use of ivies and hardy perennials.

then driven home with a heavy hammer using a dolly to prevent damage to the box on top. Care must be taken to ensure that each support remains vertical and in correct alignment with the others as they are put in place. Double check with the spirit-level as you proceed. Any space left around the spikes should be packed tight with earth or, to make doubly secure, filled with concrete.

Do not rely on your eye when setting the spikes: ground that looks level may vary by a significant amount between any given points.

The second type of post-support, those with flat flanges, are useful where pergola posts are going to be erected on concrete or other hard made-up surfaces. These surfaces are likely to be level, but this should be checked and allowance made for any deviance. The post holders are fixed to the solid ground by means of bolts.

1 Having carefully marked the position of each post-support and the exact siting for the bolts, drill holes sufficiently deep and wide to house each bolt comfortably while allowing it to project just proud enough from the surface to take the width of the support flange and at least the full width of the retaining nuts.

2 Mix a strong mortar 3:1 ratio of sand to cement.

3 Cement the bolts into the holes with each poking through its post-support hole.

4 Allow the cement to dry completely before securing the supports by screwing nuts firmly to bolts.

5 Once the concrete has set, proceed with installing the pergola posts, taking care not to exert undue pressure on the housings.

THE PATHWAY

The width of the hard pathway should not be less than some 90cm (3ft); it would look better at 1.2-1.5m (4-5ft). Pathways may look best in a natural or natural-looking material such as York stone, or – more realistically – imitation York stone, but carefully laid pavers are a good alternative. Economy is possible by laying a paved way 90cm (3ft) wide and making good the

ERECTING UPRIGHTS FOR PERGOLAS AND SCREENS

UPRIGHTS WITH PURPOSE-MADE METAL POST-SUPPORTS

Metal post-supports come in two basic designs. The first type is basically an open metal box fixed on to a long four-flanged point for driving deep into the ground. The second is a similar open metal box but this is set on a square metal base that has been drilled with holes to take bolts. The whole thing is intended to be attached to hard surfaces, such as concrete or decking, via anchoring bolts.

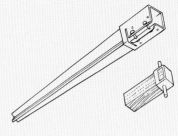

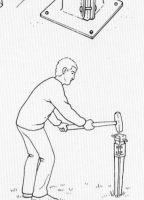

1 Make a pilot hole using a crowbar and a heavy hammer. Aim to keep your hole strictly vertical.

2 Insert the spike using a removable 'dolly' on the top to prevent damage to the support as you hammer it home.

3 Check the spike regularly with a spirit-level to ensure that it is going straight into the ground vertically.

4 Drive the spike in until the box is at ground level but ensure that the final height of each support is the same.

UPRIGHTS SET INTO CONCRETE

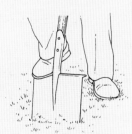

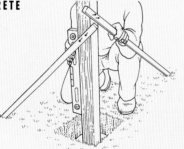

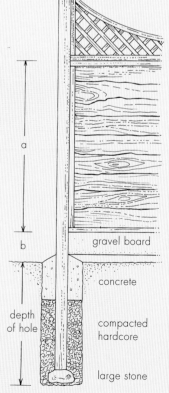

1 Dig the hole using a spade or an auger. Mechanical augers can be hired for big jobs.

2 Prop the post in the hole, check alignment and add temporary support.

3 Ram hardcore into the base of the hole and around the post, follow with concrete.

4 Trowel the concrete around the post, finishing with a slope for drainage and neatness.

The best way to erect a post for trellis or fencing is by setting it in concrete. The method is quite straightforward, the most important thing being to have a hole that is an adequate depth for the height of the post. Measure the height of the panels of trellis or fencing to be erected (a), add the height that the panel will be above ground level (b). The depth of the hole should be half of this total.
Add about 150mm (6in) if extra height is to be added (for example decorative trellis on top of a larchlap fence). Stones and hardcore should be used to fill ⅔ of the hole which is then finished off with concrete. Most do-it-yourself stores sell concrete mixtures that are suitable for use in the garden.

a

b

depth of hole

gravel board

concrete

compacted hardcore

large stone

SOME PERGOLA PLANTS

Clematis
Hedera (ivies)
Humulus (hops)
Jasminum (jasmine)
Lonicera (honeysuckles)
Parthenocissus (vines)
Rosa (roses)
Vitis (grape vines, decorative and fruiting)
Wisteria

remaining width with washed pea gravel kept in place with a line of pavers, edging stones or strong wooden boards. In every case it is necessary to strike a balance that will satisfy the demands of aesthetics, the practical use of the pathway, and the temperament of the bank manager.

PLANTS FOR PERGOLAS

The choice of what to plant on and around pergolas is very wide. Almost every climber is a candidate and some less obvious shrubs can be tied to, and trimmed around, the posts. The first consideration is whether to plant the whole pergola, and whether to use one species or cultivar or to exploit the possibilities offered by a wide selection of plants which may then make the structure colourful and interesting through the year.

There is no doubt that a pergola devoted to a single plant variety will have a sense of unity that a mixed planting misses. With little loss of unity the single choice could be converted into a double: plant a rose and there will be the temptation to add clematis. However, there are other considerations in having just one plant

type. A pergola given over to a deciduous vine, such as *Vitis cognetiae*, will look splendid in the growing season, wonderful when the plant is in autumn colour, but in the winter months could do with the backup of a series of the evergreen ivies. A single mature wisteria will be breathtaking in blossom but it will take more than a couple of seasons to grow the full length of the pergola; in the meanwhile it makes sense to have other, more quickly maturing, items to give interest.

The Covered Patio

The patio moves somewhat closer to being an outdoor room (see p.18) when pergola-like overhead beams, together with some climbing plants, are added. Before you cover the whole patio, consider how often you will need to escape from the sun: in Britain this is unlikely to be a very frequent occurrence so it may be a mistake to cover the whole patio; rain drips can be annoying! A useful compromise is to have perhaps two or three sides of the patio marked with upright posts, linked at their tops with crossbeams, at 1.5-1.8m (5-6ft) intervals. This

A country garden with a formal pergola clothed in vines that produce good crops for wine-making. Vines are decorative in leaf, and in winter the bare, twisting stems will provide an interesting contrast to the severe lines of the pergola.

The deservedly popular Clematis montana forms a useful screen and is now on its way up the adjoining wall.

TRELLIS SCREENS

Trellis screening with scrambling plants, archways, gateways, steps, curving paths and beds/borders, and partial screens formed by walls or bushes, all invite us to explore beyond to what is hidden or hinted at.

gives the opportunity to add some rafters if required, either parallel to one side or going diagonally across the corners. For an enhanced sense of privacy without blocking out too much sun, some of the space between the uprights can be filled with trellis to give extra climbing areas for plants.

Screens

There is nothing new in having screens within a garden. Screens are a less rigid, less formal way of dealing with boundaries than fences. They can also be used to mask unsightly objects or to contrive partitions within the garden itself

which can help to create the illusion of a greater space. The screens may be partially of stone, brick or solid wood. Alternatively, the artificial can be eschewed and a screen of shrubs in mixed groups can be planted and allowed to grow naturally or perhaps being kept lightly pruned.

TRELLIS

Screens can be augmented by trellis or more or less completely made out of trellis. Trellis used within a strong framework makes a pleasing screen and good support for plants. It can be invaluable for making partial blinds at right angles to main vistas. Encouraging plants to go up the partial screens will lead to the effect required – our eyes will also go up. Such screens can be effectively used not only opposite each other but staggered down the vista.

RUSTIC AND WOVEN WILLOW SCREENING

Old-fashioned rustic screening, formed of larch or other wood, with or without its bark, can play an important part in garden design. Because the material is rustic, it is sympathetic with nature and thus meets plant growth halfway, even if it is used in formal shapes.

Rustic screening must be as securely erected as any other artifact. Use pieces that are at least 10cm (4in) in diameter; spindly poles do not even begin to look effective. Prefabricated units made of larch poles are widely sold. They are about 1.8m (6ft) high by either 90cm (3ft) or 1.8m (6ft) long. Before erection they should be thoroughly treated with preservative to give them a reasonable lifespan. It is advisable to install them in concrete: although they offer little in the way of wind resistance themselves, when clothed with plants they will be under

Trellis lends support and a sense of form to the successful screening produced by roses 'Galway Bay' and 'Clair Matin' accompanied by honeysuckle. Violets run along the border below.

considerable stress and need to be securely anchored. For this reason it is far safer to plan them in a curve or with some right angles to provide greater stability. One straight line will be like a huge sail against the wind, as were the fences mentioned on pp.45-46.

Recently there has been a vogue for woven willow screening. The benefit of this is that it contributes to and maintains the natural feel of a garden. It will also often last until shrubs and other plants get established and can provide their own shelter. Willow screens are not cheap to buy, and to make them you need plenty of willow wands and plenty of patience. On the whole they look best as units not more than some 90-120cm (3-4ft) high.

FORMAL SCREENS

Rustic pole work or woven willow obviously look ideal in a cottage-type garden. In more formal surroundings they may be incongruous. Where formality rules, machined-wood screens will look much better. They could even be erected with a brick or stone base and pillars. A suitable colour paint will finish the effect.

Prefabricated units are a popular and satisfying solution. Usually the uprights – the posts – are of 10 × 10cm (4 × 4in) timber and can be 2.7m or 2.1m (9 or 7ft) high. They are sunk into the ground in concrete or slotted into metal bases to give them added rigidity and a longer life (see Pergolas, pp.52-58), for how to construct the bases). The rafters or cross beams are normally narrower, 10 × 5cm (4 × 2in), and may have decorated and shaped ends. The cross beams may be notched to allow the rafters to fit into them. Rafters and crossbeams come in a variety of lengths.

A very successful climbing plant is the golden hop, Humulus lupulus 'Aureus', here running up some trellis. It dies down for the winter but sprints into growth with the spring – its vigour amazes as surely as its limy shades please.

QUALITY OF PLANTS PURCHASED

When buying direct from good garden centres or specialist nurseries you can see what you are purchasing. Avoid plants that seem to have been living in their containers a very long time and are hopelessly root-bound. Although the quality of plants at garden centres varies considerably the standard of most reputable centres is good.

Take care with mail order. Special offers advertised in the national press can be disappointing but most specialist nurseries who work by mail order depend on repeat orders, and their reputation is important to them so they will be unlikely to send second-rate stock.

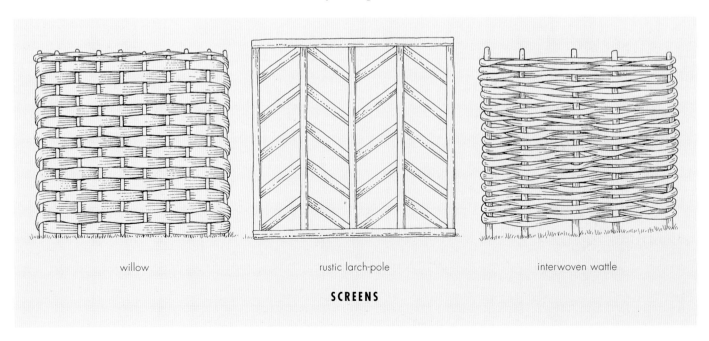

willow   rustic larch-pole   interwoven wattle

SCREENS

Framed trellis that is made in modules to use with the main structure sizes can be square or rectangular, but may have one side curved into a concave or convex line. There are plenty of other shapes, too – it is like man-size pieces of a child's construction toy. Remember your Meccano set!

GROWING SCREENS

Tall hedges can act as screens, but this role is often better played by groups of shrubs. The variation of leaf colour, flowers, habit and character of the actors is more interesting and the eye will be attracted from one to another as the months pass. The varied heights, positions and forms of a good mix of shrubs will tend to retain interest for longer than a hedge whose primary aim is, after all, to create a boundary and form a psychological as well as a physical barrier to whatever is being disguised. And screens are less work than hedges!

If the planting is not only cosmetic but also to form a windbreak it is likely to be more successful if the aim is to filter by degrees, rather than block entirely. A screen may be effective if only a metre deep but it can be made much deeper and this would allow for a range of herbaceous plants, shrubs and trees – from a low foreground, sloping up into the sky. Over this

ARBOUR

A secluded arbour provides a focal point.

train climbers such as *Clematis montana*, which will clamber up to the topmost reaches of high trees – 6-12m (20-40ft) or more.

Arbours

A major theme of most gardens is, or perhaps should be, a sense of peace and quiet. It is easy to imagine how the old-fashioned arbour could be an ideal way of boosting this atmosphere. It provides a haven, a proper place to sit, rest and

The energetic spreading and lolling Ceanothus thysiflorus *var.* repens *monopolizes a bench at Wolfson College, Oxford. Perhaps everyone there is too busy to sit but, hopefully, they can pause to admire the generous display.*

63

more effective if lesser side pieces of trellis with shorter supports were added to each side adding to the overall width of the arbour. The trellis used to fill in the arbour sides should be substantial. The closer the mesh, the greater the shelter from wind and, with plant growth over it, there could be a favoured microclimate inside for you to enjoy.

Gazebos

With a gazebo the architectural stakes take a jump forward. Not quite a summer house, a gazebo is still a piece of architecture, well beyond the somewhat casual construction that is an arbour. Like the arbour, it will be a focal point and will need to be well-sited and bear close examination.

Again, like the pergolas and arbours, prefabricated units are available. A unit that would make a reasonable gazebo consists of six sides, each 1.8m (6ft) in width.

A mini-gazebo or an arbour acts as a frame, giving height to an Egyptian vase planted with sempervivums and providing a shoulder for the rose 'Handel' to lean against.

contemplate, as well as being a focal point, up which plants can be grown, and probably working in well with any plans to form secluded corners in the garden. My feeling is that an arbour is pointless unless sensible seating is provided – it may be rustic but it ought to be trustworthy and reasonably comfortable.

Although size and depth depend on the scale of the garden and personal desires, the seating should be sufficient for two people to sit comfortably. As with the other structures mentioned so far, using prefabricated units makes life easier and they are readily available in a range of sizes.

This attractive and brightly coloured gazebo would fit well into many a garden scheme.

You can work a shallow arbour into the rest of the garden design. It is perhaps best fitted in with other woodwork that is nearby; by itself it may look gaunt and would then be

Posts, Tripods and Arches

Single posts can be placed strategically in the borders to support plants such as rambling roses. These need to be securely fixed as described for pergola supports (pp.52-58). Once they are holding the considerable growth of some roses, they will be subject to strain in high winds.

Plants of lesser stature or muscle can be trained up tripods. At their simplest these can be formed from three strong bean sticks or canes. Somewhat more elaborate and permanent tripods designed of willow can be made or purchased. Any of these will happily give the upward help needed for sweet peas and similar plants. A word of warning: don't underestimate ornamental gourds. These can be very robust and eventually produce a considerable weight of fruit. If you are going to amuse yourself in training them upwards, make sure that the support matches their strength. We have had branches

A substantial metal gazebo adds formality to the knot garden at Bourton House in the Cotswolds, making a vertical contrast to the low horizontal patterns of the knot garden.

broken from shrubs and trees by rampant gourds.

Decorative tripods or four-sided units rising to a point can be bought or made. The framework is usually constructed from timber 4-5cm (1½-2in) square and latticework is used to fill the spaces in between, being attached behind the uprights. The taller the support is, the stronger the timber used to make it needs to be. The uprights have 30cm (12in) clear of lattice work at their bases so that these can be pushed into the ground and firmed in.

ARCHES

In our garden rustic screens are made from poles that are approximately 10cm (4in) diameter. Some were purchased as prefabricated units 1.8m (6ft) square with the top 1.2m (4ft) criss-crossed with split timbers. Taller units – 2.1m and 2.4m (7ft and 8ft) high – are available. These units can be linked in groups by running single poles some 1.8m (6ft) long between their

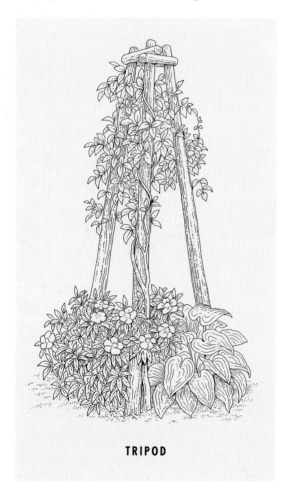

TRIPOD

Simple arches justifying themselves splendidly with a selection of rose cultivars, the whole being given extra point and formality by the precise pebble path flanked by low lavender hedges.

tops. This allows some extra flexibility for the type of shrubs that can be grown and creates simple archways. Make sure that they are wide enough to allow through machinery such as sit-on mowers. So-called 'rose arches', of similar rustic wood as the screens, can also be purchased in units to be assembled at home. The ones we use are 2.4m (8ft) high, 1.2m (4ft) wide and 70cm (28in) deep once completed.

An even less elaborate semi-screen can be erected using a series of single posts up to a height of around 2.4m (8ft) and linking them with chain or rope in loose loops. It is possible to train some extrovert and acrobatic plants to reach along these loops with a little help. Roses with stretching stems may be encouraged informally sideways and, once these get going, clematis can follow.

A simple and effective rustic wooden pole arch supports the rose 'Climbing Iceberg' in true cottage-garden style.

An archway made of willow is the happy climbing frame for runner beans and courgettes. Beauty and utility married in fruitful harmony.

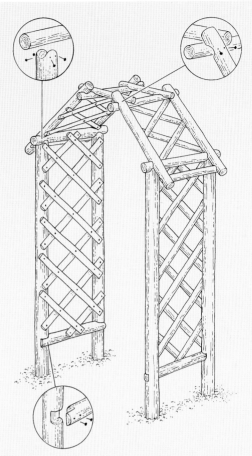

MAKING A RUSTIC ARCH

You can buy rustic poles from most wood yards. Some will strip off the bark and run a saw down two sides to give straight surfaces. Wood yards also supply poles split down the centre to produce a half-sphere cross-section. These are useful for the decorative interior supports.

Make the arch in five parts: two sides, two sloping tops and a centre roof. Join all pieces together at the site. Allow enough length for inserting the uprights into the ground. They are probably best put into metal housings or secured with concrete.

First make the two sides using the full-sized poles with one straightened edge facing inwards. Add the decorative criss-cross pattern using the split-pole wood, with the flat surfaces facing inwards. Remember to allow an overlap for the two sloping parts and cut the ends where they will meet the top to an appropriate angle, the interior angle span being something in the region of 135°. Simple joints can be made, as shown, for additional stability and neatness, or simply use nails. Drill pilot holes in appropriate places for the nails.

CARPORTS

Very clearly the first job of the carport is to protect the car. To encroach on its structure may enhance its appearance, but must be done with some care since it would not do to add to the amount of detritus dropped on the vehicle. Although you should be safe with climbers such as *Vitis coignetiae*, fruiting vines are more likely to be problematical – in fruit they attract birds and insect life and this will lead to juice spillage, either directly or via the birds' digestive systems. Roses can be attractive, provided the thorns can be kept clear of both driver and vehicle; fallen petals over the car may or may not add to the image you are aiming for.

SUPPORT CONSIDERATIONS

Now the walls and fences are in place, it is time to provide the plants with some practical assistance in their never-ending task of decoration. Decent support is almost as important as well-prepared soil.

Among the plants that are usually grown up and against walls and other structures, the self-clingers are vastly outnumbered by twining and scrambling plants that will need help in their climbing ambitions.

Temporary Support

There are very many shrubs that grow well by fences and walls. Some of these are lax in growth when young but most gain rigidity with age as leading stems thicken to form backbone or the pattern of branches becomes so dense that a sort of co-operative endeavour keeps them upright. Such shrubs will, therefore, require help in their early years but after this should be able to cope on their own. A single, strong stake may suffice for each; more diffuse growth can be helped by placing three posts in a triangle around the plant and then encircling the structure with wire, string or netting.

Permanent Support

Permanent or semi-permanent supports need to be pleasing to behold, or virtually invisible, as well as practically efficient. A series of wires stretched on a wall can be almost lost to the eye, especially when running parallel to the brick or mortar courses. Larger-scale wall supports need to complement the wall and its other fittings, such as drainpipes, windows, and so on, so that they enhance rather than detract from the façade. Usually, it is the bolder trellis-type arrangements that are most visually successful; the lightweight rather spindly affairs look temporary and will probably prove so.

Any supports, hooks or other plant holders that are added to a wall should be fastened with care. Far better to err on the side of security than run the danger of underestimating the loads and stresses likely to occur. What may seem sufficient when first fixing an arrangement like a hanging basket, window box or trellis can become woefully inadequate as conditions change. A hanging basket increases to many times its original weight as plants grow; add to this the effects of being rain-sodden and blown by a strong wind, and the stresses on its attachment point increase dramatically. The same applies to window boxes. It is easy to envisage serious accidents if these installations should slip their moorings. Trellises to which fully grown, clambering plants are attached offer any wind a real opportunity; like those trellis constructions in the middle of the garden, they can behave like the sails of an ocean-going yacht. It is best to be safe, assume maximum

VALUE ADDED

When making a choice of shrubs, trees and other plants, consider their everyday appearance in form, habit and leaf cover as well as the flowering effects. Then consider all seasons of the year and give extra points to those that have other festive times. Many will have attractive seedheads, interesting bark, fruits or autumn colours.

Left: the vivid blue flowers of Ceanothus impressus *are beautifully set off by the red brick wall behind.*

Right: Clematis 'Perle d'Azure' covers the wall with the discrete help of a section of plastic netting. Below are Sedum spectabile *and* Phlox *'Starfire'.*

gales, heaviest snowfalls, monsoons and acts of God, and add some extra safeguard with proper sized nails, screws or other support.

Masonry and Special Nails

Specially hardened masonry nails can be driven into walls to give secure tying points to hold plants like climbing or rambling roses that do not need a complete system of stretched wires. Consider using special masonry nails which are particularly strong and can be driven home into most surfaces, leaving only the head a little proud so that wire or other tags can be bound around and used to hold plant material. All nails are only as good as the material they are hammered into: crumbly mortar will secure nothing. Vine nails are not so readily available but can still be purchased. These are very discrete and it is possible to buy them with soft

metal flanges attached to the heads. Once the nail is hammered in place, the flange can be curled around the stem that needs supporting.

Wire Supports

Running lengths of wire between screw eyes is one of the easiest ways of providing a lasting and secure climbing frame for wall- or fence-mounted plants. Wire is usually stretched horizontally at intervals of 25-30cm (10-12in). Wire of 2mm (1/16in) calibre is normally adequate. The completed horizontal wire runs are held a couple of centimetres or so from the surface of the wall and are perfectly adequate for tying-in most climbers; however, there may be some that will be helped by vertical wires. Such verticals can be arranged by fixing wire to the lowest run and then running it around each of the upper wires. The vertical should not be loose, but

SHRUBS HELPED BY EARLY SUPPORT

Abeliophyllum distichum
Buddleja alternifolia
Chimonanthus praecox
(wintersweet)
Chaenomeles (japonica)
cultivars
x Fatshedera lizei
Garrya elliptica

The straight lines of this path are emphasized by the neat curbs of box hedging, the white 'Angelique' tulips, marshalled into formal lines, and the neat, painted fence. The double-flowered wisteria (W. floribunda 'Violacea Plena', also sold as 'Double Black Dragon' and 'Yac Kokyuryu') brings a touch of magic to the whole with its switch towards the vertical dimension.

SUPPORTS FOR PLANTS AND WIRES

on irregular surfaces such as stone.

6   Install rawlplugs and eyes as before.

7   Secure wire to an end metal eye by making a loop through the eye and then tightly twisting the shorter wire length and the longer wire length together to give at least 2.5cm (1in) tightly coiled.

8   Play out and cut enough wire to stretch the length of the total run. Allow at least 30cm (12in) extra to use when tensioning the wire and for winding it back on itself at the far end.

This striking display has been made by containers with Clematis sieboldii, Fuchsia *'Checkerboard' and* Pelargonium *'Lord Bute'.*

there is no need for tension. Intervals for vertical wires are dependent on plants to be secured but are likely to be 60cm-1m (2-3ft).

The wire support system described here is designed to be permanent. If there is going to be a need to detach them from the walls, you can adopt a variation of the method suggested below for removable trellis. A strong metal or wooden framework would have to be attached to battens on the walls by a series of screws or bolts that can be undone when necessary.

1   Having decided on the length and height of wall to be used, mark the end points of each wire run with pencil or chalk and using a spirit-level if necessary so that they are neatly horizontal and each coincides with good brick or stone or sound mortar.

2   Drill holes with a 6mm (¼in), or more, drill bit to accommodate rawlplugs.

3   Push in the rawlplugs then screw in strong metal screw-eyes, the eyes of which are not less than 1cm (½in) diameter. Vine eyes could be used. Screw one set of eyes in a vertical line at one end of the run.

4   Repeat steps 1 to 3 at the other end of the run, having double checked that the prospective holes are at the same level as completed ones. A string tied around the lowest installed eye can be stretched and temporarily fixed at the other end while checking the level with a spirit level. Alternatively you can trust your eye or the brick course levels.

5   Mark similar sets of holes at equal intervals between the two end sets, around 1m (3ft) apart. Taut string that is stretched between the two end sets will help to indicate where the holes should be made when you are working

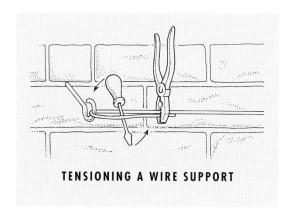

TENSIONING A WIRE SUPPORT

9   On a short run, of say 2-2.5m (6-8ft), there will be only three eyes to a run. Feed the wire through the central eye and then tension it by pulling it tight, creating an end loop and inserting a metal rod (a screw driver will do) between the two wires of the loop. Clamp the end of the wire and the main wire of the loop with a pair of pliers and twist the metal rod around until the wire is really taut. For longer runs of wire it is easier to use a small tensioning unit available from DIY stores and specifically made for the purpose.

Netting Supports

Plastic netting can be used as an alternative to wiring a wall or fence. Netting is available in several forms ranging from the very lightweight, used for protecting vegetables and bush fruit from less determined forms of bird life, to heavy, almost rigid, products with 5cm (2in) squares and normally coloured either dark green or brown.

Lightweight netting may be useful as a temporary encouragment for young climbers that, once they have got going, will be able to manage to grip without aid. It can enable clematis and other climbers to get quickly into the branches of trees or shrubs.

The heavier grade netting can be wrapped around the uprights of pergolas to support climbers. It does this job well and looks neat and unobtrusive. Stretched on a frame of wooden battens, it could be used as screening or fixed to walls. A useful and versatile product, it can be an easier alternative to wall wiring and is almost as long lasting. Also in its favour is that

it looks considerably more pleasing than the chicken wire or chain-link fencing that is often used in similar roles.

Trellis

It is usually more economical to use prefabricated trellis, already treated with wood preservative, than to make your own, although there may be some awkward spots that will have to have it custom-built. The usual offerings in garden centres and do-it-yourself stores are either lightweight – in wood or plastic – or heavy.

The lightweight range is in a compact form and pulls out concertina-wise to form a fretwork

That splendid old-timer Clematis 'Nelly Moser' in company with a rose ably supported on a wall by concertina trellis.

that is usually used as a diamond pattern. The lightweight wooden trellis cannot normally be expected to have a long lifespan but can last surprisingly well if used as the filling in a strong calibre framework to which it is securely attached, preferably by strong wire staples rather than nails, which tend to split the wood. Treatment with wood preservative will also extend its life. The similar product made out of plastic and usually coloured white may have a somewhat longer life but has little else to recommend it in place of the more natural-looking wooden article.

The heavyweight wooden trellises are usually made of 2.5cm (1in) square timber, arranged in a 15cm (6in) grid. It looks smart and is long lasting; longer life may be encouraged by judicious strengthening of the whole with 4-5cm (1½-2in) nails to back up the wire staples that are fired in by the manufacturers.

While trellis can be directly fixed to walls, it is usually much better to attach strong vertical battens to the wall first, using substantial rawlplugs and screws, and then to fix the trellis to the battens. The extra couple of centimetres or so that the trellis is held away from the wall

In sunless sites a wall can be made decorative by the imaginative use of trellis, here given extra theatrical atmosphere by the use of large terracotta urns planted with variegated ivy and shapely conifers.

HANGING PLANTS

Perennials
Hedera (ivies)
Parthenocissus
(Virginia creeper)
Vitis (grape vines)
Lysimachia nummularia
(creeping Jenny)
Vinca major (periwinkle)

Annuals and Half-hardy Plants
Thunbergia alata
(black-eyed Susan)
Tropaeolum majus (nasturtium)
Pelagonium, trailing ones
(geranium)
Lobelia, trailing varieties
Petunia, trailing varieties

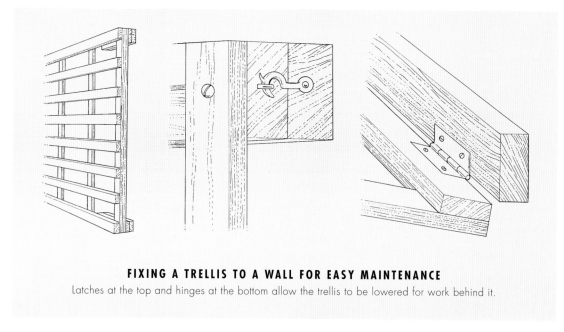

FIXING A TRELLIS TO A WALL FOR EASY MAINTENANCE
Latches at the top and hinges at the bottom allow the trellis to be lowered for work behind it.

English public houses often boast fine displays of hanging baskets and containers. This one in the West Midlands is a good example.

will provide more bird-friendly nesting sites. I recommend strong brass screws for the job. They do not rust and can be used repeatedly, especially if care is taken not to burr the screw top. A refinement is the use of hinges along the bottom edge of the trellis. Once the upper screws are released, the trellis and plants can be carefully leant away from the wall, which will be a great help in the future if work on the wall is necessary. The time for doing any such work is autumn and winter, so as to be outside the breeding seasons of birds and when the plants are less lively.

Ties

Most clambering, scrambling and leaning shrubs can be tied-in to trellis, wires or other supports with plastic- or paper-covered wire, which may be bought as cut lengths or in coils. Both these are very inconspicuous – not something that can be said of the farmer's 'friend', orange plastic baling twine. Major branches deserve the type of plastic ties that are used for holding young trees to their attendant posts.

MAINTENANCE

If initial installation is carefully done and the materials are treated to give them long life, the amount of maintenance on any of the supports described above will be minimal. It is worth checking ties of important plants after exceptional gales and it is prudent to make sure that all seasonal installations, such as the brackets for hanging baskets, are rigorously checked before reuse.

HANGING BASKETS AND WINDOW BOXES

Hanging baskets and window boxes are a way of enhancing a wall or fence and have the benefit that they can be changed through the season to provide all-year round display, or in the case of window boxes, if they are large enough, they can make a permanent feature. The larger the basket or box, the more effective it is likely to be in terms of display, the greater the opportunities it will offer in terms of impact and the easier the plants within it will be to maintain.

Hanging baskets can be secured to walls with brackets; they could also be hung over hooks screwed into overhead structures such as pergolas. Obviously, such hooks must be strong and should be screwed into the vertical sides of strong wooden beams some centimetres from the lower edge or, even better still, into the centre of the upper horizontal sides of such beams. Alternatively, you could secure some wire/chain around the beam and attach the basket to that. Do not, in an absent-minded moment, just screw the hook into the underneath horizontal surface – any such screw will pull out under the increasing weight.

With window boxes, again, the first concern must be safety: all containers much be anchored without a chance to slip. Many window sills and balconies have a slight slope so any window boxes can be supported underneath to keep them level if necessary. There should be two or three anchor points, not just a single one.

A wooden window box will be easier to keep attractive if it has a plastic or metal box inside it that is used as the container. It can then be maintained more easily, simply by removing the inner box. This also allows you to plant up a second or even a third series of 'lining' boxes that can be grown on elsewhere and then placed in succession in the wooden box as they reach their peak. Another advantage is that the means used to secure its position can be checked more efficiently.

Watering

Always consider watering when positioning baskets and windowboxes. Low ones can be kept moist with a watering can. Higher ones will need steps, a long lance on a hose pipe or a pulley system. Sometimes it makes sense to incorporate a plastic tube (such as the sliced off top of a plastic bottle) in the basket when making it up so that water can enter a temporary reservoir and then permeate the compost. Where there is going to be a considerable number of baskets or window boxes it is best to install an automatic watering system.

Naturally, preparing the baskets and window boxes well in the first place is going to be the most important factor: a punctured plastic lining will help hold water but allow some drainage and the compost should be water-retentive. Water-retention is enhanced by gels that soak up water which is then gradually made available to the plants. I am a little chary of giving a whole-hearted endorsement to them as, in my own domestic tests, I was uncertain that they really increased the performance of our baskets. The compost used should contain plenty of humusy material to help retain moisture; this will also help to maintain the desirable airy, open structure.

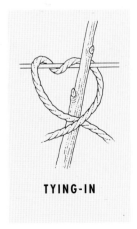

TYING-IN

Left: hanging baskets and other containers creating the often-cited 'riot of colour'.

PLANTING & CULTIVATION

Let us be bold – assault walls and fences with leaves and flowers, embrace them with plant growth. Then, not yet content, let us festoon pergolas and drape arbours with all manner of climbers and twiners.

With appropriate plants and sensible planting, there need be no huge problems for plants near walls or fences. Most troubles are going to arise from lack of water, something that will be aggravated by heat on walls that face the sun. The soil below more shady walls can also become very dry. However, all around the house is a potential drought zone as the foundations and lower walls of the house can leach some of the moisture and sensible builders may have made some effort to take water away from the house so that there is less danger of rising damp and associated troubles. (Incidentally, do be sceptical of

the advice tendered by 'experts' on rising damp when they are using meters that offer readings with a movable pointer. The measurement this type of meter indicates is the conductivity of electricity and nothing else. True, the presence of water will increase conductivity but, nowadays, house walls very rarely suffer from any excess moisture in the form of rising damp.) Builder's rubble and rubbish in the soil may also make the area dry. The closer the plant is to the wall, the more likely are its growing problems. As elsewhere a healthy plant starts with a huge advantage in resisting diseases and other nuisances.

A sunny fence can help trap and reflect heat as will other erections but not on the same scale as the walls. However, a fence facing the direction of the predominant rain-bearing winds may produce a minor rain-shadow on its lee side, a strip of ground noticeably less watered than elsewhere. The taller and more solid the fence, the more clearly defined this drier area may be.

The temperature of soil in beds in front of walls that face the sun can rise in summer months to levels that inhibit growth and this, in tandem with the lack of water, will be disastrous for plants particularly vulnerable to such stresses. On the other hand, a curb on growth may be a good thing: once the spring rush of sap has resulted in fresh wood, the rationing of moisture will help to programme the plant to provide a higher ratio of flower to growth buds than would have been the case otherwise, and the wood will start its ripening process earlier.

While soil close to buildings is often very dry for long periods, it will occasionally get flooded by persistent heavy rain that drives against the

Right: a brick wall, steps and a gravel path provide a strong framework for the upwardly mobile Clematis 'Jackmanii' and a mass of herbaceous endeavour, including phlox and white Chrysanthemum maximum.

Left: the largest-leaved vine Vitis coignetiae, in its autumn finery; the colour of its dress changes from day to day.

walls and runs down. Many plants are adapted to such conditions: part of their root systems can quickly change from apparently inert tissue to active working units that can make use of the sudden bounty. *Iris unguicularis* is one such that is happy close to a sunny wall where it can be very dry, though a newly planted specimen will need extra watering until fully established – as will most new wall plants.

In wet districts and especially in moisture-retentive soils, extra care is needed to ensure that any surplus water drains away from house walls and that the damp course is not broached. In very wet areas it might be worth considering adding drainage to any planting. Trenches may be dug near the house; they can be half filled with rough rubble that is covered with plastic netting before being topped up with soil. The bottom of such trenches should slope gently away from the house. However, it is very few houses that are in such threatened, sodden sites. Most of us will have to work to encourage water retention by soil that is near buildings. Generous amounts of organic matter need to be incorporated, perhaps excavating the original to allow a balance of a third or a half by volume of humus, the remaining being grit and loam. (Rotted turf may be used as the equivalent of loam.) When these new ingredients are thoroughly mixed, the whole can be allowed to settle. Then it may need topping up to bring it to the original level. The surface can be given a thorough mulch to trap the moisture – 7-10cm (3-4in) of shredded bark will do a good job; alternatives are well-rotted compost, cocoa shells or an inert layer of gravel/rock chips. This mulching is important but may be delayed if a full-scale planting plan is about to be carried out. Once this is completed the whole can be tidied and the mulch put on as a bed cover.

*Boston ivy,
Parthenocissus
tricuspidata, growing
up walls at Dinmoor
Manor, an attractive
building and garden in the
wide countryside not far
from Leominster,
Herefordshire. The
climber looks almost as
venerable as the building.*

PROBLEMS FOR THE HOUSE?

Normally, as has been mentioned in earlier chapters, wall plants will help to keep the house warm and dry. There is now less worry about walls clad in ivy or other creepers: they do far more good than harm – if they do any harm at all! However, one should be careful not to allow soil to ride high against the wall so that it broaches the damp course, something that could be masked by plant growth.

Strong growing climbers such as Virginia creeper and its relatives, as well as ivies and clematis, can grow over the window frames and into the gutters remarkably rapidly. One must be vigilant and try to maintain a zone that is free of growth around such spots – at least 10-20cm (4-8in) is appropriate. Be ahead of the game. We take a Stanley knife across the line of our *cordon sanitaire* a few times in the year. It almost takes more time getting the ladder out and moved than the job itself, but if the gutters are reached by the creepers the job becomes much more involved. After leaf-fall it is worth checking gutters and downpipes for loose leaves and debris.

Ceanothus and other shrubs can seem determined to encroach on window space. It is wise to have such dense and fast growers some distance from windows. They can be kept in order with a power trimmer or shears.

Where there are wide areas of wooden-boarded walls which need periodic painting, avoid planting self-clingers, which will ruin the surface with their aerial roots or suction pads. Obviously the same applies to rough-cast walls that need regular repainting. Perhaps, for the latter, you could take the decision to forgo the painting and allow for permanent all-over cover of plant growth – one less job to be done.

Even allowing for the beauty of the functional and an eye for abstract forms of art, the aesthetic appeal of most downpipes and other items of outdoor plumbing is strictly limited and it seems a good idea to mask them. In this it is prudent to plan carefully in order to limit the amount of dead foliage and debris that will get deposited in the guttering and impede the work of the fall pipes. The latter must not be allowed to be sabotaged by branches going behind them; in youth these look thin and innocent but quickly thicken out and loutishly elbow the fall pipes out of alignment and free of the wall.

Planting Plans

Here are a few guidelines on planting a wall or fence:

✻ Decide how much of the wall you want to cover. Is it sensible to grow right up to the guttering? Is there going to be a mix of self-clinging kinds and those that will need some support?

✻ Make a short list of evergreen and deciduous climbers. Select those that you think will be compatible and can hold their own in competition, or can be easily kept in order. *Jasminum nudiflorum* will grow in among other things such as the climbing *Hydrangea petiolaris*.

✻ Try to include one or more small trees if at all possible. The smallest garden can include one tree, even if it has to be in a large container.

✻ Choose one or two character climbing or rambling plants for each of the main walls. These are likely to be flowering kinds such as wisterias, roses and honeysuckles.

✻ Have a shortlist of auxiliary climbers and other plants that will make a show while more formidable characters grow into their role. Such things as the climbing nasturtium, *Tropaeolum peregrinum*, the Canary creeper, or *Cobaea scandens*, the cup and saucer plant, will be useful, decorative and interesting.

✻ Make a list of the shrubs that you would most enjoy near each of the walls. Do not forget to include some of the ones that will look well in the winter.

✻ Include one or two shrubs that you may have felt are of questionable hardiness but unquestionable interest. They can be very rewarding and worth a slight gamble. Among climbers, consider the evergreen *Stauntonia hexaphylla* with its handsome pinnate foliage and refined flowers. From free-standing shrubs choose some of the South American kinds, not just *Choisya ternata*, which has proved its hardiness and value, but the lantern tree, *Crinodendron hookerianum*, with its dark, evergreen cloud of foliage and fleshy red flowers.

✻ Between the shrubs, and benefiting from the walls, one must include the bulbs, particularly those that will flower during the winter months.

Left: when in full bloom, wisteria must be the most wonderful of climbers, as it is here in perfect contrast with the brick walls. It may look as old as time but wisterias grow quickly and after a handful of years will be blooming freely.

Right: huddling together in wintertime on a wall is the very popular duo, the winter jasmine, Jasminum nudiflorum, and Cotoneaster horizontalis.

SMALL TREES

Trees are needed for height and for atmosphere. In restricted spaces any oversized tree is going to be a continual embarrassment. Some small but proper tree-shaped trees include:

Acer palmatum – shrub sized for many years but when it acquires tree status it is very lovely.

Aralia elata – strong growing with fine foliage, particularly the variegated forms.

Eucalyptus paucifolia subsp. *niphophila* – fine evergreen foliage and interesting bark.

Eucryphia all.

Malus sargentii and other ornamental apples such as 'Red Sentinel'.

Prunus × *subhirtella* 'Autumnalis'.

Rhus typhina, Sorbus forrestii, Sorbus vilmorinii.

Planting and Aftercare

The first decision to take is how close to position climbers and scramblers to the object – wall, fence, tree – up which they are to grow. Some old-established roses look as it they must have been installed with the stock jammed against the support. This is probably a deception, the base of the plant having matured and thickened to achieve such tight juxtaposition. While we want our plants to grow upwards, this is best done by planting them 30-38cm (12-15in) from the wall or 1m (3ft) or more from a large tree. Any closer and the ground is likely to be desert dry a lot of the time. It is possible to plant closer to most fences, posts or pergolas, where artificial drought is unlikely.

The first season or two are usually the most critical ones in any perennial's life. Newly planted items have to get their toes into the new soil and establish an extensive root system to support the top growth with liquid nourishment. Keeping these specimens supplied with adequate water is even more important against a wall than in the open, the site being likely to be much drier and to lose any dampness quicker. Root systems near walls often have to be particularly wide and deep ranging; the catchment area for moisture has to be extensive because of the comparative scarcity of water. Do not stint on the initial watering: it takes huge amounts of liquid to saturate a relatively small volume of soil.

Top growth of plants whose original home is a warmer foreign clime can be a touch tender and they are more vulnerable in their youth, particularly to wind and cold.

Neighbouring plants may give some shelter and protection. The walls and other structures will help, but in time of intense cold, garden fleece will help insulate the vulnerable tissue. In areas subject to severe cold and strong winds young plants can be cocooned in jute sacking or plastic netting until more clement weather returns. Sheets of plastic are less safe. They may

A shrubby ensemble with taller shrubs sheltering lower ones. On the right is the winter-flowering cornel Cornus mas, *which is capable of making a considerable tree, in the centre is the large-leaved* Vitis coignetiae, *to the left is a form of* Hydrangea hortensis, *and below is the creeping St John's wort,* Hypericum calycinum.

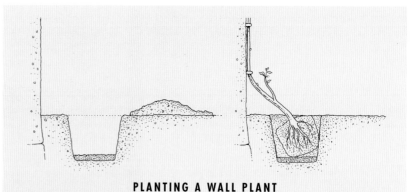

PLANTING A WALL PLANT

1 Make a generous-sized hole in well-dug soil that has been enriched with plenty of humus. Turn the well-watered young climber out of its pot and place it in the hole so that the main stem leads more or less directly to the wall or fence to be climbed and the roots point away from it in as wide an arc as possible.

2 Return good soil around the plant and firm it in so that when finished the plant sits in the soil at the same level as it did in the pot. If it is a clematis the original plant soil level should be some 10–15cm (4–6in) below the planted level – a stratagem that gives it some defence against clematis wilt.

The Requirements of Different Plants

TRAINING

All self-clingers are best led to the wall from at least 22cm (9in) away and then fixed to the surface so that the stem makes firm contact with it. Sometimes this can be done with adhesive tape, while at other times one may be reduced to leaning bulks of timber against the fledgling climber. Not only does this help the plant to secure itself to the surface with fresh aerial roots or suckers, but, having got this fingerhold, the plant seems to gain in confidence and exhibits this by immediately bursting into growth.

Clematis montana var. rubens gets everywhere. Here it is clambering irreverently over an unusual modern copper archway in a San Franciscan garden designed by Keeyla Meadows. Larger-flowered Clematis 'Ernest Markham' is also beginning to reach upwards.

add stress by being blown hard by winds and, inside, fungus and other diseases and pests can be encouraged if the wrapping remains in place for an extended time.

Wind can accelerate the rate of transpiration and in dry cold weather, especially when temperatures are below freezing, the loss of water from the foliage can be faster than replacement liquid can be brought up from the roots. The detrimental effect of such conditions is occasionally starkly illustrated by hedges of conifers left looking severely burnt on the windward side. Judicious planting can ensure that one shrub will help shelter a neighbour and as plants get bigger, the outer parts will shelter inner ones of the same plant and later the outer parts can be pruned away. Even shrubs apparently badly damaged can make a quick recovery when growth restarts.

Upwardly mobile plants usually need something to lean on or cling to; *Cotoneaster horizontalis* will get its back against a wall and edge its way up layer by layer. Winter jasmine (*Jasminum nudiflorum*) and forsythia (*Forsythia suspensa*) will be most effective with a full-scale trellis or wire support system. Clematis and such need something to wind leaf-stems or tendrils around.

Wall roses can often give their best results if main branches are brought down closer to the horizontal each year-end. This encourages fresh growth from lower down the branches, reducing the lengths of bare stem, and it also stimulates flowering. The procedure may be easier done in stages to allow the plant some time to accommodate the new position, which will initially cause some strain.

Rampant growers are going to be a constant nuisance unless they are given a suitable spot with ample room for development without the need for constant curbing. Restricted height below a window may be suitable for shrubs such as the quinces *Chaenomeles speciosa* 'Simonii' and *C.* × *superba* 'Crimson and Gold' which rarely want to get above 1m (3ft) but will go at least twice as wide. While these would not normally be thought 'rampant' growers, they can grow steadily and like most quinces are amenable to a regular pruning programme. They will bloom more prolifically if kept quite close to a wall. These and other wall shrubs that need repeated pruning, such as close-clipped pyracanthas, ceanothus or euonymus forms, need to be accessible so it is sensible not to make life too difficult by planting strong dense shrubs in front of them.

SITE PREFERENCES

The somewhat more tender shrubs and plants will benefit from some frost protection and will be better on sunny walls than the cold, shady ones. Camellias may be perfectly hardy but their flowers, like those of magnolias, are not proof against frost. The blossom is best sheltered by nearby walls and shrubs; if lightly touched by frost the flowers and buds stand a better chance

of survival if they are allowed to warm up gently somewhere out of the early morning sun. The warmth of walls will greatly benefit slightly less hardy shrubs; they will show their appreciation by ripening their wood, maintaining their health and flowering well. Frost-tender, quick, jack-in-the-box annuals have to be kept potted up under glass until the chances of a frost are no longer likely; against a warm wall they can be given temporary protection if a particularly late frost threatens after they have been planted out – even a sheet of newspaper will do a lot to help.

Cultivation Considerations

Plant health is best looked at as a whole. We want each plant to be growing so that it is capable of its maximum beneficial effect. While in youth, this will mean putting on more growth and forming a good framework for its future life; as it matures, the rate of growth should slow down and the efforts of the plant should be directed towards flowering and fruiting display as well as continuing to provide a healthy cover of foliage. The regime to promote youthful growth differs a little from that for adulthood. Higher nitrogen content in the soil aids early effort; later potassium (potash) will promote flower production, fruiting, leaf colour, wood ripening and general health.

Most of the plants mentioned in this book are going to live out their lives on walls, fences or other structures, or so close by such constructions as to be under the influence of them.

Walls

With walls, important effects on plant growth and health are derived from the ability of bricks and other building materials to store and reflect heat; the soil temperature and its moisture content are the other two main influences on plant growth. Provided some attention is paid to avoiding the worst extremes – by directing water to very dry areas when necessary – then the plants respond to the wall's influences in

With a background of high trees, this wall is almost lost behind clambering and upward-thrusting growth. Contrasting herbaceous plants flank the gravel path.

two ways: growth can be accelerated by the warmth, and the growing period can be longer and more fulfilled here than in the open. These effects may be more obvious in younger plants that have got established but are still some seasons from full maturity. As the plants fill out their rootrun, they will be limited on one side by the wall's foundations, and in other directions are likely to be influenced by soil temperatures that are still warmer than those in the open, together with a dryness that may be emphasized by rapid drainage. This will have a braking effect on too-rapid growth. For all sorts of shrubs and climbers, as they have extra heat on their more mature wood, the tissues are likely to be ripened fully and a much higher proportion of flowering buds to growing buds are produced in these favourable conditions than on the comparable plant in the open garden scene.

These physical conditions are one of the main causes of increased flower power; the balance of nutrients in the soil available to the plants is another, with potash being a lead player in this role. Flowers are followed by fruits and here many of the plants on warm walls, and in other favoured microclimates, will often fruit freely whereas elsewhere they can remain virtually barren. Plants that will benefit in this way include the passion flowers, which are wonderful and extraordinary in bloom and can look properly exotic when hung with their fruits in long bottle or gourd-like shapes. Quinces will have their dark stems burdened with hard, fat fruits closely-clasped and becoming more decorative as they develop, perhaps becoming freckled before taking on golden tones for the winter, their surfaces becoming somewhat sticky and exuding the typical quince scent. Even the Virginia creeper on the warmer walls can have a huge number of tiny and round purple fruits – grapes for the doll's house – and those falling to the ground can result in a rash of young plants.

CLIMBERS AND SHRUBS FOR DRY SPOTS

Astragalus tragacantha
Atriplex halimus
Aucuba japonica
Caryopteris
Cytisus (brooms) in variety
Genista (brooms) in variety
Hedera (ivies) many
Helianthemum (rock rose) in variety
Lavandula (lavenders) most
Parthenocissus all
Rhus (sumach) many
Teucrium fruticans
Vitis (vines) all
Yucca

PEACHES, NECTARINES, APRICOTS – A SPECIAL CASE

It is easy to be tempted to grow a peach tree against a sunny wall and then enjoy the splendid fruit that comes straight off the branch – something far removed from the usual, poor-apologies-for-fresh peaches bought from shops. Try the variety 'Peregrine', but with this and all peaches watch out for the fungal disease leaf-curl. An attack of leaf-curl is a most horrible thing to see as it causes the leaves to become distorted with hideous blisters in jaundiced yellow and orange-red. Thankfully the fungus is easily beaten.

The way to do this is to prevent spores from landing on the bush through the winter months and this is where the wall-training comes into its own. Train the tree close to the wall as a fan, that is with branches radiating from one low point and closely clamped to the wall in a 'fan' shape. Then fix a batten horizontally on the wall above the top-most growth. Next hang a curtain of strong plastic or close-woven nylon sheeting from the batten and fix it in place by nailing another batten to the first one, lengthwise over the plastic. Make sure there is enough curtain for the bottom of the plastic to reach the ground then wrap and fasten this lower end around a bottom batten which will weigh the sheet down. To keep it steady and close to the peach tree but allow for ventilation, the low batten is attached to a few ground pegs. Use the curtain to cover the peach tree from leaf-fall till spring when the leaf and flower buds begin to burst. It can then be removed or rolled up and tied together for the growing months.

Nectarines and apricots need similar cosseting, as they are subject to the same disease.

Peach, Nectarine and Apricot Cultivars

Peaches:	Nectarines:	Apricots:
early – 'Duke of York'	early – 'Early Rivers', 'Elruge',	early – 'Early Moor Park'
midseason – 'Peregrine',	'Humboldt'	midseason – 'Late Moor Park'
'Royal George'	midseason – 'Lord Napier'	
late – 'Dymand'	late – 'Pineapple'	

Plants and Dryness

The health of plants reflects the health of the soil in which they are growing. Root growth can be very extensive both in distance and intensity depending on the conditions of the soil and the need to supply the top growth with enough liquid to grow and to make good losses due to transpiration. A plant's need for moisture is so obvious that it can seem ridiculous to dwell on the point, but a mental acceptance that there is a need may inhibit one's physical action to supply it. If a deficiency in water is acknowledged then a plan should be followed to avoid problems for the plants growing where it is too dry.

Either one must decide to grow only those plants that can cope with really difficult near-drought conditions or one must increase the moisture afforded to the area and make sure that there is plenty with still enough held in reserve. In Britain south- and west-facing walls are likely to receive more natural rainfall but will also be the warmest. Sites close to walls facing away from normal rain-bearing winds can become very dry, especially from late spring onwards. Winds bringing rain tend to come from one sector of the compass and tend not to drop big loads of water in the wind/rain-shadow of the house.

Quite a number of climbers and some shrubs come from places in the wild where they can be

Against this wall is the unique Moroccan broom, Cytisus battandieri, often known as the pineapple tree, the tight flower bunches being scented of pineapple. It is accompanied by a ceanothus and oriental poppies.

subject to long thirsty periods. Climbers are often wood or forest plants that may experience serious competition for available moisture through the growing months, particularly after the early spring. Ivies are drought-resistant. Some of the *Parthenocissus* creepers are adapted to conditions that would beat many others. I have seen them growing in heavily wooded areas of America where everything was tinder-dry. Vines, once they have got their extraordinarily extensive root systems in place, seem to be able to cope with rainless months without turning a hair or leaf.

Mulching

There are five good reasons for mulching. Firstly, it will form a layer that rain can pass through and it helps to retain the moisture. The mulch will mean that all the soil is available for plant roots; the original top couple of centimetres or so would previously have been too liable to dry out, now it is very much a part of the action. Secondly, provided the material used for the mulch is free of weed seed, and the soil is clear of strong perennial weeds, the layer will tend to inhibit weed germination; such weeds that do appear are easily pulled out of the loose material. A third benefit of organic mulches are the twins – a source of food and an improvement of the soil structure. The fourth effect is the cosmetic one – a tidy appearance provided by a mulch layer of uniform colour and texture can make a good background to show off the plants. Finally comes the insulation effect of mulching. This means that the top few centimetres are a lot less liable to violent fluctuations of temperature than they would be without such a cover; a happy mean is maintained, neither too hot in summer nor too cold in severe winter weather.

Many materials have been tried as mulches.

Rotted Compost

Rotted compost provides physical cover along with a source of food and an upgrading of the soil structure as it gets integrated. As with other bulky mulches, its success depends on an even and relatively thick layer being used. Poorly made compost with some parts not fully rotted may add to the weed seed bank, which means more work.

Peat

Before realization of the ecological damage done by the heavy exploitation of peat beds, peat was a popular, easy, weed-free product that performed all the functions and improved soil conditions as worms worked it in to the top centimetres. Strong, textured forms were favoured, not the dusty 'rhododendron' peats.

Shredded Bark

We have used shredded bark in two gardens and found it a very good mulch for conserving moisture and inhibiting weed growth. It rots down slowly so that a 7-10cm (3-4in) cover will last three years. During this period it can happen that a large proportion of the soil bacteria get involved in the rotting process, leading to some initial loss of nitrogen in the soil below. This can be made good by applications of fertilizer.

Shredded bark comes in various grades. Rough, large pieces take the longest to rot down and make effective mulches in areas planted up with shrubs and where the slightly less elegant appearance is not so important. Medium graded sizes are likely to be the more popular. They look good and act well.

It is sometimes possible to get a fine, almost dust-like material, that is sieved out of the other grades. I have not used this but I imagine that it rots down rather more quickly; I have seen it in wood yards and it looks as if it could blow around a bit.

The other main product in this category is semi-rotted bark. Straight out of the bag, this can have an acrid-acid odour which is soon dispelled. The colour is darker and obviously the material is some way towards total disintegration and absorption in the soil. Unless you are concerned to get a slightly darker colour, there seems nothing to be gained from using this rather than the usual medium-grade bark.

Shredded bark is certainly a visually pleasing

material and works very efficiently if applied at around the 7-10cm (3-4in) thickness. Against the lawn and at edges it can provide continual small work opportunities; birds love scratching around it and can fling it about with no regard to the aesthetics of garden design. Making the layers thinner towards the lawn edges or creating low physical barriers may help to stop this nuisance while you work on training the birds.

Cocoa Shell

More expensive than shredded bark, cocoa shell is an even-sized product of pleasing colour and appearance. It initially has a smell that stimulates the taste buds of chocaholics. It tends to bind together lightly, so remaining in place more efficiently.

Wood Chips and Sawdust

Felled or fallen trees and branches provide a material rather similar to the shredded bark, but it is paler and is less attractive. It could be used in less visited spots and perhaps towards the back of wide borders. Sawdust certainly inhibits weed growth but is not the most useful of materials. If you have access to considerable quantities at a cheap price, it may be used in the compost heap, provided not-too-heavy doses are incorporated at any one time. Continual applications of this material over many years may eventually lead to an unfortunate increase in unfriendly fungi and bacteria.

Gravel, Rock Chips, Stones

Completely inert, mulches made of stone products are nevertheless well able to cap moisture in the soil and allow in fresh water easily. They keep the soil moist and cooler and can look good and give an even, easily maintained surface. In a very dry garden in my youth, stones were used very effectively. Since then we have used the popular washed pea gravel and find it a worthwhile material. Inevitably, worms and other forces will bring some soil up to mix with the gravel and so a light top-dressing may be needed every so often, but this is not a frequent obligation. Granite chips can look rather dead in comparison with pea gravel; rock chips of such material as the golden Cotswold stone

will look bright and garish to start with, but become more sober as moss and algae growth take some hold.

Polythene

Polythene can be a very effective mulch, particularly on completely unplanted sites and in vegetable gardens, and it can be covered with a thin layer of one of the other mulches mentioned above to make it more pleasing to the eye. Once permanent weed is eliminated from a site, the soil should be levelled after which a sheet of black polythene can be laid down. This is anchored in position with a scattering of soil or

An unusual ensemble with, among others, Nicotiana 'Lime Green' in front of Clematis *'Victoria' with* Thalictrum delavayi *and verbena.*

a thin layer of shredded bark. The polythene has to be punctured to allow rainwater through and will obviously need to be cut open to accommodate the planting of shrubs and other plants.

Membrane

Specially manufactured as thin sheets that are very much better than straight polythene, membrane allows rainwater through easily but keeps the weed seed under control and performs a semi-sealing act for the soil. It can work over a long period and allows the planting of shrubs and plants that can then establish good root systems in a more stable soil environment. Once spread over cleaned and levelled ground, it needs to be anchored by a scattering of heavier material: the choice is normally between shredded bark or pea gravel.

Other Mulches

In special circumstances there may be other materials used for mulches. I remember walking over the aromatic ground of a friend who could get hold of the waste product of the nearby factory – dedicated to making instant coffee – rich, dark, spent ground coffee beans.

Another possible mulch material that may be available to some is bracken. Farmers will probably welcome someone willing to harvest what they regard as a space-wasting weed. If you can get large quantities of bracken, it does render down through the shredder into a useful mulching product. However, the mature fronds are difficult to manage and can be full of spores which may be carcinogenic. If you can only get hold of it at this stage, it will need rotting before use. A much more worthwhile product is the end result of using bracken as animal bedding. Their waste will make it rot it down much more easily. If the choice is yours, the prime time to

A bold pergola with roses, in particular the vigorous climber 'Rambling Rector', which is capable of reaching right across the rafters.

harvest bracken is when the stems are fully grown, but the fronds have not unfurled; taken then and used for mulch, it provides an organic material very rich in potassium. If you are not ready to use such young bracken, it is still very well worth harvesting and using in the compost heap.

The most readily available organic waste for most gardeners is lawn mowings. Spreading these thickly, directly on the ground, will usually result in a strong thatch-like layer that turns water away and also takes quite some time to rot and become part of the soil. Thin scatterings are more likely to be readily absorbed by the soils, but such thin doses cannot be counted proper mulches. The best use of cut grass is to compost it with other materials and then use the end product.

COASTAL SHRUBS

Atriplex halimus
Aucuba japonica
Berberis darwinii
Berberis x stenophylla
Brachyglottis
Bupleurum fruticosum
Escallonia macrantha and others
Euonymus japonicus
Hippophaë rhamnoides
Olearia haastii and others
Phormium
Rosa canina
Rosa multiflora
Tamarix
Ulex europaeus
Yucca

Watering

Before we think about plant nutrients, the importance of water must be emphasized, particularly as a high level of nutrients can be counter-productive in very dry conditions. Plants drink. They do not eat, barring the few insectivorous ones and even these exceptions reduce their captured animal life into a liquid stew before dining.

In areas of high rainfall, soil water may be kept at acceptable levels, even near walls and other structures, where there are generally much drier local soil environments. Elsewhere, it may be necessary to supplement nature's bounty with watering cans, sprays, hosepipes or some more regular arrangement. Trickle irrigation is a real boon. The amount of water can be carefully regulated, either manually or by a built-in time clock control which will release the water for an appropriate period when it is needed. From a main supply, water is passed, via a non-return valve, through narrow-gauge pipes on the surface or just below the soil, to exactly where it can be most profitably used. It is allowed to drip out of small nozzles (usually adjustable) just clear of the soil surface so next to nothing is lost

in evaporation. (For more details see Useful Information p.250.)

Acidity and Alkalinity

Garden soil or made-up compost can be tested with a kit available from garden centres to find out the pH level, a measure of its acidity or alkalinity. The neutral balance between acid and alkaline is 7: higher numbers indicate mounting alkalinity, lowers ones reveal acidity. The kits are simple to use. A small soil sample is shaken up with the chemical indicators and the resulting colour is read off against the colour chart to give the pH value. There are similar indicator kits to measure the presence of nitrogen, phosphorus and potassium salts in the soil. In this case the colour charts indicate one of the following results: surplus, sufficient, adequate, deficient, depleted.

Most plants manage within a moderately wide band of pH levels; most gardens are around neutral and as the majority of plants can cope with somewhat acid or alkaline conditions, there are relatively few problems with this. Possibly the most desirable of soils are either neutral or slightly acid. Extreme pH levels are rare but soil near walls may be more alkaline than that of other parts of the garden due to rain moving over old mortar and builder's rubble. Continual watering with very hard water will also deposit increased amounts of alkaline salts into the soil.

Plants needing markedly alkaline or acid conditions to flourish may have to have the soil tailored to their needs. Those of us fond of a less strenuous life will try to grow what the soil suits, but there are many gardeners who cannot resist the desire to grow the more tricky things. There is always the rhododendron-fancier whose soil is chalky, and someone to whom the rhodies and their kin are a pathological phobia is occasionally going to be blessed with an estate on acid ground. There is a law that encapsulates these probabilities! (See p.94 for hints on how to alter the pH of your soil.)

CHANGING THE pH OF YOUR SOIL

Acidity can be corrected by the addition of lime, but to try to move any large bulk of soil one complete pH number level is a major operation; moreover, it is more difficult moving from very alkaline towards neutral or acid, than from a moderate acidity to neutral or lightly alkaline. Conquering alkalinity can be a long-term job, the healthy way being to add copious amounts of organic material repeatedly over the years.

If we are going to tinker with the acidity or alkalinity of soil, then against a wall is a sensible spot to make the attempt. It is best to try to designate a fairly broad area for treatment as trying to maintain a small volume of soil at a markedly different pH level to the dominant natural one is an almost impossible Canute-like task.

Take in several square metres and attempt to create some physical barriers between treated soils and the surrounds. If there is a path or other obvious boundary parallel to the wall it may be possible to excavate a trench and make a partial barrier by laying a thick polythene sheet vertically for a depth of 45-60cm (18-24in). This will inhibit some movement of soil water into the quarantined new soil mix. Against a wall, you will at least not suffer major intrusion of alkaline or acid salts from the wall side – unless it is a very

ancient one with old mortar which may provide a source of rainwater-borne alkalinity. Some arrangement may have to be made to maintain the moisture of the wall bed artificially in order to avoid 'contamination'; trickle irrigation can be effective and economic. Re-check the pH of the altered bed each season to make sure that the surrounding soil water is not defeating you.

To move from acid to neutral or alkaline conditions scatter lime powder to make the ground white, up to 100g (4oz) per sq m/yard, and work into the top soil. Test the pH not sooner than a month after application. Repeat dosage every three months until the required pH value is established but, again, do not test for several weeks after any application. When you think you have achieved your goal, wait and test again a few months later before starting on any planting of plants disliking acid soils.

The only reliable way to move from somewhat alkaline to slightly acid conditions is by the repeated generous application of humus material. It is easier to live with the natural pH levels; any tinkering that may be undertaken will be considerably easier if there is only a relatively small level of acid/alkalinity to adjust.

TRACE ELEMENTS

The following trace elements are important for plant health:
Boron (Bo)
Chlorine (Cl)
Copper (Cu)
Iron (Fe)
Manganese (Mn)
Molybdenum (Mb)

Nutrients and Feeding

The main plant elements and the ones quoted as percentages on the manufactured general fertilizers are nitrogen (N), phosphorus (P), potassium (K). All these elements are important; nitrogen and potassium work in tandem, the presence of one helping the other to work efficiently. Most soils contain enough N, P and K for plant growth, but the levels will probably need topping up regularly for optimum results.

Nitrogen's most obvious role is the encouragement of leafy growth, it is most in demand when the plants are growing fast. An excess can lead to sappy tissue that is an easier prey to fungal diseases.

Phosphorus, while needed for leaf growth, is particularly important in stimulating healthy

root formation and is, therefore, vital for seedlings. Later in life, the plants need it in the production of seed and fruit. As well as helping to build up a plant's resistance to cold and diseases, it will also help offset too-heavy doses of nitrogen. Excess phosphorus may cause premature develooopment, perhaps signalled by yellowish foliage and a hardening of growth tissue. A lack of phosphorus is indicated by an unhealthily dark colouring of the leaves, and slow growth.

Potassium is important in the manufacture of plant starches, sugars and strong tissue fibres. It helps steady growth, indicated by healthy green colours, and is especially useful in stimulating fruiting, increasing disease resistance and promoting all-round health.

Calcium and sulphur are other major elements that are needed in fairly large quantities but most soils contain adequate supplies. A range of other elements are also necessary for healthy growth: these are usually present in small amounts but more than enough for the plants.

FERTILIZERS

The fertilizers on sale in garden centres range from single element kinds such as sulphate of ammonia (N), sulphate of potash (K) and superphosphate of lime (P), to the many proprietary multi-element ones. Established in the Second World War and still a popular standard,

National Growmore has equal amounts of the three main elements present: N 7%, P 7%, K 7%. There are other similarly balanced proprietary general fertilisers. Those recommended for tomatoes are high in potash (K) and are useful for bulbs and many other plants. Among the many popular brands available, Phostrogen contains N 14%, P 15%, K 30%, Maxicrop Seaweed contains N 5%, P %5 and K 5%, Miracle-Gro's formula is N 15%, P 15%, K 30%, Vitax Q4 contains N 5.3%, P 10%, K 10% with trace elements boron, copper, iron, magnesium, manganese, molybdenum. It is one of the few to

A herb garden is given form by the neat cobbled path and the railings, their upright lines and looped tops giving a unifying formal framework for the varied foliage of the herbs. These include the dwarf lavender 'Hidcote', shrubby germander (Teucrium fruticans), ginger mint, curry plant and marjoram.

95

LAYERING – THE CHEAP AND EASY OPTION

Most shrubs can be easily increased by layering low branches. This is an operation usually best done after leaf fall and comfortably before spring.

1 Choose a branch and make sure it will reach the ground.

2 Work the soil into a friable state and add grit and humus.

3 Remove the leaves from the 10-20cm (4-8in) length to be buried.

4 Scratch the lower side of the wood of this length with a knife and dust with rooting powder.

5 Cover the layer with soil and peg it down with a wire loop or hold it down with a brick.

6 The new plant is normally well advanced after twelve months. Strong new growth will usually signal the fact that the layer is well rooted. Sever it from its parent and plant it up in its new permanent site.

Even if you do not need more specimens for your own garden, the new plants can still be useful presents or 'swops', and this is a trouble-free way of getting stock of the more unusual things.

guarantee these extra elements which are needed for healthy plant growth but are normally in adequate natural supply.

Slow-release fertilizers in pelleted form are normally used for plants in pots and other containers. They are designed as one-dose feeds to support plant health for a whole growing season. Osmocote has a formula N 14%, P 13%, K 13% and will release controlled amounts through the season.

Organic fertilizers can be rich in certain elements. Bonemeal is high in phosphorus at 17% and nitrogen at 3.5%. Dried blood is particularly high in nitrogen at 12%.

Dry fertilizer applications are dependent on moisture to dissolve the nutrients that they contain and make them available to the plant roots. For more immediate results, liquid feeds are effective and can sometimes also be used as a foliar feed, perhaps in the same application.

Specific foliar feeds can be bought that have different balances of the fertilizer elements.

WHEN TO FEED

Feeding plants is similar to the technique of feeding babies, known as 'feeding on demand'. Having established that the soil to be planted has no real deficiencies, or having made any deficiencies good by appropriate doses of dry fertilizers, then the practice of 'little and often' is regarded as the better choice than any 'once and forever' attempt. This particularly applies to those applications aimed at replacing or boosting the potash content of the soil; potassium salts are highly soluble and will leach out of the topsoil quickly. A methodical gardener might consider managing four light applications of potash a year: very early spring, late spring, late summer and mid-autumn.

The most efficient periods for applying

The roses 'Compassion' and 'Phyllis Bide' trained up a wall in the pool garden at Redenham Park, Hampshire. There is a wide selection of rambler and climbing roses available, many of which will bloom for many weeks or even months.

general dry fertilizers are likely to be very early spring, just when things are getting ready to go into rapid growth, and again in early autumn. High potash fertilizers should be applied mid-summer, or towards its end, so they can do their job of aiding the formation of fruit, the ripening of wood and the formation of flower buds. Between spring and autumn, in the somewhat unlikely event of any extra feeding being deemed necessary, liquid feeds are most beneficial. Foliar feeds also fall into this category. Some of the proprietary brands advise feeding once a week on their instructions: this is for the rearing of young plants. The 'little and often' recommendation normally means two, three or four times a year.

Maintenance

Having ensured adequate food and moisture, what remains among the more mundane jobs is weeding, although in the presence of good mulches this can be a very light workload. As always, a weed plucked in time can save ninety nine.

PRUNING

What can be more demanding than weeding is the trimming and pruning of the plants to ensure that none overflows its rightful place. In this it may be prudent to exercise some dictatorial powers: occasionally, instead of pruning, it might be necessary to sacrifice a shrub to allow room for its neighbours. The aims of pruning are to keep growth within check, to encourage the development of flower buds and allow the stems to get well ripened before winter. Shrubs trained against walls can be pressed back by repeated trimming with shears or a power tool, until all that is left is neatly machined growths. The same shrubs, given the benefit of a slightly looser rein and pruned perhaps only once or twice a year, might be more pleasing to many eyes and will certainly be less work. We prune our winter jasmine hard to the wall once flowering is complete and then, through the

year, a pattern of new stems is allowed to build, arching away and down from the wall, ready for another long winter display of blossom. Wisterias are pruned hard in late summer to remove sappy extraneous growth and leave rather bare, strong, grey stems with plenty of short spurs from which will come the flowers next year.

REPLANTING AND REPOSITIONING

Newly planted borders and beds may have been kept lively with short-term plants – annuals, biennials and quick-growing shrubs such as brooms and tree lupins. As the permanent plants begin to fill out and take control, these temporary tenants may be removed. If we wish to continue growing them, then it is necessary to plan quarters for them elsewhere.

SUPPORTS

It is prudent to check annually all wall-fixed installations. Ties for shrubs and trees ought to be checked, too, as it is amazing how quickly plants can outgrow the original ones. Often the increased rigidity of the now more mature plants means the ties can be dispensed with altogether.

THE FUTURE AND THE PAST

Much gardening is done on an *ad hoc* basis – there may be long-term plans, but very often we simply feel our way. Some lucky breaks are built on and expanded, as other less satisfactory projects are abandoned. The best 'plan' for unplanned gardens and gardeners is to try to look objectively at the whole every so often, judge it and decide on improvements, then we are likely to have a successful garden. Mistakes are made in the best-regulated regimes. It is difficult to order nature – trees or shrubs outgrow their places, may become diseased or even die. We have to be prepared to remove and replace. All this also ties in with what was said earlier (pp.14-15), the gardener's views may change: the young family grows up, the play area is not needed until the next generation comes along, the sandpit can become a pond, the swing can give way to screening and more climbers.

AERIAL LAYERING

Some shrubs are short on useful low branches to bed to the ground for layering. The answer is to select a smallish branch for layering and proceed as follows:

1 Choose a twig with about 20cm (8in) growth beyond the spot from which you aim to produce roots.

2 Remove leaves from the future rooted area, scratch it and dust with rooting powder.

3 Enclose this section with moisture-retaining material, such as peaty compost held by moss, and keep this in place by tightly bound and tied polythene. The aim is to keep the twig moist.

4 The layer can be left for a whole growing season, or you can carefully undo the bandage and introduce more water if it is needed, then rebinding.

5 At the end of the season unwrap the layer carefully to examine it.

6 If rooted, the layer can be severed from the parent, potted up and grown on for some months before being planted out in its permanent place. (A strongly rooted layer could be planted directly into a prepared garden site.)

CLIMATES & MICROCLIMATES

Planting plans depend on plant hardiness, and hardiness depends on climatic conditions. When plants are positioned near walls and fences, we are able to influence the conditions they experience – we can create microclimates.

Weather

I am writing in Britain, and Britain has interesting weather; it is a mainstay of our social intercourse. The maritime status of the British islands means that they have relatively warm air that is moisture-laden from the influences of the surrounding waters. The seas and the Gulf Stream in the west temper the climate and enable the British to grow a wide selection of the world's flora. Britain has milder winters and cooler summers than much of Europe and Asia, where the land masses and differing latitudes result in weather patterns that are more extreme and more stable. Weather patterns in much of North America also follow this more extreme pattern with longer, drier summers and colder, more persistent winters. Coastal areas and New England are less extreme. The more staid continental land mass climates are the opposite of what New Zealand experiences; here, there seems a different weather pattern every few miles! – much closer to the island experience of Britain.

The three main factors in any climate are likely to be temperature ranges, moisture fluctuations and wind effects, and within this macroclimate there are many microclimates. Rainfall maps give some idea of the differences in volumes of rain between different areas. Temperatures, too, vary very considerably. It is the winter ones, combined with winter moisture to a greater or lesser extent, that determine which plants will survive. Average minimum temperatures can be used to give a guide to what plants will be hardy in your area.

Altitude also influences temperatures. The usual reckoning is that for every 300m (1,000ft) extra height, the mean temperatures drop by 0.5°C (1°F) which may not seem a lot, but can make a big difference to the length of the growing season. Some plants that are grown with little difficulty at low levels become more difficult or impossible as the altitude increases.

THE EFFECTS OF FROST

In mild places, such as the south-west of England, even if frosts are experienced, they are likely to be of much shorter duration and less sharp. Most plants can withstand a short period of cold. From –1°C to –4°C (30°F to 27°F) is frosty but will not begin to do real damage to plants for a period of minutes, say 10-15 minutes, as leaf cells are surrounded by relatively strong tissue and the cell contents are not pure water but filled with chemicals, which will partially inhibit immediate freezing. However, if these temperature levels are maintained for 2-3 hours, damage can be extensive. Obviously, the greater the number of degrees of frost the greater the danger.

When plants experience really prolonged or hard frosts that penetrate low into the soil followed by thaws in a repeating cycle, a considerable amount of damage will be done to the root systems. Most plants subject to frost above ground adopt a deciduous lifestyle, or die down to resting rootstocks as found in herbaceous plants. For these it is the late frosts, which come after early leaf growth, that can do a lot of damage above ground. Some plants can be killed, while others will lose their new growth and have to start again, a real check to their progress.

At Mottisfont Abbey, Hampshire, the walled garden contains the famous National Trust collection of old roses. On the wall are 'Ferdinand de Lesseps' and Rosa multiflora. Below them are penstemons and foxgloves.

PLANT HARDINESS ZONE MAP

The hardiness zone system shown here was developed by the United States Department of Agriculture. Zones have been developed based on average annual minimum temperatures in various areas. Each plant is given a hardiness rating based on these zones. A plant may also be grown in all zones warmer than the one indicated for it, or in microcli-mates within cooler zones. By the same token, some plants supposedly hardy to your zone may not survive in your garden. This is particularly true towards the upper and lower limits of each zone. Gardeners living outside the United States of America can estimate their equivalent zone by calcu-lating their own average minimum temperature.

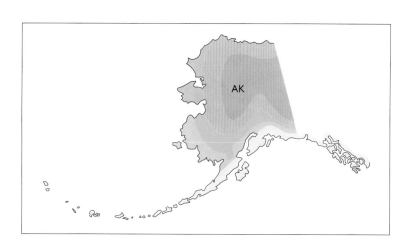

		Fahrenheit	Celsius
Zone 1		below -50°	below -46°
Zone 2		-50° to -40°	-46° to -40°
Zone 3		-40° to -30°	-40° to -34°
Zone 4		-30° to -20°	-34° to -29°
Zone 5		-20° to -10°	-29° to -23°
Zone 6		-10° to 0°	-23° to -18°
Zone 7		0° to 10°	-18° to -12°
Zone 8		10° to 20°	-12° to -7°
Zone 9		20° to 30°	-7° to -1°
Zone 10		30° to 40°	-1° to 4°
Zone 11		above 40°	above 4°

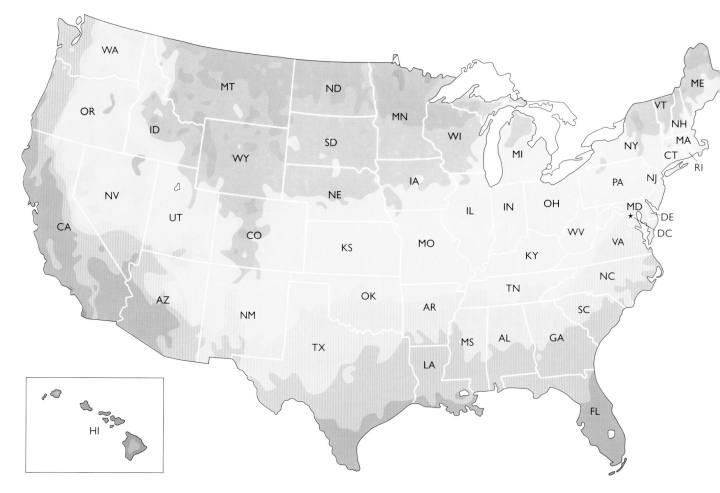

Types of Frost

Frost can take several forms. A hoar frost is produced when water has condensed and frozen from a moisture-laden atmosphere. This causes ice crystals to form wherever the moisture is found – leaves, cobwebs, wires and other thin structures are edged with ice patterns. After the thaw, foliage can be badly damaged. Tough leaves such as laurel and holly will withstand the frost but sappier ones will be defeated.

A black frost occurs when the atmosphere is dry and, in the absence of free moisture, leaves and stems freeze and are turned black.

A ground frost occurs when the temperature of the soil reaches below freezing point. A light ground frost that does not last a long time may not do extensive damage; it could even be beneficial in killing off small weeds. A severe one that penetrates some way into the soil is dangerous; damage can increase the longer it persists. A clear sky and still air facilitate a bad ground frost. The cold air is heavy and builds up at soil level. Shrubs and trees on the borderline of hardiness, and those with wood that has not ripened to a healthy hardness, will be damaged. Newly planted and young plants are more vulnerable to severe damage than established ones.

Plant Hardiness

Hardiness of plants is not something that can be marked off at some point on a linear scale: there are too many factors to consider. The assessment of hardiness, and the behaviour of a wide range of plants under different climatic conditions, is a problem that confronts all gardeners, and gardening authors. No special claims are made for the eclectic system adopted here.

One of the problems is that not all plants are obviously hardy or not hardy. It can be safely assumed that exotics, such as arboreal orchids, from very warm places are not hardy; in northern temperate zones they cannot be grown outside. On the other hand, some native plants, such as the hollies in Britain, seem able to withstand anything. Then there are those plants that will flourish in favoured mild areas but would be impossible in colder parts. Plants on the borderline of hardiness are especially difficult to classify: some may survive in the microclimate of a garden, particularly near walls where they have the shelter that gives them an extra cushion against the cold.

When looking at hardiness, it should also be remembered that every plant is different. A species may include clones that are notably more hardy than the standard. These variations are one reason why it can be profitable to raise long-lived plants from seed and discard all weaker individuals; many shrubs can be raised and got to flowering size relatively quickly. Seedlings of species or hybrid shrubs and other plants start life virus free; even in a small population it is usually easy to pick out worthwhile individuals that look good and outdo their siblings in health and hardiness.

As the plants are reviewed in chapters 11-17, some care is taken to suggest the candidates most likely to be successful if included in gardens with particular climates. Some allowance has been made for the less severe winter weather we seem to have been experiencing recently, a phenomenon that has made the growing of many Mediterranean and some South African plants a matter of relatively carefree ease in some British gardens. In my garden South African osteospermums may well come through the winter and start blooming in spring and carry on for months.

MEASURING HARDINESS

Precisely defining and promulgating hardiness is not an exact science: all plants can be killed by weather conditions. But, if we are going to put money on certain plants, it would be helpful to have some idea of their form. So we turn to the tipsters.

There has been a lot of work done in this tricky field. The two major protagonists are the Royal Horticultural Society in Britain and the United States Department of Agriculture. They have come up with hardiness ratings for plants

SHRUBS FOR ALKALINE SOILS

Those gardening on limy soils often think longingly of rhododendrons and camellias, which are impossible or can only be tried in large containers. However, plenty of shrubs are particularly good on alkaline soils. Try some of the following:

Abelia triflora
Berberis x stenophylla
Buddleja davidii
Hydrangea petiolaris
Indigofera heterantha
Osmanthus x burkwoodii
Philadelphus all
Prunus
Xanthoceras sorbifolium

The popular rose 'Constance Spry' at Mottisfont Abbey, Hampshire, encouraged to go up the wall much higher than it would manage in the open.

and these are given with the plant reviews later in the book. Although the two systems do not completely dovetail there are no important discrepancies.

The US Department of Agriculture first published their work in the 1930s. This divided the United States into seven hardiness zones, based on weather statistics and absolute minimum temperatures, collected over twenty years. Later the number of zones was increased to the present 10, with zone 1 being the Arctic and zone 10 being tropical; thus, the higher the number, the less chance of frost and cold. This system describes climatic conditions likely to be met in any particular area and one chooses plants to survive within these specifications.

The system sponsored by the Royal Horticultural Society is centred on the character of the plants and operates within 4 ratings of hardiness. In this system, the higher the number, the more hardy the plant. It scarcely needs pointing out that it is excessive cold rather than

excessive heat that is the determining factor of the ratings. The four ratings are defined briefly as follows:

H4 – Hardy outside. Can stand temperatures down to –15°C (5°F).

H3 – Hardy in some regions, and/or in particular sites or positions outside and able to withstand limited periods at –5°C (23°F), frost-hardy.

H2 – Half hardy, can manage temperatures down to 0°C (32°F).

H1 – Tender, may be damaged below 5°C (41°F). Plants may need heated glass.

The British system is much simpler, but this reflects the fact that, as mentioned above, conditions in Britain are very much more uniform than in large continental masses. To understand the differences in the zonal ratings: the US zone of 8 is equivalent to 7 in Britain, while 9 would be 8.

Sunshine and Shade

Plants need light, but relatively few need long periods of direct sunlight. In the wild, many climbers grow with the support of trees. They are naturally in some shadow and are sometimes very significantly shaded. This makes garden planning easier. There are some plants that will manage well enough on or in the shelter of shaded walls and fences where light and moisture are rationed.

Even in open areas the influence of sunshine can vary. The height the sun reaches in the sky in summer, compared to that which it reaches in winter, is hugely different. Thus, the angle at which the sun's rays strike level ground will vary; the shallower the angle (when the sun is lower in the sky) the wider the spread of the available sunlight and direct warmth. This explains why, in the northern hemisphere where the sun goes from east to west on a southerly passage, land sloping to the south and meeting the sun's rays more directly, will warm up in the spring markedly more quickly than ground that slopes away from the warming rays. Any

unshaded vertical projection, walls, post, pergolas and so on, will offer the sun a very direct target and will harvest light and warmth efficiently.

A sunny wall or fence will have the sun's rays striking it fairly directly for much of the time during the summer months. When the sun is lower in the sky through the autumn and spring months, the wall will absorb a considerably higher proportion of the available heat than the ground below. Once a wall is warm, the heat is retained relatively efficiently whereas this is not so with a wooden fence. Even a white wall, reflecting much heat, will warm up. This warmth and that which is directly reflected by the wall or by the ground will help the woody tissue of any plant near the wall to ripen more efficiently than it would in the open, and this ripening process and a percentage reduction of sappy tissue will facilitate the formation of a higher ratio of flower buds to growth ones. This ripening of the wood also helps to make the plant hardier and more resistant to cold weather.

The more methodical of us, when planning a garden, may take notes of the sunshine hours that different areas of the garden enjoy, and will note the influence of surrounding buildings and large trees. Sometimes the removal of just one branch of a tree can let in a lot of light and improve the overall prospects for plants formerly in deeper shadow. Beds that are flat can be raked to a slope to get more warmth.

Rain and Rain-shadow

We live close to the Malvern Hills. Here, and in other hilly areas, rain-laden clouds are blown across flatter land to the foot of the hills which they are then forced up. As they rise they are encouraged by changing pressures and temperatures to drop rain within a pattern that reflects in part the form of the hills. Rainfall is significantly less on the leeward sides of such natural barriers.

Local rainfall figures are usually readily available in public libraries; however, the actual volume of rain falling on a square metre/yard

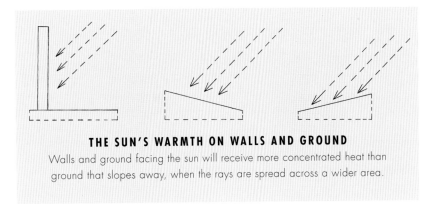

THE SUN'S WARMTH ON WALLS AND GROUND
Walls and ground facing the sun will receive more concentrated heat than ground that slopes away, when the rays are spread across a wider area.

will vary considerably within a few paces. The amount of rain falling directly on the soil under a dense tree – a yew, holly or an established conifer – will be almost zero. On the leeward side of such trees there will also be only small amounts; the same happens in the lee of large fences or house walls, which prove a barrier to sloping rain. This effect is like a rain-shadow and means that even after prolonged precipitation there can be a major strip of ground left gasping for water. Climbers and other plants that have established themselves successfully in such places will have grown far-reaching root systems to collect plenty of moisture even if their base is dry. Newly planted specimens need to have their liquid needs taken care of. Either consider some special watering until they are established, or only plant those plants that are able to manage in these conditions.

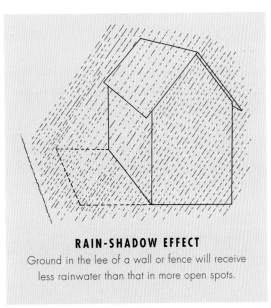

RAIN-SHADOW EFFECT
Ground in the lee of a wall or fence will receive less rainwater than that in more open spots.

Wind and Wind Tunnels

Strong winds can cause damage. This is more likely to happen to plants in the open or to the rear of solid garden walls or fences, than to those growing on or close to house walls. Wind also dries out the soil surface and increases the rate of transpiration of plants (see p.86).

Having determined from what quarter the predominant winds come, one can break its force by a series of barriers. Solid fences or walls will only displace the area of concern as the wind will rise over the barrier and curl around behind it devastatingly. The best aim is to break the force of the wind by degrees: a line of trees on the boundary will filter the main force and, before this, one or two partial barriers of shrubs, will further reduce the force (see also Screens pp.60-63). It has been estimated that a good hedge some 1.5m (5ft) high will cut the force of a wind by a half, not only immediately by it, but for a distance of up to 8m (25ft) to the leeward side.

Wind tunnels are a more specific form of wind problem. They are often caused by adjoining buildings channelling the wind into narrow confines making a draughty and unhappy spot for plants. Such sites are best given a similar treatment to that adopted for main wind – filter the effect – though here trellis and such structures are perhaps better as a first line of defence, before introducing the hardier of plants.

Microclimates

Although the hardiness ratings and zones already detailed give some indication of the plants' likelihood of survival, microclimates near house walls and in built-up areas (see below) may make conditions more favourable for plants than the map zones might suggest. Plants in an open, rather wet situation may succumb to winter cold when others of the same sort survive only few yards away. In my garden

The back of a house at Fulham Park; the extrovert growth of the main plantings in this city-centre garden is augmented by bulbous Eucomis bicolor *and petunias in containers.*

we can often easily manage plants given a British rating of H3 with only a perfunctory bit of attention to winter frost precautions. In milder areas even those plants that are listed as H2, sometimes regarded as plants needing unheated glass for part of their life, may well succeed outside.

At microclimate-level considerable variations can be found within a small garden. In any one spot the balance of factors influencing the microclimate can change as work is carried out in the garden: shrubs being planted here, walls being built there, water features being added – all have an effect. The mean temperatures at the base of a sunny wall are very different from those of one that faces away from the sun. The temperature at the base of the wall and at the gutters will be quite different, with a range of readings in-between. With hardy plants careful consideration of these factors is not needed, but it may be important with those plants that are a little more tender or with blossom that can be damaged by frost.

FROST POCKETS

Frost pockets, where freezing air gets trapped, causing isolated areas of extreme cold, are notorious microclimates. The cold air, being heavier than warm, flows downhill and if it meets a barrier, or cannot find lower ground, it gets trapped. This can happen on a relatively small scale; gardeners with large sloping gardens are best advised not to grow major hedges across the contour without leaving wide gaps for the downward flow of cold air.

BUILDINGS

Those living in the centre of cities and larger towns may think longingly of the space and fresh soils of those who enjoy rural surroundings. In some ways they undoubtedly have an arguable point, but one benefit they have above their country cousins is artificially affected climates with mean temperatures, round the year, perhaps two or more degrees above those in the country. They can consider growing even more tender plants than those living in the country. The climatic problems of the small town or city garden can result from wind tunnels and the lack of direct sunlight (see above).

THE EFFECTS OF HEAT AND SHELTER

Walls or other structures facing in different directions experience widely different temperatures as a result of how much sunlight reaches them during the day. When taken at the same time on a summer's day, thermometer readings near a sunny wall can be as much as 12°C (20°F) higher than those on a shaded wall. Red brick will absorb lots of heat and retain it for a long time; they work like storage heaters. Brick and stone walls are the most ready absorbers of heat. Wooden ones are less efficient. Walls or boards painted white or pale colours will reflect much of the heat offered them and this heat will be dispersed nearby.

Plants seem to cope with temperatures up to around 35°C (95°F) but, at these high temperatures, the leaves of many will wilt as they fail to find the reserves of water to keep them turgid as they cannot keep pace with the rate of transpiration. To prevent further water loss the stomata of leaves, through which transpiration takes place, may partially close. Some plants from hot countries have leaves that curl up on themselves for protection; a lot have hairy or waxy surfaces which help to reduce water loss. These plants

SOIL TEMPERATURE

Spring growth is as much, or more influenced by soil temperatures, than air warmth; sandy soils tend to warm up earlier than clays and loams, but it is the well-drained, humus rich, worked soils that keep the warmth longer at the end of the season.

In this wall border Stachys byzantina, *with its rabbit's-ears leaves,* Hedysarum coronarium *and geraniums are planted below* Clematis 'Rouge Cardinal' *to form a pleasing contrast with the rich golden ham stone.*

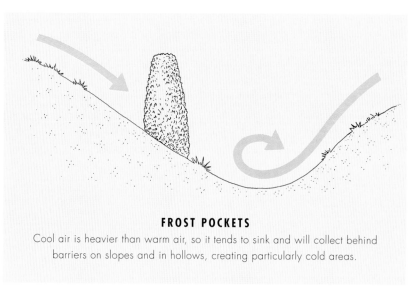

FROST POCKETS

Cool air is heavier than warm air, so it tends to sink and will collect behind barriers on slopes and in hollows, creating particularly cold areas.

Clematis armandii
'Apple Blossom' growing
around a gateway at
Greystone Cottage,
Oxfordshire, a two-acre
garden in a woodland
setting.

In one of London's many hidden gardens, the luxuriant growth of shrubs and climbers masks the boundaries above abundant healthy herbaceous plants.

will manage better than others in hot weather on the warmer walls. See the individual chapters dealing with the different wall zones for specific problems and solutions.

The rigid surfaces of walls and fences provide sure footholds for the self-clinging climbers that in the wild will have to make do with trees and rock faces. The wide masses of Virginia creeper (*Parthenocissus quinquefolia*) or of ivy that are found on favoured wall sites are virtually unparalleled in the wild. The same applies to many of the twisters and scramblers that are given wall support by means of a system of wires or trellis. In gardens there is not the same sort of competition from other plants and the conditions are not so difficult; this allows many plants to advance beyond their normal wild potential. In addition part of the success of wall plants is due to the shelter they are offered. Even in strong winds, they are not likely to suffer hugely, the edge of the wind's power being blunted by the cushioning effect of still, or nearly still, air close to the wall and half trapped by the plant growth.

Close to the wall it is understandable that extra warmth will influence growth, but the beneficial effect spreads further and, if there are other walls and fences around the garden, these too can trap warmth. In a small garden much of the plot can thus become a favoured area. The walls absorb the heat through the day and will release some during the cooler night. This effect occurs not only in the summer but through the autumn and, less efficiently but more importantly, in the warmer days of winter.

Part Two
THE SITES

The Three Sectors

Shaded Sites

Sunny Sites

This garden in San Francisco was designed by Sonny Garcia. Its clever multi-level planting includes Clematis montana var. rubens and Cantua buxifolia.

THE THREE SECTORS

Now you are ready to exploit the beneficent effects of walls, fences and other structures, from the cosy low environment which is around your toes, to the airy upper reaches that are above your head.

By dividing the wall or major fence into three parts, or sectors – the base, the middle (a prime site) and the higher reaches – we can begin to explore the different aspects and opportunities afforded by them. While there are no exact lines to be drawn between one sector and another, there are differences. The conditions that plants encounter at the base of a wall are not the same as those faced by plants halfway up or on a balcony or window sill. The main variable factors are temperature levels, light intensity and exposure to wind. These will also change considerably in the different directions that such structures face. Those facing the sun are likely to show the widest variations of each sector. All these factors should be allowed for in any planting plans.

Sector One – the Base

The base of any wall, particularly major walls, gives the most sheltered conditions in the garden, with soil and air temperatures above those of the surrounding area. This site will suffer less buffeting from wind, unless it is in a wind tunnel (see p.104). Soil care will usually be basically trying to maintain a high humus content to enrich the nutrient value and help to create reservoirs of moisture. Light intensity will depend on the aspect of the wall and the surrounding buildings and plants, including trees.

HOT AND SUNNY

Walls with a sunny aspect allow the widest choice of candidates. The wide variety of plants that can be grown here will include the whole gamut – herbaceous, bulbs, subshrubs, shrubs

and trees. Although it is, of course, possible to grow those plants that would be quite happy in the open garden, the choice can be widened considerably to take in a huge range of plants that are just a touch tender and may, or may not, manage in more exposed spots. The latter is a range of plants that I would not, in my youth, have thought the least hardy: we do seem to be in the middle of a climate change that may bring its own problems, but also offers us opportunities for success with plants that were less

A fountain of the silvery leaves of Artemisia absinthium with Centaurea gymnocarpa and hardy chrysanthemums. These plants are happy in the rather dry warm site by a wall below a Boston ivy, Parthenocissus tricuspidata.

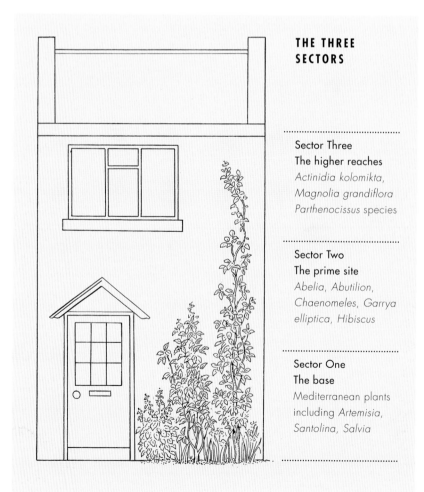

THE THREE SECTORS

Sector Three
The higher reaches
*Actinidia kolomikta,
Magnolia grandiflora
Parthenocissus* species

Sector Two
The prime site
*Abelia, Abutilion,
Chaenomeles, Garrya
elliptica, Hibiscus*

Sector One
The base
Mediterranean plants
including *Artemisia,
Santolina, Salvia*

The warmth of this wall encourages Nerine bowdenii *bulbs as well as the yellow-berried* pyracantha *and* Rosa glauca. *This rather informal piece of gardening is brought into focus by the pedestal mounted on the wall.*

likely to have survived long a few decades ago.

The first selection of non-natives that could be candidates for the base of the wall are the Mediterranean ones. These are plants accustomed to warmer weather and probably long periods of water shortage. There is a range of bulbs that get underway with the first autumnal rains and can provide early flowers before other things get into top gear. Shrubs and herbaceous plants from this part of the world include many that have silvery foliage, usually as a result of a layer of fine hairs which have the effect of reducing water transpiration.

From the other side of the world comes the second set of possible candidates for the site. They also use the silvery foliage ploy as a defence against heat and dryness. A well-known exponent from New Zealand is *Brachyglottis* (*Senecio greyi*) 'Sunshine' and several of its relatives. The floras of New Zealand and Australia are quite distinct from European ones; they never seem to lose their strangeness to European eyes. The bottlebrushes (*Callistemon* species) are shrubs that are unlikely to flourish in the open but can be very satisfactory in fertile soil under the protection of sunny walls. They are evergreens with their bottlebrushes in brilliant reds or pale yellows.

Another set of plants that might be happy with a sheltered wall base are those from South Africa. Getting to know some of the wonderful flowers indigenous to that part of the world,

through holidays or delving into floral guides, certainly makes one wish to try them. Some, such as *Nerine bowdenii* and *Amaryllis belladonna*, have long been grown in Britain and places with similar climates. Favourites for their florescent-pink autumn flowers, they grow easily once established in a warm spot near a wall.

Other bulbs and corms could include the small *Gladiolus* species and their hybrids. More adventurous gardeners might try some of the fascinating watsonias, which look like dainty cousins of gladioli. They are often 1m (3ft) high but some are capable of almost double this. The curious *Eucomis* species with their pineapple-like flowers can be successful. Agapanthus species and cultivars look as if they should be bulbous but they are really possessed of thick-rooted, tough rootstocks; they will often flourish in the open but are best with some wall-reflected warmth.

Mexico and South America are perhaps more rarely sources for outdoor plants for gardeners in the northern hemisphere, though the Mexican orange blossom, *Choisya ternata*, has been grown in Britain for a long time both by walls and in the open. It is a shrub that will delight in late spring with its masses of heavily scented white posies but can also come into quite generous blossom in late autumn. The Chilean bellflower, *Lapageria rosea*, and the coral plant, *Berberidopsis corallina*, are two others that ought to be considered.

SHREDDING

If you use a shredder the resulting flaky material, which looks somewhat like shredded bark, can be added to the compost heap or used as a mulch. Any raw colour will soon tone down. The material will have all the beneficial effects of a bark mulch and will eventually be incorporated into the topsoil.

MEDITERRANEAN BULBS

Allium callimischon
Allium moly
Allium narcissiflorum
Colchicum various
Crocus various
Cyclamen various
Fritillaria various
Galanthus various
Narcissus several including
N. tazetta
Scilla various
Sisyrinchium various
Sternbergia lutea

Climbing foliage forms a backcloth to an impressive urn planted with helichrysum, below which is the strongly contrasting sculptured foliage of Hosta sieboldiana 'Elegans' *and a selection of balls of box.*

Contrasting herbaceous and shrubby growth against a wall. The yuccas are particularly effective with their sword-like leaves.

COOL AND SHADY

Walls and fences that face away from the sun are going to be cooler than those that bear its full brunt, but still have more equable air and soil temperatures than the open garden. At their base a collection of ferns could be amassed, some perfectly hardy and others that can benefit from a little protection (see pp.126-128 for more fern ideas). A range of bulbs mix well with ferns, snowdrops and cyclamens being especially attractive and adaptable. Try also dwarf *Narcissus cyclamineus* hybrids, some of the less rampant scillas and winter aconites.

Sector Two – the Prime Site

As we move upwards to about 1.8m (6ft) above the ground, conditions change: plants still benefit from the reflected and stored heat of walls warmed by the sun but have more light and air. Leaf growth of shrubs and climbers reaching here can be more impressive than below where branches can be crowded. Many climbers will have established a trunk below and now begin to spread themselves. Here gardeners can begin making use of the wall to give backbone to shrubs that have been trained upwards. Such plants may be trimmed to size at this level. Those with higher-reaching branches can be persuaded to bring down their growth to more sensible altitudes; climbing roses can be bent over with the idea of stimulating fresh growth and flowers more within reach.

The middle section is visually important. It is vital to plan the best use of it. Like arrangements on shelves in a supermarket, it is at eye level and, just below that, we should display those items to which we want to draw most attention. It is at this height that we look first in the garden, especially near walls. Most of the shrubs that are suitable for growing against walls are between one and three metres (3-10ft) high, and even the larger ones growing to, and above, the three-metre level will spend much of their lifespan reaching up from this lower level.

While the upper reaches of the walls are going to be mainly occupied with climbers, possibly augmented by hanging baskets and window boxes, the first two metres and the ground in front will probably be mainly taken over by shrubs. These will be chosen for their intrinsic value as foliage and flowering plants, but they will play a part in forming a benign environment for the higher climbers by giving improved frost cover around their bases, as well as, perhaps, giving some extra shelter to those low growers, such as bulbs, at the base.

Choices for this prime site should include a

balance of evergreen and deciduous shrubs, giving extra points for those that provide interest through the winter months. Make sure that space is allowed for those climbers and, more specifically, shrubs that are going to be planted against the wall and trained upwards to the higher reaches. It might be a mistake to include such easy things as the forsythia cultivars as these are undeniably brilliant for a few weeks in spring but become really rather ordinary, or even nondescript, for the rest of the year. A camellia can look wonderful in bloom and has a quality dress of foliage out of bloom. *Garrya elliptica* is useful as it begins to festoon itself with catkins in the autumn and is then decorated through most of the winter. True, its evergreen foliage can be rather dark and matt – decorous rather than exciting – but something may be made of this by contrasting it with neighbouring plants such as the bright-foliaged euonymus cultivars or a boldly variegated ivy.

Foliage is often undervalued. Here we have a medley including the low silver-white Artemisia absinthium in the foreground together with the opulent vine Vitis coignetiae covering the wall.

Sector Three – the Higher Reaches

Sector three is only likely to occur on the walls of houses and other tall buildings. All the way up to the guttering at roof level the wall can be covered with climbers and trained trees and shrubs. Their lower parts and roots will be tucked away at the very favoured base of the wall; their upper parts may get a larger share of the wind and cold, particularly in the winter when they could be subject to cold, or even freezing, winds. This exposure could mean that they suffer some damage to foliage and stems but it would have to be very bad weather with several degrees of frost to do much real harm as the wall will still act as a protective shield.

If there is some dieback on plants growing at this height, it is normally made good very quickly in the spring. Even relatively tender plants, that might have a lot of their top growth 'pruned' by the winter, will soon recover. Sometimes, after a particularly bad winter, you might find what seems to be a real tragedy – the whole plant looks dead – but do not lose heart. A few decades ago we had a very severe winter and everywhere in our Worcestershire garden there seemed to be dead bushes. A substantial *Garrya elliptica* had every leaf killed and the wood was apparently also lost. Although we sawed the dead wood off a few centimetres from the ground level and burnt it, the digging out and disposing of the remaining corpse was left for a while. Before I got round to this task new shoots had appeared on it, and by the end of the season we had a respectable-size shrub again. The moral? Do not be too quick to bring in the demolition gang.

A major candidate for the upper sector, due to its amenability to being pressed up to and pruned against a wall, is *Magnolia grandiflora* probably using 'Exmouth' form, though there are quite a number of fine cultivars from which to choose. This is an evergreen of stately presence. Its highly polished laurel-like foliage

The red brick walls make a good background for the blue-flowered Ceanothus impressus, *the tall limy-green* Euphorbia wulfenii *and the lower-growing* E. polychroma *and* halimium.

looks good all round the year and it provides huge, white, upright bowl-shaped blossom in late summer to autumn every year from a few years after planting. *Magnolia delavayi* with massive, slightly corrugated leaves can be as majestic, and is well worth growing as a foliage plant alone. Both can be trained to the wall by being tied back and sparingly pruned.

More neatly tailored tall shrubs can be grown quickly up most walls. Among these the heavily berrying pyracanthas must be considered. Few shrubs can be so bright for the months from autumn through the winter. Evergreen ceanothus cultivars can be given frequent haircuts and made to fit almost any shape. A bold flat column reaching up the wall can look very well and will provide a mass of blue blossom. If

you dare to try it, you could aim for two or even more matching columns. If so the same cultivar should be used for each column. The tricoloured foliage of the deciduous *Actinidia kolomikta* is most unusual; the shrub/tree takes little pruning to make a wide framework over the wall and can reach almost any height desired.

Integrating the Three Sectors

There is no need to make heavy weather over plant integration as everyone's needs are going to be different. However, it does make sense to try to tackle the planting in some order and to attempt a visualization of what the planting will look like when fully matured. Trellis or stretched wire may need to be attached securely to the walls before too much planting is effected.

The major players to cover the wide expanses of the wall up to the roof – if we aim so high – are best chosen and planted first. Suitable contenders for the upper wall vary from the wisterias that will, in relatively few years, give a sense of almost ancient fixity to the rampant Virginia creeper tribe. Remember that the latter are late-ish into leaf, will find the gutters to twine around and after a magnificent autumn display will provide loads of leaves to cart to the compost heap before leaving the wall bare except for the tracery of their branches through the winter. It may be a mistake to use the warm sunny walls for such easy plants: keep these choice spots for the less hardy. Ivies should not be despised. They will grow well in the coldest spots and do not need the best of soils.

Once the self-clingers have been planted, the leaners such as *Magnolia grandiflora*, pyracanthas, *Euonymus fortunei* and *Ceanothus* forms should be strategically placed so that their mature size does not interfere with windows or other areas that it is important to keep clear of growth. Winter jasmine and forsythias can be added where they are wanted, and some of the lower reaches of sunny walls given over for the colourful quinces, *Chaenomeles* forms.

Next come the plants, such as *Cobaea scandens*, cup and saucer plant, that are interesting and beautiful but don't know if they are perennial or annual. Cobaea can be grown as a relatively modest climber or, in sheltered spots, as a substantial clamberer, reaching 3-6m (10-20ft). The big-leaved *Pueraria thunbergiana*, Japanese arrowroot, is another plant that has the same split personality. It makes a rampant climber in milder areas. I would grow it for its leaves alone, but it is also one of those plants whose immense energy one can admire as worthwhile in itself. It does have 30cm (12in) racemes of scented flowers in episcopal reddish purple shades, too – attractive even if they are inclined to be half-hidden by the exuberant foliage.

Important free-standing shrubs, such as camellias and garrya, can then be stationed. Beneath and beside these come the smaller shrubs and in warm pockets the bulbs – nerine, *Amaryllis belladonna*, narcissus, gladioli, sternbergia, cyclamens and snowdrops.

SUPPORT PLANTS

The stronger-growing wall plants can become hosts to many forms of climbers. Have a trawl through those listed on pp.166-187, but beware of such energetic characters as the wonderful *Clematis montana* family. Do not do without them but give them a real challenge elsewhere – how about the top of that × *Cupressocyparis leylandii* that is scraping the sky? As well as the large-flowered clematis so often seen with roses, the honeysuckles might strike up a meaningful duet.

In areas where the newly planted shrubs look very small, the gaping spaces may be clothed with some of the quick-growing, climbing annuals (see pp.235-241). Nasturtiums will make you recall moments of your youth in their growing and climbing easy colour and life. Climbing gourds can be amusing, and attractive, too. As the shrubs grow, the reliance on the annuals will diminish, but they can still be worth giving some chance to shine; some will grow over shrubs without overwhelming them.

The South African Nerine bowdenii *is here very much at home with lavender and clambering Boston ivy.*

SHADED SITES

There is no need to feel wary of shaded sites; there are far more plants that are entirely happy to spend their lives in partial or complete shade than there are those that revel in undiluted sunshine.

Shady sites are those that either never get the sun, such as a north-facing wall in the northern hemisphere, or those that get the morning sun but are then sunless for the rest of the day, such as those that are east-facing.

The first mentioned has the coolest, most shaded conditions. This might be thought a major handicap but it is not necessarily so. Many climbers and shrubs suitable for growing up walls are found in woodland conditions in the wild where they may not feel that much sun hitting them directly. Another feature of this site is that, despite being cool it may also be quite dry. The wall or fence may create a rain-shadow (see p.103).

A third feature of this cool site is perhaps a little less obvious. The predominant winds in much of Britain are from the south-west and other quarters, rather than from the north; therefore the plants growing on or by the north wall are not likely to be buffeted by too much wind, although, when the cold north winds do blow, they will have their cobwebs blown away. Even then the wall will save them from feeling the full force of the north wind.

An east-facing site is likely to be a little warmer than a north-facing one as it may get some sun in the early morning. It can be cold, it can be dry and it may be windy. On the other hand, it may be sheltered and offer a protected home to many plants.

The average temperatures of the wall or fence and its environs are likely to be cool rather than warm. However, there should be no real worries about temperatures as long as this coolness is borne in mind. On walls that only get the morning sun there is less chance of the bricks soaking up heat, storing it and releasing it during the colder periods of the night and in cool spells, which is important for plants towards the end of the winter and in spring when they are in growth and more vulnerable to cold damage. The ripening of wood at the end of the growing season will normally be satisfactory but may be less thorough than on sunnier walls. There are likely to be fluctuations in temperatures though the day, but they are not going to be as extreme as those on the other walls.

Like the north-facing site, in Britain, the ground that is close to the house on the east will lie in the rain-shadow and may escape the main load of any shower or storm. Hence it may be

Right: in this quiet corner a statue is draped with golden hop, Humulus lupulus *'Aureus', and chaperoned by* Iris pseudacorus *'Variegata' and* Geranium pratense.

Left: an Italian statue, contemplating warmer climes, is comforted by the vine, Vitis coignetiae, *and the* Hydrangea *'Ami Pasquier' in the foreground.*

necessary to arrange for extra moisture or at least to ensure that the soil has moisture-retaining qualities. Humus, in the form of peat, compost or any other form of organic matter, will help to provide food as well as acting like a sponge in retaining water.

Over Britain winds from the east are not as frequent as those from the south or west. However, through the winter months, any winds from this quarter can be very cold and will test the hardiness of any plant. Persistent strong winds in freezing conditions can badly scorch evergreens such as conifers. In built-up areas it is unlikely that much wind damage will be experienced, though, as the wall will act as a cushion to break its main force.

Plants for Cool, Shady Sites

There are plenty of plants from which to choose for cool, shady sites. Ivies are legion; there are only about a dozen species but these have a huge number of distinct forms, cultivars and varieties. At present there are around 400 cultivars of *Hedera helix*, the common ivy, on sale. The large-leaved vine, *Vitis coignetiae*, will manage here and look opulent in maturity and magnificent when donning autumn dress.

Climbing flowering shrubs for a shady spot can include many splendidly coloured ones that can dispel any notion of the site being a dull, cheerless place. Many of the large-flowered clematis hybrids such as the old favourite 'Nelly Moser' will be happy here, together with forms of species such as members of the rampant *C. montana* clan and the species hybrid *C. × jouiniana* 'Praecox'. Honeysuckles will also thrive. More exotic things such as the coral plant, *Berberidopsis corallina*, and the Chilean bellflower, *Lapageria rosea*, are perfectly happy, as is the climbing hydrangea, *H. petiolaris*, together with its look-alikes *Schizophragma hydrangeoides* and *S. integrifolium*.

At the base of the wall you can have ferns with grasses and a collection of bulbs.

The robust and justifiably named Rosa multiflora *and* Clematis × durandii *climb above white forms of foxglove,* Digitalis purpurea, *a popular shade-lover. A number of roses and clematis are happy in the shade.*

INTRODUCING LIGHT AND COLOUR

The sunless wall may need some artificial light-ing, or rather lightening by means of bright-foliaged plants, as well as the shining flowers, so it is best to give the dark ivies a miss and go for the brighter-variegated kinds. Some such as the golden-leaved *Hedera helix* 'Buttercup' may not be quite as bright a gold in the shade of the wall but can still be cheerful, as can the popular 'Goldheart'. Cultivars with silvery-cream varie-gation are helpful, too: 'Glacier' is a very popu-lar one. Like 'Buttercup', coloured forms of the larger-leaved species may not be quite as vivid as in sunny spots but will nevertheless lighten the aspect; *H. colchica* 'Dentata Variegata' or *H. colchica* 'Sulphur Heart' are worth a try. The golden hop, *Humulus lupulus* 'Aureus' will be limy green rather than gold, but then in very bright sunshine the leaves can get burnt.

The many fine forms of *Euonymus fortunei* are excellent in shady areas and can be trained to grow up walls, perhaps as far as the gutters. Their bright cream or golden variegation can provide one of the most cheerful bits of colour

This shady corner is created by a tree up which grows a column of ivy. Below it are ferns, Hydrangea serrata 'Preziosa' and other shade-happy plants, like Pulmonaria saccharata Argentea Group.

on a shaded wall and it is there throughout the year, perhaps becoming even brighter and more colourful in the cold of winter.

Major quantities of flower colour can be introduced by using clematis and roses. There is a natural tendency to associate both these important plants with lots of sunshine. However, many of them will do well with quite a bit of shade and these will certainly brighten the aspect.

Evergreen Choices

It may be thought wise to pick more evergreen than deciduous plants, especially as the whole point is to ensure that any lurking suspicion of dullness through the long winter is defeated. *Jasminum nudiflorum*, winter jasmine, which has the appearance of being evergreen because of its green stems, can be especially valuable in this season, lightening up the dark with its flowers of bright primrose. In really mild areas with neutral or acid soils one could try *Agapetes macrantha* which has interesting, hanging urn-shaped flowers of white, usually made pink through red patterning, in winter. *Jasminum polyanthum* is often thought of as a conservatory climber that can start blooming after Christmas in Britain and seemingly go on forever. In milder areas it will bloom in shady sites from late spring to early autumn with its pink-budded, white-opening flowers gushing out their sweet scent. In areas with very severe winters, the scrambling *Solanum crispum* is usually recommended for a position in full sun, but elsewhere it can be worth a try in less sunny spots. The preferred cultivar 'Glasnevin' will bloom from early summer until the end of early autumn, and maybe well beyond this.

There are also some more exotic-looking plants that can be invited around the corner to the most shaded site of all. One is the Chilean coral plant, *Berberidopsis corallina*. The generic name was given because of a passing similarity of its flowers to those of *Berberis*, beyond which there is no relationship between this monotypic genus and the multifarious berberis clan. *Berberidopsis* is a lover of moist, humus-rich soils. It can grow up a wall for 5m (15ft) or more and decorate itself for a long time through summer into autumn with plastic-looking, drooping swags of bead-like deep red flowers.

Deciduous Choices

There is a rush of energy that imparts a liveliness to deciduous plants that is less obvious in the evergreens. *Parthenocissus* creepers rush the wall and scale it by leaps and bounds, then at the end of the year after the glorious finale with fiery autumn colours, all the leaves come down in a rush, too. The hydrangeas and schizophragmas are tough plants that are best pressed tight against a wall when first planted. Once they have got a grip, they grow well, but they are at their best after a few years when they have established a wide wall territory and begin to flower more freely.

It is worth considering some of the less frequently seen climbers, even if they have a reputation for slight tenderness. In very bleak areas

EVERGREEN CLIMBERS

The plants listed here are hardy climbers and wall shrubs suitable for a cool shady wall.

Akebia quinata
Azara microphylla
Berberidopsis corallina
Cotoneaster many
Euonymus fortunei cultivars
Hedera species and cultivars
Holboellia coriacea
Holboellia latifolia
Itea ilicifolia
Kadsura japonica
Lapageria rosea
Lardizabala biternata
Pileostegia viburnoides
Piptanthus nepalensis
Pyracantha in variety
Solanum crispum

A rough shed made beautiful by the popular ivy Hedera helix *'Goldheart' and honeysuckle* L. ×. tellmanniana

DECIDUOUS CLIMBERS

The plants listed here are hardy
climbers or wall shrubs suitable
for a shady site.
Those marked * either have
evergreen relations or are
evergreen in their effect.

Akebia trifoliata
Aristotelia tomentosa
Berchemia racemosa
Celastrus orbiculatus
Chaenomeles in variety
Clematis species and hybrids*
Codonopsis convolvulacea
Cotoneaster horizontalis
Forsythia suspensa
Fuchsia 'Riccartonii'
Hamamelis in variety
Humulus lupulus 'Aureus'
Hydrangea petiolaris
*Jasminum nudiflorum**
Kerria japonica 'Pleniflora'
Lathyrus latifolius
Lonicera x *americana*
Lonicera caprifolium
Lonicera periclymenum
Lonicera x *tellmanniana*
Lonicera tragophylla
and others*
Parthenocissus tricuspidata and
other species
Rosa 'Albéric Barbier'
Rosa 'Mme. Alfred Carrière'
Rosa 'Maigold'
Rosa 'Parkdirektor Riggers'
Rosa 'Sympathie'
Schizophragma species
Tropaeolum speciosum
Vitis coignetiae

it is foolhardy to try really tender things, but plants such as the akebias are normally perfectly hardy. *A. trifoliata* is one of the best of deciduous climbing plants to go up a shaded wall, although its early flowers could be caught by a severe late frost. It is a deciduous, earlier-flowering relation of the more widely grown *A. quinata*, which is evergreen by inclination, but is sometimes forced, by hard winters, to drop its leaves. The tripartite theme of the leaflets is echoed by the flowers with three purple petals most clearly seen in the much larger female ones at the

bottom of each spray than in the projecting groups of small male ones. It is a plant to grow between two sheltering evergreen species, perhaps *Garrya elliptica* or a mahonia and *Berberidopsis corallina*, which, like the akebia, does not like being disturbed once planted.

Shrubs

Do not ignore the commoner shrubs for this site. They are probably common because of their solid, reliable, yeoman qualities. A standby for

An archway formed naturally by the winter-flowering Garrya elliptica in the Dingle Garden, near Haverfordwest, Pembrokeshire.

EVERGREEN SHRUBS

Aucuba japonica
Berberis x stenophylla
and others
Buxus sempervirens
B. sempervirens 'Marginata'
Camellia species and hybrids,
when sheltered from early
sunshine
Choisya ternata
Crinodendron hookerianum
Daphne in variety
Drimys winteri
Eleaagnus pungens
Escallonia macrantha and
various others
Garrya elliptica
Ilex in variety
Illicium anisatum
Lomatia myricoides
Viburnum tinus
V. x burkwoodii and similar
hybrids

*Sea buckthorn, Hippophaë
rhamnoides, is a very
hardy shrub, useful in
many difficult sites and
decorative with berries for
months through the winter.*

such shady places that are also plagued with poor soil is *Aucuba japonica* in one of its variegated forms. *A. japonica* 'Variegata' or one of the other clones can manage well in the most unlikely spots, forming rounded masses of healthy, polished foliage in rich green marked with bright golden variegation. It will hold the fort and look well in shade or sun, in poor soil or good and in dry or moist conditions.

Another toughie is *Hippophaë rhamnoides*, sea buckthorn, which can be found around the coast of Britain. It is used for windbreaks in these coastal areas and may even be employed, along with marran grass, to stop sand dunes from drifting. Its silvery foliage during the growing season is pleasing enough; the bright golden berries of autumn and winter are a very long-lasting decoration.

CAMELLIAS AND THE EARLY MORNING SUN

Although they will grow perfectly well, are certainly hardy enough for the conditions, and will enjoy the partial shade and shelter from searing winds, camellias would not be at their best where they get the early morning sun. This is because of the flowers, which tend to form and open from midwinter onwards. Because such a site does not get so much of the sun's heat, it will be more subject to frost, and the flower buds will be more susceptible to frost damage because their frosted parts will be exposed to the early morning sun and be defrosted too quickly, ending up mushy and coffee-brown. In other spots any flowers that are cold and lightly frosted may be safely thawed out and little damage will be done.

The *C. sasanqua* cultivars will be happy to grow in full sun, although, like all camellias, they take a little while to establish and need soil that is free of lime and preferably just on the acid side of neutral.

Ground-level Plants (sector one)

If a carefree regime is the aim, it is sensible to rely on the shrubs and climbers to provide the dominant interest and then to cover the ground with creeping plants that will help keep weeds at bay. The evergreen *Pachysandra terminalis* will grow to some 10-15cm (4-6in) in height and soon extend to create a dense growth of fleshy, rich green leaves. Its tidy habit makes it well worth considering even though its tiny white flower spikes, which appear in spring, are nothing to get excited about. Another possibility is *P. terminalis* 'Variegata' which creates a brighter effect with its cream variegation. In wider areas the tough *Vinca major* 'Variegata' will dash about with splendid vigour – it may need checking at times. The bright green leaves are margined creamy-white. Even more rapacious is the evergreen scrambling bramble *Rubus tricolor* with its heavily embossed, highly polished dark green leaves. In dry areas a reliable option is the useful spurge, *Euphorbia amygdaloides* var. *robbiae*, which will provide dark green leaf cover, augmented for months through the late winter and spring with sprays of lime-green flowers.

The ground below a shady wall can be a good site for shade-loving ferns. Try to include some

MAHONIAS

Mahonias are a trustworthy lot that certainly manage well in cool spots out of the sun where their fine foliage and flowers can be appreciated. Most kinds are suitable.

Mahonia aquifolium is useful in very poor soils and conditions. *M.* × *media* hybrids such as 'Buckland', the famous 'Charity', 'Lionel Fortesque', with more vertical flower sprays, and 'Winter Sun' all have magnificent evergreen, more or less flat-ironed, pinnate leaves decoratively and sharply armed with spikes and good yellow blossom from late autumn into winter. *M. nervosa* is splendidly tough, tidy and respectable with its neat holly-like leaves.

The fine series of hybrids *M.* × *wagneri* of which 'Moseri' is outstanding, having foliage that is flushed red or pink all round the year. *M. japonica* and the hybrids can look very distinguished, but even the underrated *M. aquifolium* can be splendid. It is a long-suffering, suckering shrub that will manage a pleasing cover over a site under-endowed with moisture and good soil.

fully evergreen species as well as deciduous and semi-evergreen kinds. In the shelter of the wall, most semi-evergreen ferns will be as green as grass through any but the most bitter of winters. Do not be too daunted by the suggestions of some writers regarding growing requirements. While the usual idea of an ideal spot for ferns is one of moist shade, and this is generally correct, there are plenty of ferns that manage quite well with some sun or shade and many will grow very reasonably in dryish soils. I have found that some types normally found in moist areas will often do well in drier soils, even if they do not grow to their maximum possible size. Hart's tongue fern (*Asplenium scolopendrium*) is considered a plant for wet or wettish places; we have it, and a collection of its mutant forms, growing happily in a dry bed. Others that we have found useful in a dryish border include the autumn fern, *Dryopteris erythrosora*, the male fern *D. filix-mas*, plus even the lady fern, *Athyrium filix-femina*. The polypodys are also very useful in

Mahonias are splendid in shady spots, the hybrid series, M. × media *being especially good with classic evergreen foliage and winter blossom. 'Lionel Fortesque' is distinguished by its vertical flower spikes.*

coloured conifers, or with a succession of flowering plants. Urns on pedestals will draw the eye up from the ground and can be used to punctuate the whole with colour from winter-flowering pansies, polyanthus or a range of potted items that can be dropped into the area as they come into bloom. It is even possible to bring a series of lilies into such an area for the weeks when they are in looking their splendid best, so long as they can get back to the sunshine after they have flowered.

Most annuals are plants that revel in sunshine. They will not normally make good plants in a shady site but, by growing some in pots, they can be brought around for a period when

Dryopteris erythrosora is a splendid deciduous fern, also known as the Japanese shield fern or the autumn fern on account of the orange colour of its young fronds.

drier soils. In the wild they often grow at the base of large trees or even on stone walls where they are likely to find water in short supply.

The ferns associate well with ivies and many grasses of which there is now such a wide choice available in good garden centres. Consider some of those listed in the margin. To give a colour-lift to the ensemble, a series of bulbs can be introduced. Obvious candidates are the many forms of snowdrops and dwarf daffodils, bluebells, scillas, and winter aconites. Windflower, *Anemone nemorosa*, together with *A. blanda*, will look attractive as will the dog's tooth violets, *Erythronium* species and cultivars.

Serendipity led us to a discovery that would not normally be endorsed by the experts. By accident we had clumps of the South African *Nerine bowdenii* develop at the base of a north wall; the received wisdom is that this needs all the sun that is available, but ours flower freely. They were, of course, shallowly planted and in well-drained soil. We have also grown camassias successfully in similar positions.

FERNS FOR DRIER SPOTS

Asplenium ceterach
Asplenium trichomanes
Athyrium filix-femina and its myriad forms
Dryopteris affinis
Dryopteris erythrosora
Dryopteris filix-mas and cultivars
Dryopteris wallichiana
Polypodium australe
Polypodium vulgare

Seasonal Additions

The whole aspect of a cool shady wall can be transformed by the addition of one or two major containers, which can either be planted up with some permanent foliage feature, such as brightly they are in full bloom. Large containers could be wheeled round with a tripod or obelisk festooned with climbers such as sweet peas, black-eyed Susan (*Thunbergia alata*), or nasturtiums. I find great success with busy-lizzies and they go on flowering well into October on a north-facing site in our part of the world. While I admit they are not my favourite plant one has to admire their colour, generosity of flower and usefulness for duller corners.

Infrastructure

Some plants in shady sites are more vulnerable to the vagaries of the climate than those in

The background of the vigorous golden hop Humulus lupulus *'Aureus' highlights the container plants, the spheres of box and the flowering* Lilium speciosum *var.* rubrum.

sunny ones. It might be wise, therefore, to consider ameliorating the worst dangers by using screens and shelters for these wall-dwellers. Shelter can include carefully chosen plants, positioned further out into the garden to provide a break against the wind.

The sunless wall may not be the ideal place for a pergola or arbour, but one or two arches could be just the thing to tie the house in with the garden and give an opportunity to lead up some interesting or attractive plant. On a wall that gets some sun in the morning a pergola might be a useful support for climbers of a tough disposition.

Paths nearby will have some influence on the surrounds, perhaps from the drainage below them or from reflecting or absorbing warmth. The first rule of path-making is to ensure that it is safe. Paving stones in a shady site should be as free as possible from wet, which will encourage moss and algae, which in their turn can cause a slippery, treacherous surface. There is usually a need to provide free-draining foundations. The next consideration could be the visual one of tone and colour. In a site that gets little or no direct sun it would probably be best to choose a light shade and a warm colour, such as red brick. An alternative is a good pea gravel mix, usually better than the cold greys or blues of granite chippings.

Care and Maintenance

In shady, sheltered areas it is helpful to trim plants regularly to prevent crowded growth which will produce stagnant air conditions that may encourage fungus diseases. We will want to maximize the effect of any bright-foliaged plant; this may mean extra feeding and curbing the growth of neighbours. Dead-heading that might be overlooked elsewhere could pay extra dividends in the shade where every extra bloom is needed. Keeping paths swept and dead foliage tidied away will help preclude any sense of a neglected area. It is always easier to spend time in sunnier spots!

SUNNY SITES

Use the microclimate created on the sunny side of walls and fences to the full.
Be bold and consider plants from tropical climes, those that would be very
doubtful starters in the open.

Walls and fences that face the sun or receive sun for a large part of the day are the most favoured ones, particularly in terms of warmth and light. It is here that we are able to try some of the plants that in other situations could prove not fully hardy. The extra protection, warmth and the consequent better ripening of wood allow gardeners to be very adventurous. We certainly ought to maximize the possibilities. The only drawback is that there could be some danger of very dry conditions occurring at times, something that happens near all larger structures but which is exaggerated by the extra warmth received by those facing the sun.

In the northern hemisphere, the wall that faces the west should be the most favoured of all. Warm and bright, it may escape some of the fiercest sun and will be fractionally less exposed to the coldest winds than most other sites.

While it would be a shame to use up favoured spots with shrubs that can do just as well in the open or on the other shadier walls and fences, the only plants that must be avoided are those that object to a surfeit of sun.

Other than the huge range of plants that can be planted on or near this site, there are the tender or tenderish plants discussed later (see pp.242-249). It is possible to enhance further the sun-trap effect and create some special spots that are even warmer than the rest of the site and its environs. For example, a wall, partial fence, or trellis that extends outwards from a sunny wall, will help block any inclement winds and enhance the shelter and warmth for some few cubic metres. Here can be planted the more exotic shrubs from South America, South Africa or Australasia, together with bulbs and other herbaceous plants from these regions and from the Mediterranean.

Plants for Warm, Sunny Sites

To provide interest all round the year in a sunny site, a wide variety of plants need to be used, including both evergreen and deciduous climbers and shrubs, as well as a good variety of bulbs and herbaceous plants along with some ground-covering ones, too. Most important is to ensure that there is a good selection of kinds that will be of interest through the winter. *Chimonanthus praecox* takes a little while to grow to a large specimen, but is certainly a good investment as it distributes its dividend of sweet perfume in the depth of the winter. *Chaenomeles* forms at the bottom of the wall will often be in bloom before Christmas and are in full flower when the leaves are unfurling; the warmth

A cheerful yellow mix of herbaceous plants. The delphinium 'Sungleam' is accompanied by the daisy flowers of Anthemis 'E.C. Buxton' and Lysimachia ciliata 'Firecracker'.

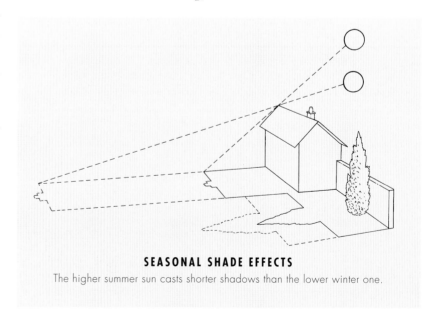

SEASONAL SHADE EFFECTS
The higher summer sun casts shorter shadows than the lower winter one.

encourages this greater precocity and freedom of flower than might occur in cooler spots. *Abeliophyllum distichum*, the creamy-white relative of the forsythia is worth a place for its late winter flowers. It is by no means as extrovert in growth as the forsythias, which one would hesitate to give space in this area. (A word in favour of *Forsythia suspensa*: its different character means that a case can be made for training it up the wall and overgrowing it with other climbers.)

Other winter stalwarts include the evergreen clematis, *C. cirrhosa* and the slightly later, larger *C. armandii*. The opportunity to grow *Iris unguicularis* should not be missed. Once settled it requires little or no care, and yet provides huge quantities of magnificent winter blossom. Not mean little flowers such as some winter bloomers offer, but magnificent creations that would make the plant a favourite even if it bloomed in spring or midsummer, with all the competition those seasons provide. The usual form is splendid but there are paler and darker violet forms as well as a number of whites.

Evergreen Choices

The evergreen element in any planting plan for a sunny wall gives plenty of scope for choice. The quick-growing and splendid North African broom, *Cytisus battandieri*, might be thought worth a place: its large silvery foliage is pleasing and the tight bunches of golden blossom smelling of pineapples are borne over a long period. It will go up a high wall and look distinctive. The splendid foliage is normally evergreen but can be dropped in prolonged periods of very cold weather.

Pittosporum forms are grown for their shining, tightly packed foliage and can be groomed to size and shape. They enjoy any extra warmth they can get, as many of those most commonly grown are natives of subtropical climes. Some of the evergreen magnolias have really large leaves and, though they can be grown on cooler walls, a sunnier aspect suits them best. *Magnolia grandiflora* against a wall will be reaching the bed-

Above: some of the sunshine of California is reflected in the blossom of Fremontodendron californicum, *here growing around a doorway. This golden wonder can be in bloom for a surprisingly long time.*

room levels in a decade and will have been providing a quota of its large white blossoms well before this. The laurel-like shining leaves make it a good contrast to most of the other smaller-leaved evergreens such as the ceanothus clan.

Olearias from New Zealand and Australasia can be good foliage plants and cover themselves with bunches of yellow or white daisy flowers in spring or summer. Top choice is *Olearia ilicifolia* from Tasmania which has very handsome foliage almost mimicking that of hollies but not quite so lacquered. It will make a rounded bush that can hide the lower leggy bits of climbers such as clematis or honeysuckle and those climbing roses that have become rather ossified in their older major branches.

EVERGREEN SHRUBS

Abelia x grandiflora
Abutilon megapotamicum
Abutilon x suntense
Abutilon vitifolium
Acacia baileyana
Acacia dealbata
Callistemon salignus
Choisya ternata
Cistus in variety
Coronilla valentina
subsp. *glauca*
Crinodendron hookerianum
Cytisus battandieri
Euryops pectinatus
Euphorbia characias
subsp. *wulfenii*
Grevillea rosmarinifolia and
in variety
Grindelia chiloensis
Leptospermum scoparium
Myrtus communis
Phlomis species
Phygelius capensis
Pittosporum various
Romneya coulteri

Deciduous Choices

There is a wide variety of climbers and wall shrubs that thrive in a sunny site. Those mentioned here are probably at their best on walls that get the sun all day, but will be happy on the slightly more shaded ones such as the west-facing in the northern hemisphere.

Actinidia kolomikta needs some encouragement to make its way up a wall and is best tied onto wires or trellis support, especially as it takes a while to get going strongly. It is never as rampant as its kiwi fruit relative, *Actinidia deliciosa*, but once established can cover wide stretches of wall and reach up some 4-5m (12-15ft) with its numerous slender stems. It is grown for its wide, heart-shaped leaves that are handsome enough in rich greens, but are even more wonderful when half or fully coloured cream or pink. It looks as if those painters in *Alice in Wonderland* who were busy painting the roses the correct colour have taken time out to play around with the actinidia. The plant in cultivation is a male with small white flowers carried singly or in twos and threes, but with each being little more than a centimetre across, the floral display is not a heart-quickening event.

There are lots of deciduous climbers and scramblers waiting to enjoy your sunny walls. You can choose from all the clematis and honeysuckle forms, the passion flowers, wisterias, grape vines, the Virginia creeper and its kin, as well as the favourite climbing and rambling roses.

Sun-lovers among the deciduous wall shrubs are just as numerous. Ones that can cope with dry, sunny wall sites include the coral tree (*Erythrina crista-galli*), the fremontodendrons, *Xanthoceras sorbifolium* and *Chaenomeles* forms. Others that are clamouring for a spot are *Viburnum grandiflorum*, the hardy fuchsias, shrub roses, philadelphus species and hybrids, *Potentilla fruticosa* cultivars, *Berberis thunbergii* forms together with other deciduous relatives,

Right: the splendid Actinidia kolomikta does a wall-covering act with its unusually coloured attractive foliage.

SOUTH AMERICAN SHRUBS AND CLIMBERS

Most of the South American, particularly Chilean, shrubs that are thought to want that touch of extra protection can be gathered by a sunny wall or fence; *Choisya ternata* is not one of these and has proved itself a real trooper elsewhere.

Abutilon vitifolium
Aristotelia chinensis
Azara various
Cestrum aurantiacum
Cestrum parqui
Crinodendron hookerianum
Eucryphia glutinosa
Fabiana imbricata
Rhaphithamnus spinosus
Solanum crispum
Sophora microphylla
Tropaeolum speciosum
Tropaeolum tricolorum

DECIDUOUS CLIMBERS

Actinidia chinensis
Actinidia kolomikta
Campsis radicans
Campsis x tagliabuana
Caryopteris incana
Clematis alpina
Clematis chrysocoma
Clematis florida
Clematis macropetala
Clematis montana
Clematis tangutica
Jasminum officinale
Lonicera etrusca
Lonicera periclymenum
Rosa species and cultivars
Schizophragma hydrangeoides
Sophora davidii
Vitis vinifera
Wisteria species and cultivars

The thick-textured leaves of Actinidia chinensis, *the climber that produces kiwi fruits. This is the useful hermaphrodite form which is able to produce its own fruit.*

DECIDUOUS SHRUBS

Abeliophyllum distichum
Abutilon in variety
Aloysia triphylla
Buddleja colvillei
Buddleja crispa
Buddleja fallowiana
Chaenomeles many
Chimonanthus praecox
Clianthus puniceus
Erythrina crista-galli
Forsythia suspensa
Hibiscus in variety
Hoheria glabrata
Hoheria lyallii
Punica granatum
Ribes speciosum
Robinia hispida
Xanthoceras sorbifolium
Zauchneria californica

Caryopteris × clandonensis, the smaller prunus, spiraeas and cytisus species and hybrids.

Shrubs

The selection of shrubs for the lower reaches of a sunny site could include a number of the less obviously hardy plants, among which are the *Phygelius* species and hybrids. *Phygelius capensis*, the Cape figwort, is often found in garden centres among the herbaceous perennials. Although it can grow up to 2m (6ft) tall, it may be cut down to the ground in a severe winter and will then grow up again. In mild areas it can make an evergreen shrub. A South African native, it has soft-textured, ovate, rather pale green leaves and very erect, narrow panicles, perhaps 60cm (24in) long, with lots of hanging tubular flowers; outside they are orange and inside and down the throats they are golden (more forms are listed in pp.232-233).

Abutilons are familiar under glass; outside they are relatively scarce but can be tried in sheltered situations in not-too-cold areas. The Brazilian *A. megapotamicum* certainly looks exotic with its hanging blossoms of red and yellow. *Desfontainia spinosa* also comes from South America. Its foliage is very like that of a holly but it has very exotic hanging blossom.

It is a plant for peaty soils in mild, damp areas where it can find a cool, moist spot. From the other side of the world, the New Zealand parrot's bill, *Clianthus puniceus*, will add a touch of the unusual and bring admiration. From Australia the bottlebrushes (*Callistemon*) are a worthy choice. *Callistemon salignus* is attractive with its very unusual flowers made up mainly of stamens in green, cream, pale yellow, pink, mauve or red.

Ground-level Plants (sector one)

Once the upper reaches of the walls have been planned and planted, along with a selection of shrubs, the seemingly lesser, more ephemeral things – the herbaceous and bulbous characters – can be considered. Despite their low growth, they nevertheless may well last as long as any of the shrubs and climbers. The larger bulbous plants – *Amaryllis belladonna*, crinums, gladioli and nerines – might be joined by smaller ones such as *Zephryanthes candida* and *Sternbergia lutea*. Agapanthus will do well here, too.

Among the musts, *Nerine bowdenii* is the only really hardy species of the South African genus. Clumps can be left intact for decades. Grown in well-drained warm soil with noses at soil level, the first bulbs planted will take a season or two to begin to show their worth; they then bloom freely at the beginning of every autumn, usually spiking up from the bare soil after the leaves have disappeared, but on occasion the foliage remains.

One size or so larger than nerines, and with maroon stems, *Amaryllis belladonna* has open trumpets of pink and white. This is another bulb that once settled is very much best left alone. The only thing to watch is that the expanding clumps do not get overgrown by shrubs. Larger again, and this time by a big margin, are the crinums. The massive leaves – they can be 1-1.2m (3-4ft) long – look like those of a lax phormium or a gigantic scilla, and betoken a large inflorescence. The usual forms available are the hybrid *Crinum × powellii* and its variety 'Album'. Stems can easily reach 60cm (2ft) high and carry up to nine beautiful silken trumpets.

Infrastructure

A path of gravel or paving running parallel to a sunny wall or fence can form an additional source of heat, the sun's warmth being absorbed and reflected. This will contribute to the Mediterranean feel of such a site, but the increased heat may bring stress to some plants. They are vulnerable to water shortage. It is advisable, therefore, to make the soil moisture-retentive with plenty of humus and mulches.

In very dry spots, it may be worth considering trickle watering lines. Pergolas and arches can be used to contribute a modicum of shade.

Care and Maintenance

Routine annual work amounts to the trimming back of the over-eager growers, checking the safety of wall-mounted trellises and so on, pruning back the flowered growth of shrubs you want to encourage to make plenty of new flowering wood for next season, and keeping an eye open for weeds and pests. Maintaining a good mulch to retain moisture is important and thorough watering may be necessary in times of droughts.

HERBACEOUS PLANTS

Anthemis tinctoria cultivars
Campanula persicifolia
Diascia species and hybrids
Dictamnus albus
Euphorbia cyparissias
Euphorbia myrsinites
Globularia various
Helianthemum various
Hordeum jubatum
Iris unguicularis
Saponaria ocymoides
Sedum various
Sempervivum various

BULBS

Amaryllis belladonna
Eucomis various
Lilium candidum
Linum flavum
Nerine bowdenii
Gladiolus species and species hybrids
Narcissus tazetta
Triteleia various
Tulipa species and cultivars

Spring at Duckyls Garden near East Grinstead, Sussex. Clematis montana grows above the tulip 'White Triumphator' and irises in a wall bed.

135

Part Three
THE PLANTS

Self-clinging Climbers

Twiners

Ramblers & Scramblers

Wall Shrubs

Base of Wall Plants

Annuals

Tender Plants

Of all wall shrubs, the scrambling Solanum crispum 'Glasnevin' is one of the most rewarding as it blooms freely for months. Here it is keeping company with the chaste clematis 'Duchess of Edinburgh', to my eye still one of the best of the large-flowered cultivars.

SELF-CLINGING CLIMBERS

In the wild, self-clinging climbers are found growing over the ground and making their way up the trunks of trees, sometimes through shrubs and occasionally up or down rock faces. They are, therefore, usually capable of growing in places that are short of a lot of direct light. Some, like ivies, are programmed to grow with energy while in a juvenile state and only to develop into their adult forms when they are well established and have grown sufficiently high, and probably into lighter conditions. Quite a number of vines show this characteristic but none so clearly and persistently as ivies with their distinct difference between juvenile and adult foliage, the juvenile growth being incapable of producing flowers and seeds and the adult growth usually devoid of aerial roots. When cuttings are taken of the adult growth the resulting plants never have juvenile characteristics: in ivies they develop into rounded bushes, normally with the undivided ovate adult foliage. The juvenile leaves of the Virginia creeper are clearly divided into three leaflets; the adult leaves are larger and in one piece with just two indentations to give the three-pointed effect.

All the plants that are reviewed here start in wall sector one and grow through sector two into sector three (see pp.112-119).

Clinging Methods

AERIAL ROOTS

An aerial-rooting climber produces a series of roots that appear along the length of its stems. These attach themselves very strongly to the surfaces they find. The commonest example of an aerial rooter is ivy.

Aerial roots form a flat bonding surface but do not penetrate the supporting surface, so are only rarely capable of doing any damage to the surface (perhaps to the powdery mortar of old buildings). They are occasionally irritating in that when unwanted growth is pulled off the supporting wall or fence, some of the aerial root growth will be left and is difficult to remove. It is usually best initially to leave this alone and allow the weather to do its work, then, if need be, to scrub the dead tissue away with a hard brush. Propagation material taken with aerial roots will quickly provide a root system and independent plants.

TENDRIL BEARERS

There is a group of plants that climb upwards by producing a series of tendrils. In sweet peas and some other members of the huge pea family (Leguminosae), these tendrils appear as central extensions of the leaf stalks. In *Parthenocissus henryana* (other *Parthenocissus* produce suckers, see below), the tendrils are produced directly from the growing stems, the tendrils appearing opposite to the true leaves. Tendrils are touch sensitive and will curl round any small object they come into contact with and thus enable the plant to climb securely. Obviously these tendril climbers need something to climb up, either other

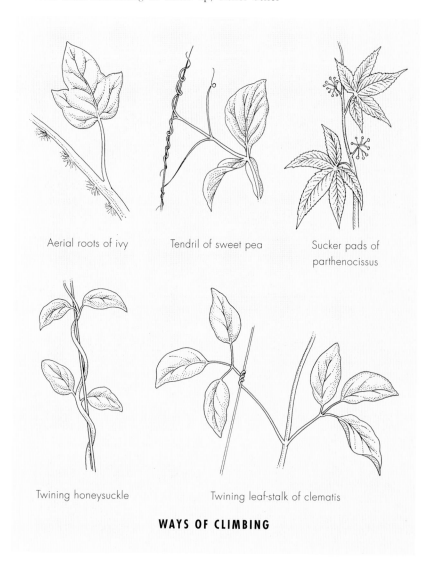

Aerial roots of ivy   Tendril of sweet pea   Sucker pads of parthenocissus

Twining honeysuckle   Twining leaf-stalk of clematis

WAYS OF CLIMBING

plants, such as shrubs, or artificial supports such as trellis or wires.

SUCKERS

Suckers may, perhaps, be thought of as a specialized form of tendril. The commonest example of a sucker bearer is *Parthenocissus quinquefolia*. As in *P. henryana*, the tendrils are produced along the young growing stems, opposite the leaves. Not every leaf produces tendrils, although it would appear that the nodal area at the base of each has the potential to do so as is the case with *P. henryana*. The main tendril stem divides quickly into a number of slender filaments, each of which has a scarcely perceivable pad at its tip. With time-lapse photography it is possible to record the movement of these filaments as they try to find a surface on which to grip. Once the tips have established contact, the tiny pad is much expanded and becomes a significant sucker, which fits so strongly to the surface that if the stem is pulled away the suckers are left behind. Like the aerial roots of ivies these suckers can be annoying on paintwork and need tackling in a similar way.

TWINING

Many climbers find support simply by twining their stems around any object they find. Twiners are reviewed on pp.152-165.

TWINING LEAF STEMS

Some plants economize, and do not produce suckers or tendrils but make do with sensitive leaf stalks which wrap themselves around objects for support. Clematis species are adept at stalk twining. This type of climber is dealt with on pp.166-187, as are those that establish themselves with thorns, hooks, spines and prickles.

A-Z Guide to Self-clingers

The most important groups of plants in this section are the ivies (*Hedera*) and the members of the vine family (*Ampelopsis*, *Parthenocissus*, *Vitis*).

Ampelopsis *Vitaceae*

These are strong, deciduous climbers of the vine family that need plenty of space. They are allied to *Parthenocissus*, but their tendrils lack sticky suction pads. The tendrils should be looked upon as an auxiliary support aid in the garden environment – especially in their youth. Tie in plants or grow them through trellis. Ampelopsis are grown for their attractive foliage; *A. brevipedunculata* can have abundant crops of berries. Like all of this family, they can be very vigorous and, while they will quickly decorate a free-standing wall, fence, tree – dead or alive, and pergolas, if grown up the house walls they can be into the gutters and under the tiles if not kept to heel. They will grow in direct sunlight or semi-shade and will cope better in dryish rather than very wet soils.

A. aconitifolia
Palmate leaves, 12cm (5in) long, are usually 3-lobed but some may have five lobes. They are dark polished green and colour up well before leaf fall. Inconspicuous flowers are followed by 6mm (¼in) round, orange fruits. Deciduous, height 12m (40ft), Z5 H4.

A. brevipedunculata
Another strong climber with 3-lobed palmate, shiny rich green leaves. The autumn fruits, which come abundantly in small bunches, start off in shades of pinky purple but ripen to clear blue. From 6mm (¼in) to slightly larger. 'Elegans' is a less muscular variety, height 4-5m (12-15ft), which may be preferred for this reason where space is limited. The dark green leaves are handsomely veined and mottled white and pink. Deciduous, height 6m (18ft), Z5 H4.

A. megalophylla
This has magnificent large, pinnate leaves with the leaflets usually again pinnately divided. A leaf can be 60cm (24in) long. They are polished dark green, with glaucous undersides giving a light grey bloom effect. Deciduous, height 10m (30ft), Z5 H4.

Grown for its attractive foliage and vigorous climbing habit, Ampelopsis brevipedunculata *can have lots of berries in the late summer and autumn.*

Campsis x tagliabuana 'Madame Galen'

This is probably the best of a series of vigorous hybrids between the two *Campsis* species and is a gardenworthy plant with attractive pinnate foliage and arching sprays of large rich pinky-orange trumpet flowers from later summer well into the autumn. The sprays may have from 5-12 blooms, with most favouring the larger numbers. If there is room for only one of these fine climbers, then this hybrid might be the best choice; it is certainly hardier than *C. chinensis*. Deciduous, height 10m (30ft), Z5 H4.

✱ Exotic appearance

✱ Bold, showy, pinnate foliage

✱ Large flowers

✱ Long season of bloom from the second half of summer into autumn

✱ Grows well on a sunny wall and is hardy

✱ Propagates from semi-ripe summer cuttings or layers in winter

Asteranthera ovata *Gesneriaceae*

A genus of one evergreen species from damp-laden forests. This needs a sheltered place, preferably free of frosts, which is cool and has an atmosphere that is not too dry. In cold areas it is a conservatory or greenhouse plant, but in mild areas it is certainly worth a try outside on a shady wall or tree trunk. Plant it in lime-free, humus-rich soil by a semi-shaded wall where it will not have to cope with harsh drying winds and the soil does not dry out. Here it will climb to 3-5m (10-15ft) high, with aerial roots, and build up a mass of rather bristly, dark green leaves of wavy outline on hairy stems. In summer the narrow-tubed flowers, up to 3-4cm (1¼-1½in) long, come singly, their attractive pinky-red colour being made more of by the 5 widespreading lobes looking like independent petals, one each pointing north, east and west with the two remaining forming the 2-lipped mouth to the south. There may be some gold stripes on the lower lip, and the throat inside pales to white. Not everyone can supply the outdoor conditions it demands, but, if you can, this is well worth trying. Evergreen, height 4m (12ft), Z8 H2-3.

Bignonia capreolata

(syn. *Doxantha capreolata*) *Bignoniaceae*

This very strong climber has large opposite leaves up to 20cm (8in) long. More or less oblong but with a wavy margin, these are dark green with a branched tendril that helps the plant's rapid rise in the world. While it is normally evergreen, bad winter weather may induce some leaf fall. The trumpet-shaped flowers indicate its close relationship to the deciduous *Campsis*. They are a bright orange-red and up to 5cm (2in) long. Grow in a warm, sunny spot to help it to bloom well, and give it some help to climb by using extra ties to trellis or wires. Once it has taken over its space, it can have new growth cut back to two or three buds from the old wood at the end of autumn or the end of winter. Enjoys fertile soil, good drainage and reasonable moisture. Evergreen, height 10m (30ft), Z8 H3.

Campsis *Bignoniaceae*

A genus of two deciduous species and a very worthwhile hybrid. Commonly known as trumpet vines, they are also sometimes referred to as bignonia. They are fast-growing woody climbers that can be grown outside but will need the warmth of walls in cold areas. They may well bloom more freely in soils that are poor and do not encourage overmuch leafy growth – they will manage plenty of the latter, even in poverty-stricken soils. Best with freely drained soil that is well watered in the growing season.

C. grandiflora (syn. C. chinensis)

This species has splendid pinnate leaves up to 30cm (12in) long and made of 7 or 9 toothed, pointed, oval leaflets. Bunches of large flowers are borne at the ends of new growths, 6-12 at a time on stems that lean out from the plant. They are rich orange or red blooms and of roughly trumpet shape but with outspread lobes. Support is needed, as the aerial roots are auxiliary rather than a complete climbing system. Deciduous, height 7-10m (23-30ft), Z7 H4.

C. radicans

Trumpet vine is a climber of exotic appeal that has been grown in Britain for over 350 years but is still not as widely cultivated as its character deserves. I have seen specimens some 13m (43ft) tall and well furnished with bloom all the way up. On the other hand, it is quite happy to be tailored to fit a much smaller space, though it will look best if not too cramped. While it is a self-clinging plant, with a series of small stem roots, ivy-wise, these are not really up to the full-time job – the weight of the growth is best given extra support; in the wild this sort of help would come from the host trees that it clambers over.

Shining, rich green, pinnate leaves, downy below, are composed of 7-11 oval but pointed leaflets with a saw-edged outline. The clusters of flowers are produced at the end of current growth towards the end of the summer and into the autumn, a particularly useful time to have something fresh to look at when almost all else seems to be Michaelmas daisies, chrysanthemums and dahlias. There are not that many flowers in a bunch but they are large, up to 8cm (3in) long, and look somewhat like huge mimulus flowers in glowing scarlet and tangerine. The warmer the spot, the more bunches of flowers you are likely to enjoy. This is a strong grower that will not want to have its roots run out of moisture, so watering will be appropriate in drought, or at least a goodly mulch cover should be given to keep the roots happy. Once established it can be given a tidying pruning in spring. This will not only keep the plant shapely, if this is what is required, but it will encourage the new, flower-producing growth.

As might be expected from such a long-cultivated plant there have been variants named: 'Atropurpurea' has rather more intensely coloured flowers, 'Flava' is a very attractive yellow, 'Flamenco Minor' is a more rarely seen, weaker plant with smaller blooms, while 'Praecox' opens flowers earlier – not necessarily an advantage. Deciduous, height 10-12m (30-40ft) Z5 H4.

C. × tagliabuana 'Madame Galen', see box.

Decumaria Hydrangeaceae

There are only two species of this genus, one evergreen, the other more or less deciduous. The flowers have very small petals but have a central mass of stamens. Both species are rare in gardens as they are somewhat tender, but they grow well enough in mild areas, such as south-west England, and in such places can be interesting and decorative growing up a tree or wall. In less temperate regions only risk them in sheltered spots on a warm wall. Open-structured soils that do not dry out.

D. barbara

Of the two, this is the stronger grower, with polished, dark green, oval leaves, each up to a respectable 10cm (4in) long – an attractive clothing. The leaves are usually dropped for the winter when the self-clinging stems can be seen to be similar to those of the climbing hydrangeas. D. barbara has lots of wide, flat inflorescences of small white flowers in the summer. Semi-evergreen, height 10m (30ft), Z7 H4.

The evergreen euonymus forms have strong, dense foliage, and many popular cultivars have bright variegation to light up a dull corner. E. radicans 'Variegatus' is an old, trusted favourite.

D. sinensis

Among the few self-clinging evergreen climbers, this is a handsome-leaved plant with polished, rich green foliage. The ovate leaves are up to 8cm (3in) long. The flowerheads are creamy white and sweet scented. Rounded or pyramidical, they measure some 8-9cm (3-3½in) across and deep. Evergreen, height 2-3m (6-10ft), Z8 H4.

Doxantha capreolata, see *Bignonia capreolata.*
Eccremocarpus scaber, see Annuals p.236.

Ercilla volubilis (syn. *E. spicata*)
Phytolaccaceae

Belonging to a genus of just two species, *E. volubilis* is the tougher of the two and should grow reasonably, especially if the wood can be well ripened. It produces tough, heart-shaped leaves, 4-5cm (1½-2in) long and a rich, glowing green with paler veins. It is worth growing for this dense foliar cover. Some support is needed for it to grow up a wall or tree trunk until the system of aerial roots bind it firmly in place. Then it will grow well and, when fully established, will produce an abundance of flower spikes which are 4-5cm (1½-2in) long and green or purplish – they are without petals. If the spring flowers have been fertilized, they will be followed by purple-black berries. Happy in sun or semi-shade with normal soils that are properly drained. Evergreen, height 8-10m (25-30ft), Z9 H4.

Euonymus *Celastraceae*

A varied genus of nearly 200 species that includes spindleberry, *E. europaeus*, one of the deciduous kinds, as well as many evergreen types. The one that is a real workhorse in the garden is *E. fortunei*, very much an evergreen.

E. fortunei

Apart from its trustworthy evergreen character, this species has much to commend it. Many forms have been named, usually those with bright variegation. The standard species is rare in cultivation. It is a dark green plant with oval pointed leaves about 5cm (2in) long, and plenty of them so that there is a thick cover of foliage. **var. radicans** is a widespreading plant that will mount walls by means of aerial roots at intervals along the stems. Its oval, tough, dark green leaves measure up to 3.5cm (1½in) long. Bits pulled off the parent plant root easily.

Left to their own devices, the named forms range from clearly prostrate to those that make dense

mounds. Some make useful spot shrubs, some may be persuaded to make hedges, others are excellent for groundcover while most can be easily encouraged to make their way up walls and fences or even through trees. They only need support initially to make sure they know which way they are required to go; some will produce aerial roots to help themselves, but they tend to make a rigid bush with the tough branches meshing together to form the equivalent of a backbone.

Their unquestionable hardiness makes them ideal for those gardening in very bleak conditions. There can be few evergreens hardier: they can even outdo

Euonymus fortunei *'Gold Spot', unlike most of its variegated relations, has its brightly lit yellow areas confined to the leaf centres.*

Euonymus fortunei 'Emerald 'n' Gold'

Like the species (see left), this is a dense-foliaged shrub, but this time the bright green of the polished leaves plays very much second fiddle to the broad marginal variegation, which is brilliant gold and can almost cover some leaves. Again the gold can be enriched with a pink flush with winter. Evergreen, up to 1m (3ft), Z5 H4.

* One of the hardiest of all evergreens
* Outstandingly bright golden foliage variegation, pink-tinged in winter
* Easy to cultivate in sun or part shade
* Can be trained up a wall readily
* Responds well to clipping
* Propagates easily from layers or cuttings

GOLDEN/YELLOW-LEAVED SHRUBS

n occasional brightly coloured
olden shrub can light up a dull
orner and will always create a
ontrast to the orthodox green-
leaved brethren. Try some of
these.

*Aucuba japonica 'Sulphurea
Marginata' and other bright-
variegated cultivars
Berberis thunbergii 'Aurea'
Choisya ternata 'Sundance'
Elaeagnus pungens 'Maculata'
Euonymus fortunei
'Emerald 'n' Gold'
E. japonicus 'Ovatus Aureus'
Sambucus nigra 'Aurea'
S. racemosa 'Plumosa Aurea'
S. racemosa 'Sutherland Gold'*

ivies. Another plus is that they will respond well to trimming, so you can form neat columns up walls if you wish. To maintain their sturdy yeoman character, they are best grown in poor, rather than rich, soil, which does not get too dry, and in full sun, although they do not object to some shade. Some of the bright variegated kinds can be used to light up a somewhat dull shady spot. In such sites the variegation might be a little less intense but it is still of a telling brightness. Evergreen, height from 60cm (24in), 5m (15ft) or more up walls, all Z5 H4.

EUONYMUS FORTUNEI CULTIVARS

'Emerald Gaiety' is a compact bushy kind with healthy, rich green leaves clearly margined with white. As with some other cultivars and also some variegated ivies, this variegation can take on a suffusion of pink in the winter months. As a free-standing bush it will grow to a height of 1m (3ft) and spread at least half as much again.

'Emerald 'n' Gold', see box.

'Gold Spot' has dark leaves with a vivid splash of gold in their centres.

'Silver Queen' is a more upright plant, easily gaining some 2.5m (8ft) in height in the open while spreading more, but, given the chance to lean on a wall, it can grow up to the roof some 6-7m (20-22ft) above. Flowers of E. *fortunei* are usually inconspicuous small clusters of cream or white, but 'Silver Queen' adds to its lightness with an abundance of these little powder puffs in the summer.

E. japonicus

This species has very dark, shiny leaves of very tough texture. It was more popular formerly, but E. *fortunei*

seems to have usurped its place, probably because this species has a susceptibility to mildew. The most widely planted and enjoyed form is probably the deep golden 'Ovatus Aureus' with its bold contrast of almost black-green and the old gold variegation. Will grow happily in sun or semi-shade, as long as the well-drained soil does not get very dry. Evergreen, height 4m (12ft), Z8 H4.

Ficus pumila *Moraceae*

More often grown inside than out, this evergreen relative of the common fig is certainly hardy in mild areas against a wall or in a sheltered spot where it can climb up any support initially holding itself in place with aerial roots. The juvenile foliage is maintained outside, and this consists of heart-shaped leaves up to 3cm (1¼in) long; if you should achieve adult leaves these will be twice as long and more leathery. Secateurs are not needed except perhaps occasionally to encourage branching in a certain direction. Probably best in fertile, well-drained soil in light shade. Evergreen, height 4-8m (12-24ft), Z9 H1.

Hedera *Araliaceae*

An evergreen genus of under a dozen species, but with many cultivars; the common ivy *H. helix* has several hundred named forms. Until one looks dispassionately at some of the variations offered by this well-known genus, it is easy to overlook its real merits: most are very hardy, their foliage is surprisingly varied in form and their colouring can enhance all sorts of places in all sorts of ways. All secure themselves to supports by plentiful aerial roots. (See the box on p.146 for cultivation details.)

Right:
Euonymus fortunei
'Silver Queen'.

Far right:
Hedera canariensis
'Gloire de Marengo'.

H. canariensis

One of the large-leaved species, this has unlobed leaves, 10-15cm (4-6in) long and 8-12cm (3-5in) wide, with heart-shaped bases. The young leaves are light green but become darker with age. The most important cultivar is **'Gloire de Marengo'** (H3) with leaves up to 11cm (4½in) long and wide. The background light green is allied to wide areas of silvery, grey-green and to variegated margins of pale yellow, which tone down to cream with age. The leaf stalks and young stems are purple-wine. It is one of the most effective variegated climbers especially on stone walls. Evergreen, height 4-5m (12-15ft), Z7 H3-4.

H. colchica

This has large, unlobed leaves, up to 22cm (9in) long and nearly as wide, though an average might be 17 × 16cm (7 × 6in). Leather-tough, they hang to make a dense cover. The species is almost a rarity in gardens but the well-known **'Dentata Variegata'** (see box) is reckoned one of the most useful of all variegated plants. **'Sulphur Heart'** ('Paddy's Pride') is almost as popular and effective as 'Dentata Variegata'. In this the centre of the leaves is shot through with gold, with the colour often extending from the base, along the veins, leaving just the margins green, the opposite arrangement to 'Dentata Variegata'. The large leaves are arranged almost like tiles, turning rain away from the wall. Evergreen, height 10m (30ft), Z6-7 H4.

H. helix

From the hundreds of cultivars of this, the common ivy, a few favourite and distinct forms have been chosen to mention here. **'Buttercup'** is undoubtedly the most brilliant of these. In the sun those leaves that

Hedera colchica 'Dentata Variegata'

This is probably top of the list of variegated climbers. Its light green leaves are marked with areas of grey-green but are boldly splashed with areas of creamy-yellow, especially irregularly around the margins. The yellow fades to near cream with age. The contrast of these colours with red brick or grey stone can be very effective. The polished leaf surfaces enhance the bright colour, which can look even richer in winter months. Evergreen, height 10m (30ft), Z6-7 H4.

❋ Bright, boldly variegated foliage

❋ Thick cover of evergreen leaves

❋ Easy to cultivate; no special needs

❋ Very good for brightening a shady spot

❋ Will drape a fence, chain-link or low walls to give a hedge effect

❋ Propagates freely from layers or cuttings

are fully exposed are likely to be a uniform gold, or at least a lime-yellow; in shade the colour is light green; heavy shade makes them lose much, if not most, of their golden character. 'Buttercup' is very effective on walls, large or small, fences or trained up posts, pillars or large urns. Seen at a distance it can be as bright as a flowering shrub. **'Eva'** is very popular for the pot plant trade because of its neat, small, three-pointed leaves but it is perfectly fine outside, where it can

Far left: Hedera helix *'Buttercup' grown over a low wall and looking like a very bright, neat hedge.*

Hedera colchica *'Sulphur Heart', the correct name for the strong ivy sometimes known as 'Paddy's Pride'.*

Popular, close-clinging
Hedera helix
'Goldheart'.

Right top: Hedera helix
'Goldchild'.

Right bottom: Hedera
helix *'Green Ripple'.*

make a pale-coloured flat wall covering. The basic
grey-green of the leaf is irregularly, boldly and attractively margined pale cream. **'Glacier'** has leaves measuring up to around 6 × 5cm (2½ × 2in) and is
another popular pot plant that is happy outside, making a striking background for bolder coloured shrubs.
The muted leaf colours are a basic silvery-green with
various patches of silvery-grey and pencilled margins
of cream. The well-lobed leaves of **'Goldchild'** have
generous, irregular creamy-gold, variegation around
margins and occasionally invading leaf blade centres.
In contrast to this, **'Goldheart'** is polished gold in
the middle with deep green margins. The leaves are
cleanly cut to sharp triangular points. The colouring
flares up the leaf, often mimicking the outline of a
maple leaf. 'Goldheart' will certainly enliven a dull
wall and often makes an effective contrast to neighbouring shrubs. **'Green Ripple'** is a rich green ivy
with well-defined, pointed-lobed leaves and pale
veins. **'Königer's Auslese'**, which is often sold as
'Sagittifolia', is a popular pot plant that is also good
outside, its foliage very heavily indented in the form
of a bird's foot. **'Parsley Crested'** has so far forgotten
its family manners as to lose its ivy outline in favour
of a rounded, crimped outline that might make a useful disguise. The leaf colouring is a rich shade of
green. Altogether it makes an interesting contrast to
other more traditional ivies. **'Sagittifolia'** has longish
leaves in the form of an arrow head. Anyone would
be forgiven for thinking **'Sagittifolia Variegata'** was a
variegated form of 'Sagittifolia'. It is not. The leaf is
of bird's foot form, with a long-pointed central lobe
and much smaller but deeply indented other lobes.
The light green is lightened further with pale cream

variegation, which is painted all round the margins
and sometimes invades more of the leaf blade. It is a
small-leaved, neat growing ivy that looks bright and
cheerful wherever it grows. Evergreen, height to 7m
(22ft), some smaller, Z5 H4.

H. hibernica

It would appear that this species is, in fact, a
tetraploid form of the common ivy and should probably be known as *H. helix* subsp. *hibernica*. It is a popular deep green ivy, especially useful for its quick
growth and large leaves, up to 15cm (6in) across and
with traditional triangular lobing. **'Variegata'** is an
interesting strong plant with leaves showing all possible degrees of cream variegation, from mere flecks to
irregular wide splashes and with some leaves almost
all cream with only a token touch of green. It makes
an interesting study. **'Deltoidea'** is another strong

CARING FOR IVY

Ivies hardy seem to need care. They are certainly easy to grow, but there are two or three points to bear in mind to get the best from them. Happy in full sun or considerable shade, they will grow freely in normal soils and can cope with dry ones better than most plants.

✻ Young plants will get away quicker if when planted the leafy growths are closely attached to the wall or other structure so that they are in direct contact. This encourages the aerial roots to develop and may be done with canes or with sellotape. Once aerial roots grab hold, the plant accelerates into growth.

✻ Established plants can be given a trim with shears or strimmer (carefully) to clear old foliage off at the end of the winter. Once the old leaves have been cut away the plant can be given a brush down with a yard broom to dislodge dead foliage. Very soon it will refurnish itself with a bright new cover of leaves.
Note: If you are trying to create a tenement for nesting birds this procedure is obviously not recommended.

✻ When plants have grown for a number of seasons and reached a considerable height, the top growth can begin to develop adult wood and foliage – usually diamond-shaped leaves without indentations. This mature wood will produce tree-like branching without aerial roots and eventually forms a top-heavy mass, which will look curious on a house wall. If this is not what you desire, it will have to be cut away.

---

plant but this time with the leaf lobes blunted to rounded margins with only a minor indication of the indentations typical of the species, it is sometimes called the sweetheart ivy. I have seen this used very effectively to fall down a containing wall and probably cut back regularly. The foliage looked neat, a rich dark colour and very healthy. Evergreen, height 5m (15ft), Z7 H4.

Climbing hydrangea, H. petiolaris.

Hydrangea *Hydrangeaceae*

Climbing hydrangeas are hardy and are tolerant of all aspects, growing equally well in each situation. Once a young plant has got its first grip on a wall with its aerial roots, nothings stops it. The deciduous *H. petiolaris* may be preferred to the evergreen *H. serratifolia*, the benefit of evergreen cover losing out to the more decorative blossom of the former species with its large lace-cap flowerheads. Like most hydrangeas they grow much better in moist than in dry soils, but they are surprisingly long-suffering – we have managed large specimens on poor, not very wet soils.

H. petiolaris (syn. *H. anomala* var. *petiolaris*)
This clings tightly to the wall or trunk with a plentiful supply of aerial roots gripping the surfaces. The leaves are similar to the large-flowered hybrids, but more modest. The older stems shed curling lengths of fawn bark. In summer an established plant will produce plenty of flowerheads in clusters almost as flat as plates, their abundance making the whole decorative in a discrete, rather than flamboyant, manner. The fertile flowers are tiny white spots in the centre of the flowerhead. They are shepherded by a ring of large sterile ones in pale cream. Young plants may spend more effort on growing than flowering, but they soon reach a reasonable size and then bloom freely. Newly planted specimens may hesitate about moving unless their stems are introduced to, and kept in contact with, the surface they are to climb: as soon as a few aerial roots are secured the plant will gallop away. The ultimate size depends on the wall space or tree size you can offer – 15m (50ft) is no problem. Deciduous, height to 15m (50ft), Z5 H3.

H. serratifolia (syn. *H. integerrima*)
This evergreen plant can be just as large and vigorous as the deciduous species with tough dark leaves up to 15cm (6in) long and strongly serrated in young growth but becoming less so in more adult parts. The rounded heads of fertile flowers are white and only occasionally have an odd sterile blossom. Evergreen, height 15m (50ft), Z9 H3-4.

Lathyrus *Leguminosae/Papilionaceae*

The herbaceous, everlasting peas seem to be second-class citizens, hidden in the shadow of their highly-bred, showy-flowered and fragrant annual cousins, but they deserve a place and once planted should return year after year with fresh new growth quickly coming from their overwintering rootstock. I do not know whether anyone has tried cross-breeding these perennial species. It would seem worth an attempt. They do best in light sunny spots, even if their roots are in shade. They enjoy a fertile, open-structured soil that does not dry out.

L. grandiflora

This will scramble up any support and produces a welcome succession of rounded, purple-pink or reddish flowers, either singly or in twos or threes, each bloom being up to 3cm (1¼in) across. Herbaceous, height 1.5m (5ft), Z7 H4.

Possibly the best of the 'everlasting' or perennial sweet peas, Lathyrus latifolius.

L. latifolius

The most popular of the everlasting peas, this species has winged stems and typical grey-green pea foliage. Bunches of 6-11 flowers range from a modest 1.5cm (½in) across to at least double this size. The standard colour range is pinky-mauve to near purple but there are true-breeding kinds such as the fine pure white **'White Pearl'** and the pink-flushed **'Blushing Bride'**. Herbaceous, height 2m (6ft), Z7 H4.

L. odoratus, see Annuals p.238.

L. pubescens

A strong climber, *L. pubescens* has unwinged stems and leaves that are darker than usual. In summer it produces a succession of bunches of 6-15 flowers coloured lilac-blue, some paler, some darker. Herbaceous, height to 3m (10ft), Z7 H4.

L. rotundifolius

A pleasing enough little plant with bunches of small flowers, perhaps up to a maximum of 11, each never bigger than 4.5cm (1¾in) across and usually somewhat smaller. The colour can be deep pinky-lilac to rusty-red. Herbaceous, height to 1m (3ft), Z7 H4.

Mutisia *Compositae*

These shrubs are not seen as much as they deserve. Daisy-flowered evergreens, they climb by means of tendrils. The underside of the foliage is usually a woolly white. While some of the genus are very definitely plants for under glass, the following will be hardy in milder areas. In cooler areas they may need a little protection, and in cold ones they may be best in a conservatory. All favour light sunny positions but with the root run shaded. They require normal healthy soils that are open-textured to give good drainage, not sodden conditions.

M. clematis

This is one of the stronger growers. The leaves are composed of 6, 8 or 10 narrow leaflets, each up to 3-4cm (1¼-1½in) long and ending in a long, divided tendril. In youth they are covered with fluffy wool but they become more or less clean-shaven later on the upper surfaces. Bright orange daisy flowers measure some 6cm (2½in) across. They are produced singly over a long period from the beginning of summer into autumn, each opening from a long bud and being semi-pendent. It is best in a sunny spot in moderately good soil. Evergreen, height 7-10m (22-30ft), Z9 H3.

M. decurrens

This is a distinct plant with winged stems and 12cm (5in) long narrow dark leaves ending in a 2-part slender tendril. The bright, burnt-orange daisy flowers

Parthenocissus henryana.

Below: Parthenocissus quinquefolia.

can be an impressive 12cm (5in) across with the 12 or so petals tending to recurve. While it can be slow to establish, propagation is fairly easy as this is a suckering plant. Evergreen, height to 3m (10ft), Z9 H3.

M. *ilicifolia*

The bright green foliage is, as the name suggests, shaped like that of holly (*Ilex*), each leaf being up to 6cm (2½in) long and, in this species, ending in a single, undivided tendril. The flowers, 7cm (3in) across, are produced from summer, well into autumn, and are pale pink with yellow centres. One of the most distinctive and useful of the genus. Evergreen, height 3-4m (10-12ft), Z9 H3.

M. *oligodon*

A rather sprawling climber with serrated, shining, dark green leaves with single long tendrils. The long-stalked flowers have 6-12 quite wide petals around the golden centre of stamens, and look like miniature, single dahlias, some 7cm (3in) across. They are produced from summer into autumn. It can be grown through a more rigidly upright shrub. Evergreen, height 1.5m (5ft), Z9 H3.

M. *spinosa* var. *pulchella* (syn. M. *retusa*)

The oblong dark leaves of this variety make a background for small pink daisies. The lower leaf surfaces are usually woolly and white. There is also a white form. Evergreen, height 3-6m (10-20ft), Z9 H3.

Parthenocissus Vitaceae

These vigorous climbers are among the most popular of climbing plants. Many walls are clothed with them. They are less often seen growing up trees where they produce informal curtains or draping, hanging branches. This latter site can be most effective and removes the worry about the thrusting stems reaching into the gutter and under the roof tiles. The autumn colours are splendid. They are sometimes rather loosely called Virginia creepers, but this name is really the property of *P. quinquefolia* alone. They are all invaluable for shaded walls but will manage well in sun. Happy with most soils, provided there is reasonable drainage.

P. *henryana*

Sometimes rather ambiguously called the Chinese Virginia creeper, to my eye this is one of the best of the genus. It has palmate leaves usually of 5 pointed, oval leaflets, up to 12cm (5in) long, with a little serration, rich green but with conspicuous pale veining in white or sometimes flushed pink. A hint of reddish-pink underlies the green and in autumn the red takes control and the plant becomes incandescent.

Colour is best on plants that are grown in some shade. In very, very cold areas it may not be 100 per cent hardy. Deciduous, height 10m (30ft), Z9 H4.

P. quinquefolia

The Virginia creeper is another palmate-leaved species, normally with 5 saw-edged leaflets just a little smaller than those of *P. henryana* and mid-green. In autumn these become vivid golds, oranges and reds. Very hardy. Deciduous, height 17m (56ft), Z3 H4.

P. thomsonii

This has dark, palmate leaves with 5 leaflets up to 10cm (4in) long. The colours vary: new young leaves are a purplish red, they become a purpled green for their mature months and then don the brightest red hues for the autumn. Deciduous, height 10m (30ft), Z9 H4.

P. tricuspidata

Boston ivy is probably the most popular and strongest growing of the genus. The large leaves vary in shape; they normally have 3 pointed lobes but 3 leaflets is a possibility. The leaves are up to 20cm (8in) long and are a polished healthy bright green. Autumn colours are golds, purples and dominant reds. Like the other species, it can produce small dark fruits; we find lots of self-sown seedlings underneath our monster plant with which we have a love-hate relationship – love when it is in full leaf and in autumn dress, hate when it needs cutting back from gutters, and an ambiguous feeling as we collect the masses of leaves after leaf fall. At least they are dropped quickly and all is grist to the compost heap. **'Veitchii'** has darker foliage that becomes very deep, purple-red with the summer's end. Deciduous, height 20m (70ft) or more, Z5 H4.

This cheerful corner has the large-leaved Parthenocissus tricuspidata (Boston ivy) *and* Vitis coignetiae *creating a curtain behind the daisy-like flowers of* Dendranthema *'Cottage Apricot' and 'Jante Wells'.*

Right: Passiflora caerulea
'Constance Elliott'.

Passiflora Passifloraceae

These exotic-looking plants have one of the draw-backs of many exotics – they are likely to be tender. Of the 500-odd species *P. caerulea* is the hardiest; it will give no problems in mild areas but elsewhere is best given a sheltered warm spot. There are named cultivars and a few hybrids that will be equally hardy. Gardeners in very favoured spots might like to try some of the less hardy types such as *P.* 'Amethyst' and the robust red *P. manicata* which has white, pointing petals and a centre of blue ringed white.

P. caerulea, see box.

Pileostegia viburnoides Hydrangeaceae

Related to the climbing hydrangeas and to *Schizophragma*, this species is the most commonly grown of four in the genus and, like its relatives, it climbs by means of strong aerial roots. It seems equally happy in sun or shade and produces a mass of tough-textured,

Passiflora caerulea

This grows rapidly with lots of 10cm (4in) long rich green leaves, deeply divided into usually 5 lobes. The flowers, 8-10cm (3-4in) across and with about 10 petals, are produced from midsummer well into autumn. They are saucer-shaped and usually basically white but sometimes tinged pale blue or pink. Within are white, purple and green zones behind a spun ring of fine white filaments; from the centre protrudes the tripartite stigma. After a warm summer many of the flowers will be followed by very decorative egg-shaped, hanging fruits in tones of orange-gold. While they can be eaten, this is not the passion fruit for sale in the supermarket (the edible ones are imported fruits of *P. edulis*, a native of Brazil). This is a climber to grow in full sun or partial shade in reasonably fertile soil that does not dry out and in a place free from the worst of the drying winds. It can be trained on a trellis or wall, through a climbing rose, up a pole or over a pergola. 'Constance Elliott' is a long-prized, sweet-scented, white form with cream or pale blue filaments. 'Grandiflora' has flowers like the type but half as large again. Deciduous, height 10m (30ft), Z7 H3.

✻ Fascinating flowers and attractive fruits

✻ Long season of bloom – and fruiting

✻ Rapid grower on various supports, artificial or natural, up walls, posts, pergolas, or over shrubs and small trees

✻ Sun or part shade

✻ Many other species and cultivars to try

✻ Propagates easily from seed or semi-ripe summer cuttings

shining, long, elliptic leaves measuring up to 15cm (6in), which look as if they should be evergreen but are not. The dense foliage mass is topped in late summer and autumn with many intricate panicles of tiny cream stars that are massed to make a pleasing, but not riotous, display. Normal water requirements, happy in most soils that are well-drained. Deciduous, height 6m (20ft), Z9 H4.

Schizophragma *Hydrangeaceae*

Plants of this genus are close to the climbing hydrangeas in habit and appearance, and useful in the same places – on walls of any aspect and to grow up large trees. Young plants should be secured to the surfaces which they are required to climb. Once they catch on they will support themselves. Similar soil requirements to *Pileostegia*.

S. hydrangeoides

A strong climber with lots of aerial roots and broad, oval leaves, markedly serrated and up to 15cm (6in) long. They make a dense, rich green cover on the wall and form a backcloth for the abundant, creamy summer flowers. The wide flattened flowerheads consist of many small, fertile central flowers and are well furnished by showy, flat, pointed, oval marginal bracts, which can be up to 6cm (2½in) long. If you decide to try this shrub consider getting hold of the clone called **'Moonlight'**; its bracts seem larger and the foliage is lightly variegated. Deciduous, height 10-12m (30-40ft), Z5 H4.

S. integrifolium

This is a similar species to the last and is the one more frequently planted although possibly just a degree less hardy – but having said that it will do well in most parts. It may be preferred for its rather larger flowerheads with their larger, oval, pointed, cream bracts, some 9cm (3½in) long, margining, and often covering, many of the small, fertile creamy flowers. Fine on all walls and up trees but may be best in some shade in the warmer, sunnier areas. Deciduous, height 12m (40ft), Z7 H4.

Vitis *Vitaceae*

When considering these deciduous vines one could be in a bit of a quandary. What takes priority, the appearance or the crop of fruit? Fortunately grape vines are attractive plants so can easily be an option for a decorative feature. In warm areas they can be positioned to grow up walls, poles or over pergolas. There is plenty of choice, for example the standard German grape **'Muller Thurgau'** or one of the early-

Vitis coignetiae

This is a magnificent large-leaved vine that is grown solely for its foliage. The heart-shaped leaves are lightly lobed, of a velvety texture, lightly brown felted below and up to 30cm (12in) long and almost as wide. The bright green of the growing months is replaced in autumn with a wide palette of golds, oranges and reds. Few climbers can look more impressive along a pergola, up a wall or over a carport, where it may manage to hold itself with strong tendrils but should be made safe with an occasional tie. Grown up trees it will reach from branch to branch and tree to tree and then produce a curtain of hanging branches – impressive enough in the summer but dazzling in autumn. Deciduous, height 15m (50ft), Z5 H4.

* Strong, healthy growth

* Goes up wall supports, over pergolas and carports and through trees

* Not fussy about soil

* Very bold, attractive foliage

* Wonderful autumn colour

* Propagates from layers

ripening French ones such as **'Madeleine Angevine'**, which has particularly attractive foliage. The cultivar **'Brant'** will produce grapes but is often grown as a decorative climber for its fine, bold foliage of 3- or 5-lobed, bright green leaves, often 20cm (8in) long, which turn gorgeous bronzes and reds in the autumn when the bunches of near-black grapes are ready for picking. All vines are best in sunny spots with roots in freely draining soil that is not over wet.

V. coignetiae, see box.

V. vinifera

This is the wine grape. There is a particularly good cultivar 'Purpurea', which has typical vine leaves, almost fluffy in youth but of firm texture, flattened and coloured rich dark shades of pinky or plum-purple. They turn deeper in the autumn, when they will be accompanied by tight bunches of dark grapes – decorative only – you will regret tasting any. Deciduous, height 6-7m (18-22ft), Z5 H4.

TWINERS

There is a wide variety within this group but all more or less rely on other plants or structures to provide the backbone that enables them to rise in the world and display their wares. They climb by twisting their stems around their support: some twist clockwise, some anticlockwise. It is an efficient method of growth limited only by the extent of the supporting material. Common examples of twiners are the climbing honeysuckles and bindweed (hopefully not too common in your garden). There is no clear-cut division between twiners and those described as ramblers and scramblers. For the purposes of this book clematis are decreed to be scramblers; although they may twine, they also scramble and help themselves up with twisting leaf stalks.

Many of the plants considered here can be invited to climb into trees and shrubs so making a double use of one site: the chocolate vine, *Akebia quinata*, is one such as are honeysuckles and even major items such as wisteria, if one has a suitable tree that is also large enough. There is something particularly gratifying about creating a successful twosome – a matchmaker's

reward when all goes well. If there are not enough trees to train climbers through, or they are already fully booked, then alternative sites include trellis (in the open or against walls), poles and pergolas. The berchemias would serve in any of these stations; the bittersweets (*Celastrus*), with their fascinating autumn fruits, might also be possible but they look particularly good supported by trees.

Chilean bellflower (*Lapageria rosea*) might be best growing up a sheltered wall or fence but it need not be one in full sun as this interesting evergreen will flourish with a little shading.

Plants reviewed here are likely to straddle all the three sectors described on pp.112-119.

Annuals and herbaceous plants
There is a selection of twining annuals, or plants treated as annuals listed on pp.235-241. Everlasting sweet peas are reviewed on pp.146-147.

A-Z Guide to Twiners

Actinidia Actinidiaceae

A bunch of deciduous, twining climbers of which the kiwi fruit or Chinese gooseberry, A. *deliciosa*, is the best-known species. They will grow in sun or partial shade, enjoying good soil and reasonable moisture.

A. arguta
Handsome when in full leaf, this strong-growing climber has widely oval leaves, 8-13cm (3-5in) long, marked with bristles. Early summer brings small, scented bunches of white flowers, like single roses, 2cm (¾in) across, in enough numbers to make it a garden feature. The form **'Issai'** is self-fertile and will produce oblong, golden, edible fruits, 2.5cm (1in) long; the plants are normally either male or female. Deciduous, height 6m (20ft), Z5 H4.

A. deliciosa (syn. A. chinensis)
The kiwi fruit is also mainly single sexed, but there is a female form **'Blake'** which is self-fertile. It is an extraordinarily vigorous climber – as anyone who has seen it clambering up Powis Castle can testify – and clothes itself with a fine cover of large, rough-textured, rounded or heart-shaped leaves, 20cm (8in) long. A series of 4cm (1½in), white flowers open in early summer; they age to cream and then yellow. By

---

Actinidia kolomikta

Totally distinct from the other species, this is a more slender-stemmed climber with smooth leaves serrated and remarkably coloured. Some leaves are a plain mid-green but many have their end halves painted bright creamy-white, usually suffused pink – they could have been dipped into a paint pot. A few leaves may be wholly white or pink. The small white flowers and oblong yellowish fruits on pollinated females are both secondary considerations. The tricoloured leaves are brightest the first half of the year. Deciduous, height 6m (20ft), Z5 H4.

✻ Unique foliage colouring

✻ Classy foliage

✻ Grows well on walls

✻ Sun or shade. One of the best wall plants for shade

✻ Propagates readily from layers or semi-ripe summer cuttings

---

PRUNING OF CLIMBERS

While different genera and species or cultivars can present their own problems and possibilities, there are some general principles to the pruning of climbers.

1 Do heavier pruning in winter when plants are dormant or at least less lively.

2 Aim to thin overcrowded growth.

3 Try to get more air to the centre of the plant.

4 Each year try to remove a proportion of the older wood to allow newer wood more room for action

5 Cut away damaged wood, cutting back to strong bud/s.

6 Shred and compost prunings.

7 Burn any prunings that might be diseased.

8 Remember the old gardening adage 'Growth follows the knife'. The idea is that you are likely to get strong growth from pruned-back stems.

the end of the summer these are replaced by the typical kiwi fruits. Deciduous, height 10m (30ft), Z7 H4.

A. kolomikta, see box.

A. polygama

For those who do not have the room for the potential giants above, this, the silver vine, could be the one to grow. It can be put up a wall or tree, or draped over a pergola. The leaves, 7.5-12.5cm (3-5in) long, are broadly elliptic or oblong with the bristly serrated margins typical of the genus. They are dark green, but when newly opened may have a bronzy cast and can be tipped silver-white; odd leaves will have white or creamy-yellow tips. Deciduous, height 5m (15ft), Z6 H4.

Akebia *Lardizabalaceae*

This is a small genus of some five species of twining climbers found on forest edges. Their hardiness is not in doubt but occasionally early flowers may be damaged by frost. The flowers are unusual and interesting and the foliage is always pleasing. *A. quinata* is the showier species. While best in sun, it will manage with some shade in normal healthy soil, but resents disturbance.

A. quinata

The chocolate vine is a strong-growing plant that hovers between being evergreen and deciduous. It has clockwise-spiralling twining stems and its leaves are composed of 5 equal, rounded, oblong leaflets, 4-8cm (1½-3in) long, smooth-edged and rich green above but with a blue cast below. The leaflets are usually fanned out in a flat, more or less horizontal plane. The 3-petalled flowers are produced in early spring, in hanging bunches, and are an unusual brownish-purple, hence the common name – although the spicy scent is like vanilla. The female flowers are 2-4cm (¾-1½in) long and conspicuous; the males are very much smaller. Fruits may follow; 12cm (5in) long and sausage-shaped, they are curious violet or purple creations often with a grey bloom. It is a plant that relishes reasonable soil and peace; it can take a little while to settle and then should not be disturbed. Semi-evergreen, height to 10m (30ft), Z5 H4.

A. trifoliata (syn. *A. lobata*)

The rounded leaflets of this species look so independent that with a glance one might not realise that the three together make the complete leaf. They have a less regular margin than *A. quinata* and are a pleasant bronzy colour when newly unfurled but soon become a rich mid-green. The early spring flowers are 3-petalled and purple – females up to 2cm (¾in) across,

the males smaller – and are liable to spring frost damage. There is an intermediate hybrid between the two species called *A. × pentaphylla*. Deciduous, height 10m (30ft), Z5 H4.

Araujia sericifera, see Tender Plants p.243.
Aristolochia, see Tender Plants p.243.

Berchemia *Rhamnaceae*

These twiners are grown for their foliage and fruit. They are useful for covering awkward spots like old tree stumps as well as draping trellis, fences or walls. They are hardy in mild areas, such as southern England; *B. racemosa* is the hardier and therefore possible over a wider area. Happy in sun or shade in normal well-drained soils.

The curious 3-petalled flowers of Akebia quinata.

B. racemosa

A twining climber of rather spreading habit with dark green, ovate leaves, up to 8cm (3in) long. Its tiny green flowers are carried in bunches about 15cm (6in) long and deep. This undistinguished summer performance may be followed by the more exciting oblong fruit. Starting green, they become red and finally black. The fruiting is more plentiful in a warm summer. The form **'Variegata'** has the same more or less heart-shaped leaves but with creamy-white variegation and is thus perhaps more decorative than the type. Deciduous, height 5m (15ft), Z6 H4.

B. scandens (syn. B. volubilis)

This species has acquired the common names of supple Jack and rattan vine and it is certainly vigorous. For most gardeners, this energy may be its most interesting feature, although its foliage is distinctive. A strong twiner, its leaves, up to 8cm (3in) long, have undulating margins and well-marked parallel veining and end in a bristly point. The insignificant itsy-bitsy green flowers should be followed by 1cm (½in) long fruits of deepest blue or black, but this is not a reliable harvest. Deciduous, height 5m (15ft), Z7 H4.

Calystegia hederacea

(syn. C. japonica) Convolvulaceae

This relative of bindweed will quickly get up trellis or any other support with its stems of heart-shaped leaves, and then produces typical convolvulus trumpet flowers in pink. **'Flore Pleno'** is double-flowered, with wavy petals that open pale pink but then become rosy. It will cover old dead trees or shrubs but is not the tidiest of plants so it is best planted where it has plenty of space in the wilder corners of the garden. Better in sun than shade and not wanting very wet conditions. Deciduous, height 7m (20ft), Z6 H4.

Celastrus Celastraceae

These hardy, deciduous climbers are too little seen; even C. orbiculatus, which most would pick out as the best and is the widest planted, is still not used as much as it deserves. C. orbiculatus is the most readily available but the others are worth seeking out. Anyone with walls, buildings, pergolas or trees in need of extra adornment should consider these strong plants, which are happy to tackle those difficult cool, shady walls. While they manage well enough in normal garden soils, they repay feeding by producing even more muscular growth. Foliage is good; the autumn fruiting is splendid. These are relatives of the spindleberry (Euonymus); their fruits proclaim the relationship.

C. hypoleucus

This is a species that may commend itself to those wanting to try these plants but frightened that ones like C. orbiculatus will be too vigorous. C. hypoleucus is a splendid thing, and no namby-pamby plant, but it is probably the least rampant of those in cultivation. The oblong leaves are some 10cm (4in) or so long and rich dark green above with surprising blue-white, silvered undersides. At the ends of the stems, in summer, are borne 20cm (7in) racemes of limy-yellow flowers, each individual being not much over 5mm (¼in). Rounded, green fruits split open to reveal the yellow-painted surfaces and red seeds. Like the other species these seedheads are persistent and abundant. Deciduous, height 7m (20ft), Z8 H4.

C. orbiculatus, see box.

C. rugosus

This species has rough-textured, boldly serrated leaves, 7-14cm (3-5½in) long. Small, green flowers may be followed by tangerine fruits with red seeds. It is very good when it fruits heavily, but this is not a regular occurrence. Deciduous, height 7m (20ft), Z6 H4.

C. scandens

This is another species that has male and female forms. Plant both and you will enjoy the fruits that split open to show orange insides and vivid scarlet seeds. The foliage is rather narrower than that of C. orbiculatus and with less regular toothed margins. The creamy flowers are of little distinction but after a good summer it can be heavy with bunched fruits and looks very fine. Deciduous, height 10m (30ft), Z3 H4.

Cionura erecta (syn. Marsdenia erecta)

Asclepiadaceae

Suitable for a sunny wall, this is a rather lax shrub that climbs by means of twining tips on the many slim stems. Its has opposite, heart-shaped, grey-green leaves, 3-6cm (1¼-2½in) long, and wide, flat-topped bunches, up to 10cm (4in) wide, of small, white flowers in summer. The flowers have 5 spreading lobes and release a sweet perfume. Best in fertile, well-drained soil. Deciduous, height 3m (10ft) or more, Z8 H3.

Clematis, see Ramblers and Scramblers p.166.

Cocculus Menispermaceae

A genus of deciduous twiners with downy stems and pleasing foliage. The flowers are small but the fruit is attractive. Those included here are hardy, others of

Ceslatrus orbiculatus
(syn. C. articulatus)

By any measure this is a magnificent plant. Its vigour and healthy foliage speak of a character at peace with itself. It is the young stems that twist; they also have pairs of spines at each bud. The leaves are usually rounded with neatly toothed outlines and measure 6-12cm (2-5in) long. The flowers are small, green technical necessities; the rounded 1cm (½in) fruits are yellowish-green but split open to reveal the dazzling golden interiors, settings for the highly polished, scarlet seeds. These are displayed through the autumn with the accompanying yellowed foliage, but are still there for months after the leaves have dropped. There are various clones in cultivation: get an hermaphrodite, which will look after its own fertilization, otherwise you will need to ensure that you have both a male and a female specimen to enjoy the fruit, which is the overriding reason for growing this species. Deciduous, height 20m (70ft), Z5 H4.

✳ Very colourful and unusual fruits

✳ Long fruiting season from early autumn well into winter

✳ Energetic twisting habit

✳ Good in shade or part shade

✳ Respectable rounded leaves

✳ Propagates without trouble from seed, layers or semi-ripe summer cuttings

the genus are not likely to be. Easy in sun or semi-shade with roots in ordinary well-drained soils, that are not liable to sodden conditions.

C. carolinus
Called the Carolina moonseed in its native land, this has attractive, more or less heart-shaped leaves that can be lobed. They are 5-12cm (2-5in) long and smooth above with white downy undersides. The small, white flowers are borne in separate clusters of males and females; sometimes, but rarely, plants produce flowers of only one sex. Fruits the size of elderberries are carried thickly in bunches, a colourful red. Deciduous, height 5m (15ft), Z7 H4.

C. orbiculatus (syn. C. trilobus)
This has similar leaves to C. carolinus but they are rather smaller, up to 10cm (4in) long. Clusters of small, cream flowers should be followed by an abundance of crowded bunches of fruit each about 1cm (½in) across and blue-black and bloomy. It needs to feel the sun on its back to fruit freely and should therefore only be used in the warmest, sunniest position. Deciduous, height 4m (12ft), Z7 H4.

Fallopia baldschuanica
(syn. Polygonum baldschuanicum) Polygonaceae

This is the mile-a-minute plant, also known as the Russian vine. It is sometimes talked of disparagingly, but this is probably only because it is so easy and grows so amazingly quickly, forming intricate masses of long intertwined branches. Planted in the wrong place, it can be a threat, but it is a useful beast for covering large unsightly buildings or objects. The leaves, up to 10cm (4in) long, are heart-shaped and dark green. The mass of branches and foliage is topped in late summer and well into autumn with an abundance of loose panicles of small white or palely pink-flushed flowers, froth and spume from the vigorous activity of the plant. This is really a pleasant enough offering. Try to look objectively at this plant – too often wrongly dismissed as second rate – but do not plant it in a site where you want discrete manners: it needs space. Sun or semi-shade. Normal soils, better dryish than very wet. Deciduous, height 12m (40ft), Z5 H4.

Holboellia *Lardizabalaceae*

These are first and foremost foliage plants, and as such are ones of quality. Flowers are a useful bonus and they can have amusing fruits. They will delve through some of the smaller trees or grow over a pergola or archway and are equally at home in sun or shade provided soil is properly drained.

H. coriacea

This strong-growing evergreen has leaves composed of 3 or 5 oval to oblong, shining dark leaflets of clean-cut outline and neatly stalked. The effect is of dignified opulence. A complete leaf is about 15cm (6in) long. Male and female flowers are carried on the same plant, in separate hanging bunches, in mid-spring. The mauve-tinted, pink male bells are just over 1cm (½in) long, the females are larger and greenish-ivory with some purple infusion. They occur more frequently on specimens grown on a warm, sunny wall, and in such a spot one may get occasional fruits – purple sausages 4-6cm (1½-2½in) long. Evergreen, height 8m (25ft), Z9 H3-4.

H. cuneata, see *Sargentodoxa cuneata*.

H. latifolia

This is not strikingly different from *H. coriacea* but can have leaves divided into 3-7 leaflets and could be somewhat less hardy. It comes into bloom earlier; the males are greenish-white and the females a mauve shade. Evergreen, height 5m (15ft), Z9 H3.

Humulus *Cannabaceae*

Hops are strong herbaceous plants, the common beer hops being not without attraction for covering a wall, fence or awkward corner in the growing months. Grows well in almost any soil, either in sun or half shade.

H. japonicus

This is included here as it is a strong grower – you can

stand and watch it grow – but it is best treated as an annual as it is likely to give up in the winter. The leaves are similar to the common hop, but with 5 or 7 lobes. It lacks the fruiting appeal of the familiar hop. Herbaceous, height to 10m (30ft), Z9 H1.

H. lupulus

This is the common hop with its rough hairy stems and roughly serrated leaves with 3 or 5 lobes. The yellow-leaved **'Aureus'** is popular in gardens. It has limy-yellow leaves, greener in semi-shade and brighter in sunshine. Herbaceous, height 6m (18ft), Z7 H4.

Kadsura japonica *Schisandraceae*

Close to the *Schisandra* species listed below, this has alternate, dark green, oval, pointed leaves, 5-10cm (2-4in) long. Scented flowers are produced singly from the leaf axils of the new growth. They are 2cm (¾in) rounded cups of 6-9 petals and creamy-white. Plants are either male or female, and both sexes are needed to produce the round, red berries. The foliage colours up well in autumn and is showy in full-blooded reds and purples. Best in half shade in any normal healthy soil and benefits from the shelter of a wall. Evergreen, height 4m (12ft), Z8 H3.

Lapageria rosea *Philesiaceae*

This is a wall climber for mild regions; its hardiness may not prove sufficient in colder areas. It is best with some shade and shelter. With ovate, pointed, tough, dark green leaves, up to 12cm (5in) long, it will twine up artificial or natural support on a shady wall and then produce a very satisfying number of its semi-pendent, long-tubed or bell-shaped flowers in pinky-red. They look succulently fleshy and are a showy 9cm (3½in) long. The Chilean bellflower is best in soil that does not dry out and which is acid or neutral. It will need no pruning. Evergreen, height 5m (15ft), Z8 H3.

Lardizabala biternata, see Tender Plants p.248.

Lonicera *Caprifoliaceae*

The honeysuckle genus is large, with nearly 200 species, but only the climbers concern us here. These must be close to clematis in the popularity stakes. There are both evergreen and deciduous species plus some that cannot make up their mind; some have the well-known perfume, other showy ones are completely bereft of what to many would seem to be one of the defining features of the plant.

Lapageria rosea.

Once planted they will last for decades. Like clematis, they are best with 'toes' in the shade, 'faces' in the sun. They enjoy reasonable soil that is not too wet. To get the best from them it is wise to cut back half the stems of a newly planted specimen to encourage branching. Thereafter, in theory, one should prune to remove older wood and thin out exuberant growth shortly after flowering. This is one of those rules very often acknowledged but equally often ignored. However, it is worth getting to work periodically, especially if plants are grown over fences or walls to imitate a hedge. Here it would be in order to prune after flowering and again later to provide a 'proper' shape. A hedge can be hugely successful at flowering time, a mass of flower and a cloud of perfume.

Those in the following list are well worth considering, even if one eventually strays no further from a form of the common hedgerow honeysuckle, *L. periclymenum*.

L. × americana (L. caprifolium × L. etrusca)

A scrambling climber with large, branched flower clusters produced early in the season and with a powerful scent. The individual flowers, up to 5cm (2in) long, are yellow, very heavily flushed with rich maroon. Both the parents are European and the hybrid is one that has been found in the wild, although it uncertain whether the plant in commerce is of wild or garden provenance. Deciduous, height 10m (30ft), Z6 H4.

L. × brownii 'Dropmore Scarlet'

A brilliantly flowered hybrid with blue-green, rounded leaves some 8cm (3in) across. It has many-flowered, whorled heads of tubular, vivid pinky-scarlet flowers with orangey interiors, each individual

Lonicera caprifolium.

flower being 3.5cm (1½in) long. It blooms for a long period over the summer but is only very lightly scented. Deciduous or semi-evergreen, height 4m (12ft), Z2 H4.

L. caprifolium

Italian honeysuckle has grey-green, rounded leaves, up to 10cm (4in) long. Summertime bunches of strongly scented flowers make whorled arrangements of cream, yellow and pink. **'Anna Fletcher'** is a common form in cultivation. Deciduous, height 6m (20ft), Z6 H4.

L. etrusca 'Superba'

This is a strong form of the Etruscan honeysuckle with flowers opening creamy-yellow but maturing to orange so that there is usually a range of shades at any one time. Smooth oval leaves up to 9cm (3½in) long. Fine in warm areas and on walls or fences in cooler areas. Scented. Deciduous or semi-evergreen, height 4m (12ft), Z8-9 H4.

L. × heckrottii 'Gold Flame'

(*L. × americana × L. sempervirens*)
This hybrid has dark, rounded leaves and scented flowers, each 4cm (1½in) long. The fragrant flowers are carried in whorls through the summer and are rich orange-pink and glowing tangerine. Deciduous or semi-evergreen, height 6m (18ft), Z6 H4.

L. henryi

Typical paired honeysuckle leaves, glossier than most and dark green, set off yellow and maroon flowers through the first half of summer, with black berries following in autumn. This is one of the more vigorous of an energetic genus. Evergreen, height 10m (30ft), Z5 H4.

Left: Lonicera × americana, *a very fine honeysuckle that, despite its name, arose from a cross between two European species.*

You cannot have too much of a good thing. Here, the popular honeysuckle Lonicera periclymenum *dances round a pool, like a corps de ballet. A bold and effective use for a favourite plant.*

Below: Honeysuckle over the doorway may seem a cliché in the abstract, but it cannot fail to please. The variety here is the paler Lonicera periclymenum *'Graham Thomas'.*

L. japonica

Japanese honeysuckle is different in character to the other species. It has ovate to rounded, dark green leaves, sometimes lobed. Flowers are borne in pairs from the leaf axils. They are white but often suffused with purple. The popular form **'Aureoreticulata'** has smaller and more rounded leaves, heavily veined in gold, making it highly decorative. It is not so completely hardy as some of the other species but should be all right in a warm spot. **'Halliana'** is an extra-vigorous plant with flowers that open all white innocence but are transmuted to deep gold with age. Evergreen or semi-evergreen, height 10m (30ft), Z5 H4.

L. periclymenum

This is the common honeysuckle of which outstanding forms can be found in hedgerows. It might be a good idea to take a small cutting of such as this was how the named forms were selected originally. **'Belgica'** (Early Dutch honeysuckle) is early into bloom, with deep pink buds opening to creamy-gold flowers but remaining red-pink on the reverses. It has a delicious fragrance, something that can build up particularly in the evenings. **'Graham Thomas'** can smother itself with white and creamy-gold flowers for long periods through the summer and autumn and is very fragrant.

'Serotina', see box.

L. sempervirens

The coral honeysuckle has large, rounded leaves, up to 7cm (3in) across, and whorls of long, tubular flowers, 5cm (2in) long, with 2 short lips. The brilliant scarlet of the exteriors gives way to a glowing

Lonicera periclymenum 'Serotina'

This is an outstanding late summer- and autumn-blooming plant with white and rich wine-red flowers making an intoxicating display enhanced by the sweet bouquet. Deciduous, height 8m (25ft), Z6 H4.

✳ Easy to cultivate in sun or light shade

✳ Richly coloured flowers

✳ Long period of bloom and freedom of flower

✳ Pervasive perfume

✳ Adaptable. For walls, fences, screens, pergolas, posts, into trees

✳ Propagates easily from layers

tangerine inside. There is no scent. It is prolific in summer and autumn and is then quickly followed by decorative glossy red berries. Deciduous or evergreen, height 4m (12ft), Z8 H4.

L. × tellmanniana
(L. sempervirens × L. tragophylla)
Round, deep green leaves are bluish-white below and large – 10cm (4in) long. From late spring well into summer a cornucopia of typical honeysuckle blossom is produced at the ends of each twig in large whorled heads. The flowers are shining, bronzy-orange, each 5cm (2in) long with protruding stamens. A robust grower but the flowers are without scent. Deciduous, height 5m (15ft), Z8 H4.

L. tragophylla
With typical paired, oval leaves, up to 12cm (5in) long, this is a bold plant that has lots of large, terminal whorls of scentless flowers. Basically gold, they are tinged with red through mid- to late summer.

Certainly one of the largest flowered and a magnificent plant. Deciduous, height 6m (20ft), Z6 H4.

Mandevilla laxa (syn. M. suaveolens)
Apocynaceae

A strong, much-branched twiner producing ovate leaves, 5-10cm (2-4in) long, with long, slender points. Draped over an archway or pergola they will display both their shining rich green upper surfaces and some of the undersides of grey or purple. From midsummer into autumn it has sprays of conspicuous long trumpet flowers, profusely scented and pure white. The narrow tubes of the flowers open at the mouth to 5 lobed circles 5-10cm (2-4in) across. A graceful, worthwhile climber for growing as a flowering foliar screen, in a sunny position with an open-structured, humus-rich soil. In cool spots it will benefit from extra mulching around the base for winter protection. Deciduous, height 4m (12ft), Z9 H2-3.

Marsdenia erecta, see *Cionura erecta*.

Menispermum canadense
Menispermaceae

Canadian moonseed is a suckering plant that is more or less woody and twines up supports such as trellis. It can be grown through tough shrubs, although care should be taken that the shrubs do not get completely subdued by the vigorous growth. With many, thin, tangled stems and long stalked, heart-shaped or rounded leaves, this is a distinctive plant. The small, limy-green flowers are followed, on female plants, by decorative glossy black fruit like small grapes or blackcurrants held until very late in the autumn or the beginning of winter. These are not edible; they are poisonous and should be kept out of the way of children. The plants of both sexes are needed to produce fruit. Every 2-3 years all the top growth should be cut away in the winter and the plant made to start again. Sunny, well-drained spot. Deciduous, height 5m (15ft), Z8-9 H4.

Muehlenbeckia complexa
Polygonaceae

This is a spreading, scrambling plant that can be a twining climber with thin, twisting stems supporting small, dark leaves. The biggest of these are only 1.5cm (1½in) long. They are oval but often so indented as to make violin shapes. Left to its own devices in the open it will make a mound perhaps a metre high, but with the help of a wall it may go three times higher, a pleasing mass of foliage. The tiny flowers are ivory-green and (if there are both female and male plants in the vicinity) may be followed by small, rounded, white fruits; however the species is usually grown as a foliage plant. Equally good in sun or shade. Any normal healthy soil. Deciduous, height 2-3m (6-10ft), Z9 H3.

Oxypetalum caeruleum, see *Tweedia caerulea*.

Periploca graeca *Asclepiadaceae*

Silk vine, like the muehlenbeckia, is also grown primarily for its foliage. It is a trouble-free plant for draping a wall, fence or pergola, but there are probably more jolly performers. Highly polished, oval or pointed leaves are from 5-10cm (2-4in) long. Clusters of small flowers are lime-coloured in bud but open chocolate-purple and have an unhappy smell. Thin seedpods and silky seeds. Sunny, well-drained soil. Deciduous, height 10m (30ft), Z7 H3.

Polygonum aubertii, **P. baldschuanicum**, see *Fallopia baldschuanica*.

Pueraria thunbergiana, see Annuals p.238.

Sargentodoxa cuneata
(syn. *Holboellia cuneata*) *Sargentodoxaceae*

A very strong-growing climber with handsome long-stalked, dark polished, tripartite leaves, each part a clean-cut oval 6-12cm (2½-5in) long. From the end of spring into early summer it produces bunches of

Schisandra chinensis *in berry.*

small, starry, greenish-yellow flowers, up to 2cm (¾in) long, formed of 6 narrow sepals, acting as petals – a floral act that lacks excitement. Plants are either male or female, the females producing clusters of berries about the size of elderberries and a purplish-blue. This is a rare plant for a warm wall and any healthy, unsodden soil. Deciduous, height 8m (25ft), Z9 H2-3.

Schisandra Schisandraceae

These are attractive deciduous climbers, S. chinensis and S. rubriflora being particularly good. The sexes are separate, so you will need plants of both to get the females to set the handsome fruits. They are best planted in semi-shaded spots on a wall or growing among other plants up pergolas. No extraordinary soil conditions.

S. chinensis
Young red shoots produce elliptic leaves of polished dark green, up to 15cm (6in) long. From spring's end into summer there are small clusters of hanging cup-shaped flowers in blush-pink. Each is about 2cm (¾in) across and female plants can subsequently produce 15cm (6in) spikes of showy, fleshy, red or pink fruits. Deciduous, height 9m (28ft), Z6 H4.

S. henryi
Triangular-sectioned shoots, winged in their young state, unfurl ovate or heart-shaped, polished green leaves, 7-10cm (3-4in) long. In spring there are small clusters of white flowers, followed on female plants by spikes of pulpy, red fruits. Deciduous, height 4m (12ft), Z9 H3.

S. rubriflora
Pinky-red young shoots unfurl longish, ovate, lightly serrated leaves, 6-12cm (2½-5in) long. The hanging flowers have long, separate stalks but are produced in small clusters, from the position where new shoots have grown, in spring. They measure 2.5cm (1in) across and are a shining crimson-scarlet; the sexual parts form a central knob like those in magnolias. Females can produce hanging 15cm (6in) spikes of red fruit. The dark green leaves turn yellow before falling. Best given wire support. Deciduous, height 9m (28ft), Z9 H3-4.

S. sphenanthera
This species has almost circular leaves, 5-10cm (2-4in) long, with minute teeth, and pendent, green flower buds that open to many-petalled orange flowers. Deciduous, height 5m (15ft), Z7 H4.

Semele androgyna, see Tender Plants p.249.

Sinofranchetia chinensis
Lardizabalaceae

This is the only species of a genus close to *Holboellia*. A rampant grower, it is only suitable where space is plentiful, so is not normally worth trying in a small, modern, suburban garden. If you have a suitable tree, grow this species into it as this is what it does in its native haunts, where it can smother large trees. Thrusting young stems and leaf stalks have a young purplish bloom that later wears off. Three oval leaflets make up leaves 6-15cm (2½-6in) long, which are not unlike runner bean leaves and are a good green above but suffused blue below. Hanging groups of small, white flowers will not disturb the pulse rate but female plants then produce bunches of grape-like, purple fruit. Females do not need a male plant in order to bear fruit. Best in semi-shade and normal soils. Deciduous, height 16m (48ft), Z6 H4.

Sollya Pittosporaceae

An Australian genus of only two species which may be tried outside only in the mild areas, such as southern and western England, and should be mulched around its base as a winter protection. Both species have been grown for many years in greenhouses. They are woody-based climbers capable of rapid growth and long flowering periods. When seen in bloom they will

Schisandra sphenanthera *in flower.*

Sollya heterophylla.

measure 5-13cm (2-5in) long and have a tailored look that is somewhat at variance with the tangled manner of the plant's growth. In mid- to late spring it bears small, hanging clusters of egg-shaped buds that open to discrete bells, altogether a refined and pleasing arrangement in pale violet, suffused white and enhanced by a pleasing perfume. Plants are male or female. Purple 'plums' may be produced, especially in warm springs and summers. This is a climber for gardeners in the warmer spots, where it is worth a sheltered place. Sun or semi-shade and well-drained soil. Evergreen, height 10m (30ft), Z9 H3.

be thought well worth this little extra effort. Plant on a warm wall in humus-rich soils.

S. heterophylla

The bluebell creeper has thin, twining stems carrying ovate or narrower leaves, 2.5-5cm (1-2in) long. From midsummer into autumn it can produce small clusters of hanging, wide, bluebell flowers in brilliant sky-blues with a central yellow nob of fused anthers, below the projecting white stigma. Needs full sun and moist soil with good drainage. Usually grown as a greenhouse plant. Evergreen, height 2m (6ft), Z9 H1-2.

S. parviflora

This is a pared-down version of S. heterophylla, smaller in all parts and with darker blue flowers. Evergreen, height 1m (3ft), Z9 H1-2.

Stauntonia hexaphylla *Lardizabalaceae*

Similar to *Holboellia*, to which it is closely related, this plant's distinguished, 3-part leaves are long-stalked with each oval leaflet sharply pointed. They

Right: Trachelospermum jasminoides.

Right: Tropaeolum speciosum, *the flame creeper, living up to its common name.*

Below right: Tropaeolum tricolorum.

Trachelospermum *Apocynaceae*

Both these evergreen species are hardy in all but the most bleak of areas. Best in sun, they will manage with some shade in well-drained soil, although they can cope with plenty of moisture in the growing months. They can be shown how to climb up trellis or other support and will then flower freely on the old wood; pruning should, therefore, be confined to keeping the plant tidy.

T. asiaticum

A dense shrub of many twining stems generously furnished with dark, oval leaves, 2-5cm (¾-2in) long. The summer flowers are 2cm (¾in) across and open white with a creamy centre, soon aging to yellow. This is regarded as hardier than the more often-planted *T. jasminoides* but is less prominently scented. Evergreen, height 6m (20ft), Z9 H2-3.

T. jasminoides

This plant is widely grown in the USA where it acquired its name confederate vine or jasmine; it is also known as star jasmine. A strong, twining climber, it has elliptic, polished, dark green leaves, up to 10cm (4in) long but more often half this length. Clusters of highly fragrant, 5-petalled flowers, about 2.5cm (1in) across, are carried freely in the second half of summer. Each bloom looks as if it has just stopped whirling round in an anticlockwise motion as the base of the petal curls round the small centre. It is grown as a greenhouse climber in cold localities. Evergreen, height 10m (30ft), Z9 H2-3.

Tropaeolum *Tropaeolaceae*

A genus of nearly a hundred species including herbaceous perennials and annuals, the best-known of which is the annual nasturtium *T. majus*. Many are not fully hardy.

T. speciosum

The flame creeper or flame nasturtium is a perennial with a substantial creeping rhizomatous rootstock. It seems best when established in moist soil rich in humus where the roots can be in shade and, as such, is a plant that is often grown more easily in cool and dampish soils, free of lime: spectacular specimens can be seen in the north of England and in Scotland. The long slender stems are happy in sun and will cope with shade. It will grow up trellis or other supports on cool, shady walls but some of the best effects are seen when it finds its own way up such hosts as box, yew hedges or even clematis. Dark green evergreens certainly set off the brilliant vividness of the many scarlet flowers, which are 3.5cm (1½in) long and with spurs almost as long again. The rather square petals do not overlap and give the flowers a rather excited, startled look. Blooming starts quite early in summer but becomes freer as the plant grows on, and will still be produced into the autumn up until the frosts. Foliage is recognisable as a nasturtium's even though there are 5 or 6 boldly fashioned lobes. Herbaceous, height 3m (10ft), Z8 H3.

T. tricolorum

This is a tuberous-rooted perennial with rounded, palmate leaves of 5 to 7 elliptic leaflets, almost

thread-like stems, and flowers from the end of winter through spring. These blooms are 3cm (1¼in) long with decorative, dark-edged, rich orange calyces, short yellow or golden-orange petals and conspicuous long, upward-pointing spurs in yellow, red or maroon. By summer the plant has died down and it stays dormant until early autumn. The trick is to keep the tubers from getting too wet in the winter, or too cold. However, there may be a place near a sheltered hedge where the tubers can be safe, or they should be planted in a coldframe or under other glass and top growth led out into a sheltered spot. Herbaceous, height 1-2m (3-6ft), Z8-9 H1-2.

T. tuberosum

This perennial climber grows quickly from very substantial yellow tubers that are splashed purple-red. The flattish grey-green leaves have 3-6 well-cut lobes and the flowers are hung out on long, maroon stalks that curve so that the flowers seem almost free-hanging and show their long spurs. Relatively small, up to 4cm (1½in) long, the midsummer to autumn flowers are cup-shaped; the orange-red sepals give way to gold or tangerine petals but are marked in the throats with brown veining. The best-known form is **'Ken Aslet'** (correctly *T. tuberosum* var. *lineamaculatum* 'Ken Aslet'!) with glowing orange flowers. The tubers grow close to the soil surface and are vulnerable to frost, which will kill them. In mild areas it may be

Wisteria sinensis adorns a wall.

Wisteria floribunda 'Multijuga' ('Macrobotrys')

All wisterias are stars, but 'Multijuga' must be the primadonna of the group. As strong and simple to grow as any cultivar, the almost unbelievably long racemes of dark violet flowers mark it out as something very special. Deciduous, height 9m (28ft), Z5 H4.

✻ Extraordinary flower racemes, up to 1-1.2m (3-4ft) long

✻ Hardy

✻ Very long-lived

✻ Excellent on walls; perhaps still better on a bold pergola or even through trees

✻ Very atmospheric

✻ Many other fine cultivars to try, including white ones

sufficient to cover them with a protective layer of chipped bark or something similar in winter; in more frost-prone areas they can be lifted and stored like dahlias, and replanted in the spring. When lifted they may be large enough to split and provide extra plants. Herbaceous, height 3-4m (9-12ft), Z8 H2-3.

Tweedia caerulea

(syn. *Oxypetalum caeruleum*) *Asclepiadaceae*

A genus now of one species (it used to have fifty but these have been reallocated to other genera). A woody climber with lance-shaped, somewhat hairy, misty-green leaves, 5-10cm (2-4in) long, quite broad, and heart-shaped at the junction with the leaf stalk. From summer until autumn it produces small clusters of 5-petalled, forget-me-not flowers, pink in bud but opening to clear blue stars before becoming purple with age. The flowers are 2-2.5cm (1in) across. Able to stand some frost, but in cold areas best grown as an annual or with plenty of protection on a wall in sun and open-structured soil. Evergreen, height 1m (3ft), Z10 H2-3.

Wisteria *Leguminosae/Papilionaceae*

Most gardeners regard this heavyweight contender as the leading flowering climber. Little wonder as it can clothe major walls, perform miracles in trees and transform pergolas. There are ten deciduous species, six of which are usually grown; two of these represent

STARTING WITH WISTERIAS

❋ Make your choice:
W. floribunda 'Macrobotrys' or *W. floribunda* 'Alba' take a lot of beating.

❋ Choose a site – a sunny or semi-shaded wall, pergola or tree. If you choose to grow it into a tree there is little need of pruning.

❋ Ensure the soil is well-drained but not liable to drying out.

❋ Plant firmly at the end of winter or earliest spring and then cut back the main shoot to approximately 75cm (30in) and any others to half their length. Tie to support.

❋ Aim to take a leading shoot upwards to the desired height. Prune back its laterals to about 15cm (6in). Attaining the full height may take a couple of seasons and then the laterals can be trained horizontally. If you want to cover a wall, you can tie laterals horizontally to the support and thereafter prune back sublaterals to 2 or 3 buds to form flowering spurs.

❋ Once the framework of branches is established, there will be too much subsequent growth. In late summer prune back all shooting stems that are not needed to further the framework, leaving up to 6 leaves on each shoot. In winter reduce these spurs to 2 or 3 buds.

❋ Maintain this strict pruning regime in following years. Pruning and restricted rootruns will maximize flower production. (Rootruns can be given some limits in a similar manner to that recommended for greedy hedges, p.48.)

the vast majority found in gardens: *W. floribunda* from Japan and *W. sinensis* from China.

Wisterias suffer from a reputation of taking many years to get to flowering stage. While it is true that a newly planted specimen will take a few years to get established, given the correct treatment new plants should start blooming quite freely in about four years, not much different from the waiting period for many shrubs, and usually quicker than most trees. It will take a little longer to cover the whole of the side of a house, but more quickly than it is rumoured. If you have not tried yet, follow the suggestions above.

W. floribunda

A very strong anticlockwise-twining climber with pinnate leaves of 11-19 spear-shaped leaflets. This is the hardiest and the one capable of having the longest flower pendents (see 'Multijuga', box). The standard, hanging, pointed racemes are 30cm (12in) long and are composed of pea flowers in pale violet but there are varying shades – some much darker, some pink and white. There are many named forms, most with synonyms. **'Alba'** is exceptional with shapely snow-white racemes some 60cm (24in) long. **'Honbeni'** has pink racemes 45cm (18in) long. Probably the most famous cultivar is **'Multijuga'** (syn. 'Kyushaku', 'Macrobotrys', 'Naga Noda') (see box). **'Royal Purple'** has racemes of 30-50cm (12-20in) in rich violet. They all look quite fabulous on walls, but perhaps the most magical effects are produced by growing plants over pergolas or along linked posts so that the flowers hang down around anyone underneath. Deciduous, height 9m (28ft), Z5 H4.

W. sinensis

Another strong grower, this has leaves with 7-13 ovate leaflets, and well-packed, hanging, tapering bunches, 30cm (12in) long, of lilac pea-flowers. **'Prolific'** is lilac-blue and blooms freely from a very early age. **'Alba'** is pure white with shorter racemes than *W. floribunda* 'Alba'. Deciduous, height 9m (28ft), Z5 H4.

W. × formosa

A hybrid between the two previous species and equally strong. As pleasingly fragrant as those of its parents, the violet flowers, in 25cm (10in) racemes, have white and yellow markings. Deciduous, height 9m (28ft), Z6 H4.

Wisteria floribunda 'Alba'.

RAMBLERS & SCRAMBLERS

Ramblers and scramblers are general and rather loose terms used to define upwardly mobile characters – other than twiners and self-clingers – that aspire to the heights but lean on others, or need some artificial aids, to accomplish their ambitions. Some need greater help than others. Climbing and rambling roses are in a category halfway between the self-sufficient and the dependent; most have strong enough branches to achieve a good degree of upward security but are all the better for some intervention by the gardener in the way of ties and pruning. The clematis are included in this section: though many are able to help themselves by means of tenacious, coiling leaf-stalks, many others are likely to fall flat on their face if not given some assistance – in some gardens some clematis are grown over the ground!

Another important genus featured in this chapter is *Jasminum*. Even covering just these three genera – rose, clematis and jasmine – is a daunting prospect as there is such a wide range of them, so I have been very selective and have picked only some of the very best to grow on walls and fences, over pergolas and up poles.

Although this is rather an arbitrary category, one thing that becomes abundantly clear is that the ramblers and scramblers are likely to be showy items; they are among the more highly bred garden favourites with many fine cultivars worthy of places in our plots. Colour and extrovert display are both more than adequately supplied by these plants. They are readily available in garden centres and nurseries, and if they are widely grown, this only reflects their good value for money and space.

Providing support for these plants is of crucial importance. For many it will make the difference between a distinguished plant and one that becomes disorganized with the result that its effect is diminished. Many of them are the type that can be severely pruned and will grow strongly to regain their ground: among these are *Jasminum nudiflorum* and *Forsythia suspensa*, which, once they have formed a skeleton of bones on the wall or other support, can be cut back after flowering so that fresh new growth is made to carry next year's crop of blossom. Most roses will respond to the knife, and need to make new wood for the flowering buds for the following season. Fruit trees pressed to the walls and trained espalier-wise need to be pruned annually to give their best in flower and fruit.

A-Z Guide to Ramblers and Scramblers

Clematis Ranunculaceae

Although the past few decades have seen a great rise in the interest in clematis, they have actually been 'hot news' from the middle of the nineteenth century and seem set to continue their rise in popularity. The small-flowered species are just as popular as the large hybrids that followed the introduction of the famous deep purple *C. × jackmanii*, raised in 1860. Their popularity is not difficult to understand. They propagate easily and are for sale everywhere. Even in small gardens there is always room for another clematis and, of course, they can be trained to any level. They can be grown in pots, up walls, pergolas, poles or over buildings or they can be planted in association with shrubs and trees, and allowed to work their way up and over them – conifers, roses, golden privet or such as *Solanum crispum* 'Glasnevin' are all suitable partners. They are not snobby, and will be as happy going

Clematis armandii.

hrough privet as a magnolia. They come in all sizes and you can find kinds to bloom in all seasons (at east two easy and outstanding evergreen species bloom in the winter). And they are beautiful – often spectacularly so. One note of caution: it is wise only to plant the robust species, such as C. *montana*, where they have room to spread.

Please note that the coloured, petal-like parts of the clematis flower are correctly called sepals.

CULTIVATION

Culture is not difficult: a shaded rootrun is what they expect in the wild and enjoy in cultivation, although they like to get their faces into the light. Many are happy in partial shade and there are few real sun-worshippers like C. *texensis*. Some are indifferent: sun, semi-shade or full shade are all the same to such as C. *montana*, C. *viticella* and C. × *jackmanii*. Even the large-flowered kinds are perhaps happiest with some shade.

Clematis appreciate an open-structured, deep and well-drained soil that does not dry out. Sandy soil is not ideal and will need a lot of additional humus. Evergreen kinds are best planted in spring or early summer, while others can be planted almost anytime except in the depth of winter.

PLANTING AND CLEMATIS WILT

As an exception to the usual rule about planting, clematis should be interred deeper than they were originally in their pot, a matter of up to 15cm (6in) of stem being covered with soil. This will do two things. It will help to keep the roots moist and cool and it will thwart the very annoying clematis wilt caused by the fungus *Asocochyta clematidina*. The latter is first seen when the terminal shoots flop suddenly. This is likely to be followed by the collapse of major areas of the plant, perhaps all that is above ground. All affected parts should be removed and burnt or safely taken out of the garden as the older wood will harbour spores. There is every likelihood of the basal parts sending out fresh growth unaffected by the fungus. This should be sprayed with a systemic fungicide to ensure the re-establishment of the plant. Some of the large-flowered hybrids are most at risk.

Because clematis is such a large and diverse genus it makes sense to impose some order on the plants for the purposes of this book. Therefore you will find them divided here into winter-flowerers, p.168, groups of similar species – Montana group, p.169, Viticella group, p.170, Texensis group, p.170, Vitalba

group, p.170, Orientalis group, p.171, and, finally, the large-flowered hybrids – early flowerers, p.172, early doubles, p.172, mid-season flowerers, p.173 and late flowerers, p.173. Species groupings are determined by many minor features of more interest to botanists than gardeners, though the form of the

PRUNING CLEMATIS

The species can be allowed complete freedom or are cut back only when they outgrow their allotted space. Pruning the large-flowered hybrids can cause some worry. There ought to be no difficulty: some gardeners bypass any problem by a display of masterly inactivity, and the clematis still perform very adequately. Those who want better results can heed the following advice for the different classes as listed below.

Group 1

Early bloomers, flowering on last year's wood. Prune as the flowers finish. Pruning can be restricted to removing weak and older wood and curbing undue territorial greed.

alpina, chrysocoma, graciflora, macropetala, montana, x vedrariensis, vertillaris.

Group 2

Evergreen clematis. Leave alone or just tidy unwanted twigs.
armandii, cirrhosa, finetiana, meyeriana, quinquefoliolata.

Group 3

Those flowering from midsummer on current growth and dying back in the winter. At the end of winter cut away dead material. This moribund tissue may go a considerable way back, even to the base.
campaniflora, x durandii, texensis, viorna, viticella.

Group 4

Those flowering from midsummer on current growth and adding to the considerable growth of previous years. These tend to build up huge tangled masses of growth above bare legs. Prune back some of the stronger stems, or reduce all stems to say 1m (3ft), making sure that there are buds left to break.
potaninii (fargesii) var. flammula, graveolens, maximowicziana, orientalis, serratifolia, souliei, tangutica, vernayi, vitalba.

Group 5

The majority of large-flowered hybrids. They bloom on short lateral shoots breaking from last season's stems – midsummer flowers with perhaps another flush in late summer or autumn. Most need only light pruning to remove untidy, dead or very weary old shoots, and will survive well enough with this attention. All pruning should be completed before any buds break. If you cut back fairly drastically in spring you will get stronger new growth and a later show of blooms.
x jackmanii, 'Beauty of Worcester',
'Duchess of Edinburgh', 'Hagley Hybrid', 'Nelly Moser', 'The President',
'Vyvyan Pennell', and so on.

flowers and sepal ('petal') pose is one important factor. The possession of stunted embryo petals (to the botanists petaloid staminodes) between the sepals and the stamens defines some groups.

WINTER-FLOWERING CLEMATIS

C. armandii

This strong species was introduced in 1900 and is easy to grow on walls or in more open sites with some shelter. It has formidable leathery, polished, dark green leaves of 3 undivided ovals 7-12cm (3-5in) long. Flowers 5-7cm (2-3in) across are made the most of by being widespread and facing upwards. They are freely produced in large clusters from the end of winter into early spring; odd blooms can open earlier. Several forms have been named, the two leading ones being **'Appleblossom'** and **'Snowdrift'**. Both are strong with wide, good-sized flowers. 'Appleblossom' is tinted pale pink, especially as the flowers age, and has foliage with a bronzy cast. 'Snowdrift' is snowy-white with rich green foliage.

To get the benefit of the blossom it makes sense to give them support up to about half their height and then perhaps train them across pergola horizontals. In the very coldest of districts one might look to grow this in a right-angle corner between two sunny walls. Evergreen, height 6m (20ft), Z8 H3.

C. cirrhosa

This evergreen is an easy, strong plant that is quite distinct from *C. armandii*, with more typically lobed clematis foliage, the leaves being perhaps 2-5cm (1-2in) long and shiny. It hardly waits for the winter to begin before producing the first of a long series of goblet- or bowl-shaped flowers, 3-7cm (1¼-3in) wide, which will continue to appear until spring. The colour is basically cream but may be freckled with tiny red dots. The scent is a bonus. It can be very floriferous, something more obvious in named forms; the blooms are produced from leaf axils in ones or twos and look outwards or down. The flowers are discrete offerings rather than gaudy ornaments; the masses of silky seedheads that decorate the plant in late spring are more showy.

There are several named forms. The oldest is **var. balearica**, which is free-flowering with freckled open bells and with more deeply cut, ferny foliage that is suffused bronze or purple in the winter. It could be grown as a foliage plant. **'Freckles'** is a popular cultivar bearing flowers splashed with reddish maroon. **'Wisley Cream'** is another fine kind, freely bearing good-sized, showy flowers. Evergreen, height to 5m (18ft), Z8 H3.

C. meyeriana, see Tender Plants p.246.

C. napaulensis (syn. *C. forrestii*)

This species grows strongly in the more favoured districts; in very cold areas it might need glass protection. Hanging flowers in groups are rather slender, long, cloche-hat shapes in pale creamy-yellow with contrasting purple stamens. They are 4-9cm (1½-3½ in) long and produced from the end of the summer until towards the end of winter. Semi-evergreen, height 10m (30ft), Z8 H3.

Left: Clematis cirrhosa *var.* balearica *is often heavily speckled.*

Clematis alpina *'Ruby'.*

MONTANA GROUP

C. montana, see also box.

This is the best known of all the species in the garden. The type is creamy-white with typical 4-sepalled flowers borne in amazing profusion in late spring and early summer, starting before the new leaves have emerged. The more usual form planted is **var. rubens** with pink flowers followed by the typical leaves consisting of 3 pointed and lightly serrated, purple-flushed, mid-green leaflets on long, purple-green stalks. Pink-flowered montanas usually have purple-flushed leaves. **'Elizabeth'** has large, rich pink flowers, 7cm (3in) across; its foliage is purple-tinged. **f. grandiflora** is a large-flowered white with individual flowers up to 10cm (4in) across, later flowers contrast with its dark foliage. **'Tetrarose'** also has large flowers. They are 9cm (3½in) across and rich pink. The foliage is larger than the type and purple-tinged.

C. alpina

An energetic species making great huddles of intertwined stems well furnished with tripartite pointed foliage but with these parts usually further divided, the central leaflet into 3 and the side ones into a major and a minor part. It begins to flower just a little later than *C. montana* and will often continue to offer a scattering of blossom later, and especially in the autumn. Instead of the widespead flat look of *C. montana* when open, the pointed buds are held in a nodding pose and the sepals only get halfway back, at a 45° angle to the protruding bunch of stamens and stigma. The type varies from pale to deep lilac-blue with a white centre and is up to 3.5cm (1½in) long. **'Francis Rivis'** (syn. 'Blue Giant') is good, with lots of blue flowers 7cm (3in) long, the sepals somewhat twisted. **'Ruby'** is optimistically named, but is a pleasing deep pinkish-mauve. Deciduous, height 3m (10ft), Z5-6 H4.

C. chrysocoma

Pale pink flowers at the end of spring and early summer and stems and leaves covered with short, dense, fawny down. Perhaps a little less hardy than the reliable C. montana. Deciduous, height 6m (18ft), Z7 H4.

C. macropetala

A very hardy, easy species with cut, pointed leaves and lots of spring and summer blossom of nodding, many-sepalled, rounded flowers, 6-9cm (2½-3½in) across. The colour varies from lilac to violet-blue. The 4 larger outer sepals are joined by the petaloid stamens and these are darker in the outer rings and

Clematis montana

There can be few gardens that will not be the better for one or more plants of this easy, strong, twisting, scrambling, free-flowering prodigy. Try to see the colour of the clone you are going to plant as there are a number of less attractive ones on sale. For a darker form try 'Tetrarose' (right) or 'Ruby'. We have two or three different colour forms together so we get a mixed effect in spring. Deciduous, height 8m (25ft), Z5-6 H4.

✳ Extraordinary freedom of flowering

✳ Choice of colour forms

✳ Rapid growth

✳ Hardiness and freedom from diseases

✳ Happy in sun or shade

✳ Good foliage

✳ Adaptable. Up wall trellis or wires, into trees to great heights, over railings, fences or low walls. Sometimes used over soil surface

✳ Propagates easily from layers or cuttings. Varies from seed

Clematis macropetala.

paler towards the central cream ones. There are several named clones. **'Markham's Pink'** is rosy with paler foliage. **'Maidwell Hall'** is a lovely blue. Deciduous, height 4m (12ft), Z5-6 H4.

C. × vedrariensis

A series of robust hybrids with pink flowers and tripartite leaves of rather dull, purplish-green and hairy below. The best clone is **'Highdown'**. Deciduous, height 7m (22ft), Z6 H4.

VITICELLA GROUP

C. campaniflora

This is a small-flowered but very prolific species close to C. *viticella*. A strong grower with neatly cut pinnate leaves, it has been rather eclipsed by the larger-flowered C. *viticella* and this is a pity as it is a worthwhile plant. Saucer-shaped flowers are white, lightly veined or suffused with pale blue or pink, the sepals gently recurving; each flower is a modest 2-3cm (1in) across. It generates masses of blossom through midsummer into early autumn. Deciduous, height 6m (20ft), Z6 H4.

C. viticella

The 3-part leaves of this species are usually further subdivided and look quite ferny. Flowers are up to 4cm (1½in) across and can be blue, purple or pink. They are borne in great profusion midsummer until autumn. The species has been grown in Britain since

the 1500s, so it is not surprising that several good forms have been selected and named. These tend to be larger and are showy in bloom, although the larger the flowers, the more the grace of the species may be under threat. **'Abundance'** is a strong grower, up to 5m (15ft), and justifies its name with lots of pale lilac flowers that are made to look deeper by the purple veins. **'Mary Rose'** is a double form in pink. **'Purpurea Plena Elegans'** is popular with lots of deep violet or purple-mauve flowers, 5-8cm (2-3in) or more across; there are 4 major outside sepals, which are sometimes green, and lots of smaller inner ones. See also **'Etoile Violette'** p.174, which is sometimes listed under C. *viticella*. Deciduous, 3-4m (10-12ft), Z6 H4.

TEXENSIS GROUP

C. texensis

This is the most garden-worthy of this group; the others are interesting and some are inclined to be herbaceous, as is C. *texensis* itself. Its divided leaves are made up of 4-8 bluish-green leaflets. There may be a tendril at the end of the main leaflet. The flower colour is unique in the genus – a blatant red, sometimes of a scarlet or purplish inclination. The flowers are bell-shaped and about 2.5cm (1in) long. It needs a warm, sheltered spot by a wall to do well and flower freely from midsummer until autumn. As might be guessed from its homeland, this species is capable of growing in rather drier soils than its relatives. It tends to die down with the winter, either halfway or, in hard weather, to the ground. It will probably do its best growing through a shrub or with other climbers when the darkest red forms can look really exciting. **'Duchess of Albany'** is splendid with deep pink, 5cm (2in) long flowers in late summer into autumn. The slightly darker central bands inside help to enrich it and its shape puts one in mind of a miniature, narrow-petalled, lily-flowered tulip. **'Gravetye Beauty'** is crimson with narrow sepals, to 5cm (2in) long, in bell shapes that later open wider. Outside the sepals are rather paler. **'Princess Diana'** is pink. It is a good idea to take cuttings of these cultivars and keep one or two plants in reserve to replace any that disappear. Tidy up by cutting back hard in winter. Deciduous, height 2-3m (6-9ft), Z5 H4.

VITALBA GROUP

One can admire C. *vitalba*, traveller's joy, in the hedgerows, but it is not a spectacular garden plant. In the garden, related kinds can be used to cover walls, fences, tree stumps and so on.

There is plenty to see in Beth Chatto's inspired garden near Elmstead Market, Essex. Here is a corner with the extrovert Clematis viticella *'Abundance' making determined advances on the rich-leaved* Berberis × ottawensis *'Purpurea'.*

C. flammula

This is rather like traveller's joy, writ somewhat larger and making a frenetic tangle. The bright, dark green leaves are pinnate, and pure white, very fragrant flowers are produced in large clusters in the second half of summer and into autumn, each individual flower being up to 2.5cm (1in) across. A vigorous, easy plant, it is ideal for covering a wall or fence, tree stumps or an ugly corner. Deciduous, height 4-5m (12-15ft), Z7 H4.

C. maximowicziana

Hugely vigorous, this has tripartite or pinnate leaves in dark green, and white, scented flowers in autumn. It will cover almost anything in a glorious tangle and is at its best, florally, in warmer gardens. Deciduous, height 10m (30ft), Z6 H4.

C. potaninii var. souliei (syn. C. fargesii var. souliei)

A strong plant with large leaves, often purplish, of leaflets up to 9cm (3in) long. It bears flurries of flowers from early summer into autumn. Borne singly or a few in sprays, they are white and about 6-7cm (2½in) wide. Deciduous, height 7m (22ft), Z7 H4.

C. terniflora (syn. C. paniculata)

Usually semi-evergreen, this species has polished, rich green foliage with, in late summer and autumn, contrasting large panicles of white stars, 2-3cm (¾-1¼in) across, followed by masses of attractive silky seedheads. A strong plant that is ideal for a place in full sun. Semi-evergreen, height 5-6m (15-20ft), Z8 H4.

ORIENTALIS GROUP

C. florida 'Sieboldii'

By no means a rampant grower, this is a beguiling character when it blooms in summer with beautifully clean-cut, wide-open bowls of creamy-white, 7-10cm (3-4in) wide. Each has a splendid rounded boss of purple stamens making it look almost like a passion flower. Deciduous, height 2m (6ft), Z7 H4.

C. orientalis

A widespread species with thick, fleshy leaves of bluish- or greyish-green, sometimes, like the young pale stems, tinged with wine colours. Many small, limy-yellow flowers are borne in large clusters. The filaments of the stamens are burgundy when the flowers fully open, and this colour may infuse or spot the downy flowers to a greater or lesser degree. This is a complex and interesting species but in the garden is bettered by C. tangutica. Deciduous, height 6m (18ft), Z6 H4.

C. rehderiana

A strong climber bearing bright green, pinnate leaves with as many as 7-9 leaflets, this blooms freely from midsummer well into autumn, its pale yellow flowers hung out like rounded, nodding bells with recurved tips. The scent is usually likened to that of cowslips.

Roses and clematis together again, this time with clematis 'Princess Diana' (which is a texensis type, and not to be confused with 'Princess of Wales', which is a lanuginosa type) and perennial sweet peas.

AUTUMN CLEMATIS

A good number of clematis species and cultivars add colour and interest to the autumn scene by their flower and seedheads. Here are a few.

C. rehderiana has lots of small, long, hanging bells in lime-yellow from midsummer until late autumn.

C flammula bears a long succession of clusters of small, starry, white flowers from summer until late autumn; also has silky seedheads.

C. x jouiniana 'Praecox' is rather like the last one – an energetic scrambling plant with lots of bunches of small long-petalled, white stars, pinky-blue in bud.

C. 'Bill MacKenzie is free with bright yellow, hanging, pointed globes opening to 4-pointed caps; silken seedheads, bright ferny foliage.

C. tibetana subsp. *vernayi* 'Orange Peel' similar to 'Bill MacKenzie' but with perhaps even thicker petals.

C. x durandii has nodding wide bells in deep purplish-blue that open to a starry shape with a boss of contrasting pale stamens.

Another good species for clothing awkward spots or running through a tree. Deciduous, height 8m (25ft), Z6 H4.

C. tangutica

The best of the yellow species, this produces a long succession of many nodding, bright gold bells, on long stalks, from late summer well into autumn, followed by silken seedheads. Sepals only curve out gently at the mouth. Much-cut, pinnate leaves are fresh green, a good accompaniment to the flowers. It is a particularly accommodating plant, growing with equal freedom in sun or shade and only needing a little shelter to do its splendid best. Some clones are better than others so it is best to buy one seen. Deciduous, height 4-5m (12-15ft), Z6 H4.

C. 'Bill MacKenzie' (possibly C. *orientalis* × C. *tangutica*)

From midsummer until late autumn, this produces nodding, golden lanterns with contrasting maroon anthers; the sepals have often been likened to orange peel for their thickness and colour – they are even thicker than those of its presumed parents. The flowers are somewhat wider than those of its parents, measuring 8cm (3in) across. It is fertile, the seedlings being attractive, but not true 'Bill MacKenzie' and not to be called such: there is enough confusion in this group without adding to it. Deciduous, height 6-7m (20-22ft), Z6 H4.

Clematis 'Bill Mackenzie'.

A series of hardy cultivars normally with wide flat flowers, 9-20cm (3-8in) wide, opening in early summer with later flushes through the weeks that follow. Simple, unserrated, oval or lance-shaped leaves or three leaflets are usually light to medium green. Prune in later winter or early spring to promising buds. These will give the first flush of bloom, others follow from new shoots. The following are among the best of the early-flowering clematis. Deciduous, height to 2-4m (6-12ft), Z6 H4.

'Bee's Jubilee' opens deep pink flowers that fade to leave a deeper central stripe on each of the 8 overlapping, rounded sepals. It is perhaps better in part shade and is a less straggly grower than many. Height 2.5m (8ft).

'Elsa Späth' is a fine plant, starting early and going on to summer with large flowers of rich purple-blue enhanced by red anthers. Height 2-3m (6-10ft).

'Nelly Moser' is one of the all-time successes. It is very free-flowering with good-sized, pink blooms that have striking wide, central stripes and red anthers. The blooms fade in full sun; flowers produced as a late summer flush are a paler pink. Height 4m (12ft).

'Niobe' is a tidy, tight grower bearing deep red flowers, 10-15cm (4-6in) wide, with pointed sepals and yellow anthers. It is free-flowering through summer. Height 2-3m (6-10ft).

'Ramona' is a strong plant bearing plenty of pale blue flowers, 10-15cm (4-6in) wide, from midsummer onwards. Height 3m (10ft).

'The President' has large, silvery buds opening to strong purple, velvety blooms that retain a silvery underside. Height 2-3m (6-10ft.)

These only differ from other earlies by having doubled flowers. While the first flush of these will have typical double or semi-double flowers, the later ones are likely to be less doubled, or single. Deciduous, height 2-3m (6-10ft), Z6 H4. The following are a couple of favourite early doubles.

'Proteus' has neatly doubled, early flowers with many layers of sepals, the colour graded towards the centre, which is somewhat paler than the mauve-pink of the main parts; the outer ring of petals can be green. From midsummer it will produce flowers that are single and pale mauve. Height 2.5-3m (8-10ft).

'Vyvyan Pennell' has well-doubled flowers of rich lilac, some 13cm (5in) across; the centre sepals are paler; the anthers are golden. The midsummer flowers are less doubled or even single, and are rather more blue. Height 2-3m (6-10ft).

MID-SEASON FLOWERERS

Hardiness and foliage is on a par with early kinds. They are vigorous, free-flowering and large-sized. The following is a selection of the most attractive mid-season clematis; they are single-flowered.

'Duchess of Edinburgh' is a robust clematis that can easily reach 3m (10ft). Its large white flowers may have some green shading and there is some doubling with the stamens making narrow petals. Large and free-flowering. Height 2-3m (6-10ft).

'General Sikorski' is free-flowering, bearing well-formed, blue flowers with creamy anthers. Height 3m (10ft).

'Henryi' produces creamy-white blooms with broad, pointed petals and contrasting deep chocolate anthers. Exceptionally large, the flowers may be up to 20cm (8in) across. Height 3m (10ft).

'Marie Boisselot' is strong-growing and has flowers up to 18cm (6in) across. White with cream anthers, they are borne from midsummer into late autumn. Height 3m (10ft).

LATE FLOWERERS

With similar foliage to the earlies and just as strong and hardy, these flower on the new growth and tend to hold their blooms outwards. The later flowerers are in bloom in summer until well into the autumn. Here are some of the best.

'Comtesse de Bouchard' bears bright pink flowers, up to 10cm (4in) across, with a suggestion of mauve, textured with channels running towards a central

Above: Clematis *'Nelly Moser'.*

Far left: Clematis *'The President'.*

Clematis *'Duchess of Edinburgh'.*

173

boss of golden anthers. It is very free-flowering. Height 2-3m (6-10ft).

× *durandii* is rather an 'odd man out', a muddle-headed plant that has only half its mind on climbing. With support it reaches 1-2m (3-6ft) only, but it bears lots of very attractive summer saucers, 6-8cm (2½-3in) wide and of deepest blue with a hint of violet, made more dashing by the central bosses of golden anthers.

'Ernest Markham' has lots of vivid, deep magenta summertime flowers, 10cm (4in) across, with purple-brown anthers; later flowers may be smaller. Height 3-4m (10-12ft).

'Etoile Violette' also has lots of saucer-shaped flowers. These are 7cm (3in) wide and deep violet with contrasting yellow anthers. They are borne from summer until late in autumn. Height 2-3m (6-10ft).

'Hagley Hybrid' is a well-known, compact, robust clematis. Its 8-10cm (3-4in) flowers, carried from mid- to late summer, are pinky-mauve with red anthers. Height 2-3m (6-10ft).

'Huldine' is free-flowering with smaller flowers. They are 6cm (2½in) wide and white with a mauve

back, giving a very pale pink effect. The sepals tend to curve back. Height 3-4m (10-12ft).

'Jackmanii' was the first of the hybrids to be introduced and is still a favourite. It can have very large numbers of velvet-textured flowers up to 10cm (4in) across and deepest purple with limy anthers. Height 3m (10ft).

'Mme Edouard André' forms silvery buds that open to wide-sepalled flowers of a deep pink that borders red, but retaining silvered undersides. The anthers are gold. Height 2-3m (6-10ft).

'Mme Julia Correvon' has open, bell-shaped flowers from midsummer until autumn. They are 7cm (3in) wide and burgundy-red. Height 3m (10ft).

'Perle d'Azur' bears saucer-shaped, azure-blue flowers, 8cm (3in) across, with somewhat recurved sepal tips; blossom smothers the plant and makes it one of the most successful from midsummer into the autumn. Height 3m (10ft).

'Rouge Cardinal' has 10cm (4in) flowers of a velvet texture in rich crimson with rusty-red anthers. A sun-lover. Height 2-3m (6-10ft).

'Victoria' is a vigorous plant with rich mauve-pink flowers 10cm (4in) across. They are very freely produced. Height 3m (10ft).

'Ville de Lyon' has 13cm (5in) flowers with very broad sepals. They are deep burgundy to carmine-red with pale yellow anthers. As the season advances, the lower foliage can die off and look unsightly, so it is best to plant a shrub in front to hide the lower parts. Height 2-3m (6-10ft).

Clematoclethra Actinidiaceae

This deciduous genus is close to *Actinidia* (see p.152) and, like them, consists of vigorous climbers that grow easily in mild areas if given some shelter and

Clematis 'Etoile Violette', a viticella-type.

Right top: The viticella-type clematis 'Royal Velours', a very prolific late-bloomer, with the jackmanii-type 'Victoria' in the garden of The Anchorage, near Bromley in Kent. It is easy to understand the popularity of such clematis.

Right bottom: The evergreen Bupleurum fruticosum, from the Mediterranean, with its pale mustard-yellow blossom in the embrace of the overflowing jackmanii-type clematis 'Perle d'Azur', a pleasing duet.

Left: Clematis 'Hagley Hybrid', a favourite jackmanii-type.

warmth. In regions like south-west England and other favoured spots, they can be grown in the open to clamber over trees or even on pergolas, but they must be regarded as half hardy in cold areas. Plant in sun or semi-shade in healthy well-drained soil.

C. actinidiodes

A pleasing clean-shaven foliage plant, this species has wide, heart-shaped leaves, up to 7cm (3in) long, on thin stalks. The early summer flowers are white, maybe blushing pale pink, 1cm (½in) across, and are borne singly or in twos or threes. Small, black berries may follow. Deciduous, height 12m (40ft), Z6 H4.

C. scandens

In contrast to the previous species, this is one with such very bristly young shoots that they look rusty brown. The bristly effect extends to the margins and midrib of the leaves, as well as the underside of the veins. The healthy-looking, oblong to ovate leaves give the plant a look altogether of an opulent bon viveur. Bunches of 3-6 white flowers, each under 1cm (½in) across, may be followed by similarly sized fruits turning from green to red. Deciduous, height 8m (25ft), Z6 H4.

Clianthus puniceus

Leguminosae/Papilionaceae

At one time, the evergreen lobster claw or parrot's bill would have to have been listed under tender plants, and it certainly cannot be given an endorsement for full hardiness in colder parts, but it is well worth trying in mild areas, such as southern England, where its base may be given some cover for extra protection if really bitter weather threatens. In cold areas it is often grown under glass as it is an exceptionally fine plant. Outside it will enjoy sunshine and plenty of moisture through the growing months, but in well-drained soil. The flowers are pea-like although the standards are completely reflexed, giving it an unusual effect: the lobster's claw is the pointed, slightly curved keel, which is 6cm (2½in) long. These interesting flowers are carried in pendant racemes of perhaps 6 to over 12 blooms, and as they are brilliant red, they really do make an impact. There is a fine pure white form, f. *albus* **'White Heron'**, while **f. albus** is white, sometimes suffused with green. The leaves are 7-15cm (3-6in) long and pinnate to the extent of having up to 24 small oval leaflets. It will make a bushier plant if the shoots of young plants have their growing tips nipped off. Like many of the pea-family persuasion, this is rarely a long-lived plant but is easily raised from seed. Evergreen, height 4m (12ft), Z8 H2.

Elaeagnus glabra *Elaeagnaceae*

This splendid but slightly rambling shrub is easily pruned to fill the area required. Tough, 3-10cm (1-4in) long leaves are meticulously polished above

Jasminum nudiflorum

The winter-flowering jasmine was only introduced into cultivation in 1844 and from that time rapidly became perhaps the most popular of all hardy winter-flowering plants. It is a straggling, loose-limbed individual that, left to itself, will go skating over the ground and leaning up against any obstacle. In gardens it is usually trained up walls, but it can be effective if allowed to spill over a dedicated piece of ground or fall over a containing wall. The 3-part pointed leaves and new stems are dark green. The flowers start to appear in late autumn and can open in succession for the first half of the winter. Each bronzy red bud opens to make a flower up to 2cm (¾in) across and with 5 or, more usually, 6 lobes. Hard frost may kill off open flowers but there are always plenty more buds to open later – budded sprays brought inside make pleasing decoration as the flowers open. The older wood produces long laterals that carry the flowers; these long shoots are best cut back to 2-3 buds after blooming to give next season's flowering wood. As plants age, one or two of the older branches can be removed to be replaced by any of the thrusting younger ones. Any twig that touches the ground will root, which is one reason why almost every garden has one or more plants. Deciduous, height 3-4m (10-12ft), Z6 H4.

✳ Winter-flowering

✳ Evergreen effect

✳ Use in sun or shade

✳ Easy to cultivate

✳ Adaptability. Up walls, down banks, on poles

✳ Easy to prune and hardy

✳ Propagates itself by layers. Will root readily from winter cuttings

but covered with brown scaliness below, as are the shoots. The tubular, fragrant flowers in the autumn are similarly brown-scaled outside but shining white inside. They may be followed by egg fruits, up to 2cm (¾in) long, which are orange, lightly spangled silver. Its lax manner of growth means many long slender stems lean over all and sundry; it is best to cut these back in the winter to encourage new strong growth. Evergreen, height 6m (18ft), Z8 H2-3.

Jasminum *Oleaceae*

This genus would reward study by anyone willing to research some 300 species, mainly climbers and shrubs, both deciduous and evergreen, from temperate, subtropical and tropical areas. The winter jasmine, *J. nudiflorum*, is very widely grown. The only species to be anywhere near as popular is the summer-

Left: Jasminum mesnyi.

lowering, white *J. officinale*, the common jasmine, with its intoxicating perfume. Do look at the merits of the others of this charming genus.

J. beesianum

This is a borderline twiner as it makes its way upwards in a twining manner to form a mass of pointed, oval, dark green leaves, up to 5cm (2in) long. Flowers, to 1cm (½in) across, are borne in groups of 1-3 on side shoots, in late spring or early summer. They are red or deep carmine-pink: no other jasmine in cultivation has flowers of this colour. The plant will usually produce many small clusters of shining black berries that last well into winter. Hardy in most parts but will need a sheltered warm spot in cooler areas. Evergreen, height 5m (15ft), Z8-9 H3.

J. floridum

A rare plant in gardens, this is a scrambling rambler with leaves of 3 or 5 oval leaflets. Long-tubed, small yellow flowers are produced in great numbers in the second half of the summer, towards autumn, especially on well-established plants in a really sunny corner or conservatory. Semi-evergreen, height 2-3m (6-10ft), Z9 H2-3.

J. fruticans

Grown in Britain since the 1500s, *J. fruticans* builds up into an erect, thick shrub with evergreen, or more or less evergreen, leaves of 3 oblong leaflets. In the summer it conjures up lightly scented bunches of bright yellow flowers at the ends of each shoot. In a warm summer these may be followed by a considerable crop of black berries each about 1cm (½in) across. Evergreen, height 1.5m (5ft), Z8 H4.

J. grandiflora, see J. officinale f. affine.

J. mesnyi (syn. J. primulinum)

Long grown as a rambling conservatory plant, this will manage well enough on a warm wall in mild areas. It looks much like the winter jasmine (see box) – although the flowers are a little smaller, they open in good numbers in the spring. They are often semidouble and their shining, rich primrose-yellow lightens the dark green 3-part leaves. Plants can grow into a massive tangle and get top-heavy, so it pays to do some thinning each season after flowering. If it had the hardiness of the winter jasmine, it would be seen more often outside – perhaps a hybrid of the two species might produce some useful cultivars. Evergreen, height 1-2m (3-6ft), Z8-9 H2-3.

J. nudiflorum, see box.

J. officinale

This old favourite is often planted close to the house so the long summer season of scent can be enjoyed freely. It will relish the warmth of the wall and in mild regions, such as south and west Britain, can prove perfectly hardy in more open sites. In cooler areas this fine plant is best given a sheltered spot on a wall. Although usually deciduous, it will be semievergreen in milder areas or in soft winters. It is best not pruned heavily and will twine its way up any support, soon meeting you at the bedroom window. It blooms more freely as it gets established and of mature years. The rich green leaves are up to 6cm (2½in) long and consist of 7 or 9 pointed leaflets. At the ends of the shoots lots of pink buds, in clusters of 6-12, open to purest white in seemingly endless succession from early summer until autumn. The long tubes end with 4 or 5 widespread lobes, some 2cm (¾in) across, to make a starry effect. **f. affine** has flowers twice the standard size and with a pinky blush. Deciduous, height 12m (40ft), Z7-8 H4.

J. polyanthum

Another borderline twining climber, this is a very free-flowering, attractive plant with prodigiously scented, narrow-tubed, pink buds that open to dazzling white stars. Many-flowered bunches, some 10cm (4in) across, appear from spring into summer. This is a mass-produced pot plant and is popular in conservatories but is also excellent on a sheltered wall in milder areas. The pinnate leaves consist of 5 or 7 leaflets. Evergreen, height 3m (10ft), Z9 H2.

J. × stephanense (J. beesianum × J. officinale)

While this hybrid occurred in the wild, plants in cultivation probably all derive from one that was raised in a French garden. This is a splendid strong climber with leaves ranging from simple elliptic to pinnate with 5 leaflets. Leaves are matt-green and can be

Jasminum officinale 'Argenteovariegatum'.

variegated or flushed creamy-white. The terminal posies are finely scented, pink stars, each up to 2cm (¾in) across, and are borne in the first half of summer. There is a second season of attraction when the black berries shine in the autumn light. It is a plant to grow on a warm wall with some shelter. As far as I know, this is the only hybrid in the genus: it would be pleasing to have further examples, perhaps melding the undoubted hardiness of some with the floral qualities of others. Deciduous, often evergreen, height 5-7m (15-22ft), Z7-8 H4.

Lycium barbarum Solanaceae

Chinese box thorn ranges from a more or less erect shrub to a wide-spreading one, usually with long, arching branches that can lean through neighbours. Its opposite leaves are up to 6cm (2½in) long and oblong, oval or spear-shaped and mid- to greyish-green. They can be accompanied by very sharp, slender spines. The funnel-shaped flowers are usually under 1cm (½in) long and borne either singly or in clusters of perhaps 3-4 in late spring. The flower colour ranges from a rich purple to lilac or pink. The more usual darker flowers will fade with age to yellowish-pink. Then, at the end of summer, showy egg-shaped, fleshy berries, each measuring up to 2cm (¾in) long, turn from golden-tangerine to scarlet. The energetic character of the bush, its density together with its foliage, flowers and berries has made it popular as a windbreak and even as a hedge plant in coastal spots. It is certainly hardy in the south and west of Britain. If used as a hedge, to keep it in order it will need a severe cut in spring, followed by one or possibly two tidying-up operations in the summer. Deciduous, height 4m (12ft) but wider, Z6 H4.

Mitraria coccinea, see Tender Plants p.249.

Rosa Rosaceae

These are the most romantic of flowers. There are roses for every site and occasion. We enjoy the species. We love the golden oldies. We get excited by the latest novelties. Old-fashioned roses such as the climbing rose 'Cockade' with its big, wide-open blooms have long been popular and evoke a strong sense of nostalgia. Many gardeners like to collect the older cultivars, loved by generations past: breeders have caught on to this and devoted much of their effort to combine the old-fashioned look with plants that bloom longer and more generously in modern gardens – and, yes, they usually have scents!

Left: Lycium barbarum, *chinese box, is an energetic, deciduous shrub.*

ROSES – CULTIVATION AND PRUNING GUIDELINES

1 Purchase good stock. If in containers avoid those with their bases rising high in the pots. Do not take any plants that look as if their tops have been cut back after making a lot of growth. We want strong new plants, not last-season's 'retreads'.

2 Take note of the potential size of the cultivar and find a suitable position; do not try to fit an energetic quart into a pint pot.

3 The rose is likely to stay put for at least a decade so it is worth digging the ground thoroughly and deeply. Take the opportunity to incorporate generous amounts of humus-type material, especially in sandy or poor, thin soils.

4 Try to plant in autumn or late winter. Spread the roots widely in a generous hole that will accommodate the plant easily without the roots having to be curled around. Return soil and firm as you go. Aim to have the plant's union of top growth with rootstock ending up just fractionally below the finished soil surface. The planting operation should only be undertaken when the soil is friable, not in sodden conditions.

5 Prune away weak and damaged top growth. Cut back the remaining firm branches to strong outward-facing buds.

6 Roses planted against a wall should have their bases 30-45 cm (12-18in) away from the wall but with the top growth sloping towards it. The roots should be fanned out to point away from the wall and downwards.

7 When they are long enough, tie new growths to proper wall supports (see pp.70-77), taking branches outwards rather than straight up.

8 With established roses, prune from autumn until spring, removing weak and damaged wood. Try over the years to cut away some of the older wood to give newer growth more space. Many ramblers can have old flowering branches cut away almost completely; there will be plenty of new growth coming from the base. With these do pruning after flowering. With climbers older branches can be brought closer to the horizontal to encourage new branching from lower down and to stimulate flowering. Getting stiff old branches lower may mean doing it in stages, some weeks apart. Prune in winter.

9 Many species and shrub roses, such as the new 'old-fashioned' English cultivars, may almost be left to nature or merely tidied up. Some of the much-flowered wood can be cut away to allow more space and air. Far-reaching and untidy branches can be somewhat shortened.

The classification of roses has become quite complex; for simplicity I have reviewed mainly those that are called ramblers and climbers. There is not space to list all those available so I have selected a few of the very best. (British readers might like to visit the show gardens of professional growers, such as David Austin, or those of the National Rose Society Garden. See Useful Information p.250-251). The list starts with a few scrambling species (below), followed by hybrid climbers (below) and hybrid ramblers (p.183).

CLIMBING SPECIES

R. banksia
The yellow form of the species – **'Lutea'** – is the most widely grown. It has fully double, yellow flowers in late spring. These are borne in hanging bunches well before those of any of the other rambling-type roses. A favourite with gardeners since early in the nineteenth century, it is especially treasured by those who have tall walls with an aspect warm enough to protect it from frost. Deciduous, height 6m (20ft), Z7 H3.

R. bracteata
One of a series of very strong species and a parent of 'Mermaid' (see p.182), this very quickly grows into a strong, tall, scrambling plant, massively armed with thorns. From summer until autumn it produces an unusually lengthy succession of singly borne, lemon-scented, pure white, flat flowers, 6-10cm (2½-4in) wide, with a boss of golden anthers in the centre, and surrounded by leafy bracts, the feature that suggested its name. Rounded orange-red hips. Very much at its best in mild areas, elsewhere it should be found a warm wall. Deciduous or semi-evergreen, height 6m (20ft), Z7 H3-4.

R. filipes, see *filipes* 'Kiftsgate' p.184.

R. moschata
The musk rose is a strong, loose-limbed plant with curved, grappling thorns and dark, polished leaves of 5-7 leaflets. Open clusters of a few creamy-white flowers, 5cm (2in) wide, are offered with their musk scent from the second half of summer until winter threatens. More or less round red hips follow. Deciduous, height 4m (12ft), Z7 H4.

R. mulliganii
This very strong plant produces good shiny foliage and smothers itself in large bouquets of single, white flowers, 6cm (2½in) wide, with golden stamens, in summer. Deciduous, height 6m (20ft), Z5 H4.

R. multiflora
A free-growing species that can be chained to a wall or allowed to swing through the branches of a tree. The leaves are 7-9 leaflets and are usually downy below; the stems are equipped with large numbers of small prickles. This can be one of the wonders of the genus when established and in full summer bloom. Individual flowers are only 2-3cm (¾-1¼in) across, but they are produced in very generous numbers in massive trusses. They are white, sometimes tinged with pink, and scented. Where the branches touch the ground they will root, so there is always plenty of stock to give away to friends who have gardens large enough to accommodate it. Deciduous, height 3-5m (10-15ft), Z5 H4.

CLIMBING HYBRIDS

'Alister Stella Gray' is a noisette rose that will go 4m (12ft) up a wall and carry on flowering from midsummer to mid-autumn. Musk-scented flowers open from long, pointed buds. They are very double, yellow

CLASSIFICATION

In Britain the National Rose Society keeps an eye on the official classification. It differentiates between climbers and ramblers using the following criteria, but some plants could fall into one or the other.

Climbers have long shoots and large flowers carried singly or in small bunches. Some bloom once only in summer but nowadays most of the newer ones offered for sale are repeat flowerers, displaying their wares from summer into autumn. Climbers also now include some roses, such as the popular 'Albertine', introduced in 1921, that were formerly listed as ramblers; 'Albertine' really falls neatly between the two stools.

Ramblers are strong climbers with long, pliable stems carrying large bunches of relatively small flowers and normally opening early in summer. They often produce strong new growth from the base, stems that will bear the best blooms of the following year.

Rosa moschata, *the musk rose, is a most vigorous climber, able to reach to the top of lofty trees.*

SHRUBS FOR HEAVY CLAY

Heavy clay conditions are probably those most grumbled about. Clay is not the easiest to garden on but, once established, plants can find it a 'bank' on which they can draw sustenance and moisture without fear of running out of funds. Traditionally roses have been recommended for such soils, and not without good reason. Some other genera are suggested. You can also try other kinds within the same genera.

Aucuba japonica cultivars
Berberis darwinii
Chaenomeles x *superba*
cultivars
Choisya ternata
Cytisus x *praecox* and
other hybrids
Escallonia 'Apple Blossom'
and others
Magnolia grandiflora
Philadelphus all
Pyracantha all
Viburnum tinus

blooms with a deeper centre fading later to near white. Sun or part shade.

'**Aloha**' is strong and can go to 3m (10ft) easily, clothed with dark green, plastic-looking leaves. From summer until autumn it produces a series of rounded, very double, rich pink flowers with a touch of salmon and with the slightly fussy, quartered-centre look of old-fashioned kinds. Each bloom is up to 10cm (4in) across and well endowed with perfume. Sun.

'**Blairii Number Two**' has an old-fashioned appearance and grows to 4m (12ft). It bears cupped, double flowers that are deep pink in the middle, paler at the margins. Good pose. Choose a light airy spot to help combat mildew tendency.

'**Casino**' is a worthwhile yellow rose with rather scanty foliage but a large number of flowers in succession from summer until autumn. The fully doubled flowers are fragrant and some 9cm (3½in) across. Grows to 2.5-3m (8-10ft).

'**Cecile Brunner**', from an 1880 introduction that sported in 1904, is still one of the most popular roses for walls, pergolas and even climbing into trees. It can go up to 6m (20ft). Known as the sweetheart rose for its delightful, precisely formed buds, it covers itself with its first flush of bloom in early summer; lesser numbers are produced later. The buds open to very full, voluptuously doubled masses of pink petals. There is little scent, but the pointed, somewhat bronzed foliage is neat and it proves one of the most disease-free of all. Few thorns. Sun or partial shade.

'**Chaplin's Pink Climber**' is an old-fashioned one, to 3m (10ft), with rich pink blossom.

'**Climbing Ena Harkness**', one of the better climbing sports, is well-branched and will be happy to go 5m (15ft) up a wall and produce a good crop of deep red, fragrant flowers of the high-pointed shape typical of the hybrid tea tradition. Each bloom is up to 12cm (5in) across. Sun or partial shade.

'**Climbing Iceberg**' is one of the more successful climbing sports. It has 'Iceberg's' polished, bright foliage to contrast with its pure white flowers, and grows to 4m (12ft). Sun or half shade.

'**Climbing Mrs Sam McGredy**' with its rigidly branching, erect habit, to 3m (10ft), and not too

Another way of exploiting the versatile climbing rose. Rose 'Blairii Number Two' is on the right and 'Chaplin's Pink Climber' is on the left.

much dark foliage, bears 11cm (4½in) shapely flowers in a rich, glowing salmon. At its best in midsummer.

'**Compassion**' makes a good, erect, sensibly branched shape, to 3m (10ft), and healthy, dark foliage. Salmon-pink flowers are produced from the first great scented summer flush to autumn; each very doubled bloom measures some 10cm (4in) across. Good for pillars or on a wall. Sun or partial shade.

'**Constance Spry**' can be grown equally effectively as an open-ground shrub rose with arching branches, or as a climber, when it will be encouraged to add to its stature; it is 2m (6ft) in the open and perhaps double this against a wall. Spicy-scented flowers, 12cm (5in) across, are carried in summer. They are a rounded, cup-shape with crowded petals in rich pure pink. The foliage is a pleasing grey-green complement. Sun.

'**Danse de Feu**' was introduced in 1954. On parade to 2.5m (8ft) high, it has strong stems and plenty of polished, mid-green leaves, together with dark scarlet-red flowers of hybrid tea form, from midsummer until autumn. The flowers fade to a duller shade. It can be spectacular, but is in competition with 'Parkdirektor

Riggers'. It will succeed on a cool shady wall.

'**Gloire de Dijon**' is an old-timer, introduced in 1853 and still highly thought of, especially as it is one of the first to bloom in late spring, and then it is rarely without flowers until everything is wrapped up for the winter. On a wall it can be left to go up to 5m (15ft) and will need little pruning. If the base gets bare, try bringing some branches down or plant something in front. The scented flowers are 10cm (4in) across, a buff-yellow with orange tones. The petals are a handsome muddle, sometimes arranged in the old-fashioned quartered style. Any lack of grooming is forgiven for the sake of the mass effect of the many small clusters. Sun.

'**Golden Showers**' stands stiffly upright to some 3m (10ft) high, with dark, lustrous leaves and plenty of golden flowers, scented and shapely in bud and then opening to a more informal cup shape, 10cm (4in) across. These are freely borne from summer into autumn. Sun.

'**Handel**', another erect grower, is 3m (10ft) high with dark foliage and double, bicoloured flowers from

This cottage provides an excellent excuse for roses. The front door is festooned with, from left to right, the cultivars 'Pink Perpétué', 'Compassion', 'Swan Lake' and 'Handel'. The old-fashioned atmosphere is enhanced by the fanfare from the perfumed trumpets of the beautiful Lilium regale.

summer until autumn. They are white with pinky-red margins. Sun or partial shade.

'Joseph's Coat' can be grown as a shrub or encouraged to go higher – up to 3m (10ft) – against a wall. A repeat performer, it has clusters of 8cm (3in) blooms in yellow suffused with salmon. Sun or partial shade.

'Mme Gregoire Staechelin' is a hugely vigorous plant, up to 6m (20ft), with an abundance of dark foliage and arching stems. Although an old-timer, it is of great value for its early, fully doubled, 12cm (5in), nodding blooms in solid cup shapes and rich pink, sometimes enlivened with red flushes. It has showy round hips later. Sun.

'Maigold' makes a modest climber of some 2.5m (8ft) but is a healthy plant with prickly stems, good strong foliage and lots of early summer blooms of somewhat bronzed gold. If these are pruned away as they fail it can produce a reasonable second crop. Sun or half shade.

'Meg' is of the strong, upright persuasion, reaching 3-4m (10-12ft). It has scented, salmon-pink flowers that are semi-double, with dark stamens making a contribution. It is a repeat bloomer from midsummer. Sun.

'Mermaid' is a famous old rose that is not absolutely hardy in cool areas. It is best on a warm wall where it can be left alone; it needs little pruning except perhaps occasionally to gently cut back some green growth to stimulate fresh branching. It becomes like a small tree some 6m (20ft) tall, with a formidable trunk and stems armed with evilly-hooked thorns and carrying leaves that are almost evergreen. Its wide, single, 10cm (4in) flowers of clear yellow have persistent orange stamens. You would be unlucky not to find an offering of flowers any time from early summer to mid-autumn. Happy in sun or light shade.

'Morning Jewel' makes a free-branching and free-blooming plant reaching up to 3m (10ft). It has polished, mid-green foliage and lots of rich pink, 9cm (3½in) flowers that are not so doubled as to disguise the gold boss of stamens. Colourful from summer until autumn. Sun or part shade.

'New Dawn' is a deservedly popular, robust rose of

This pergola is almost lost under the roses 'New Dawn', to the left, and multiflora, which are accompanied by a variety of herbaceous plants. It is a good example of how air space above our heads can be used.

arching form, to 5m (15ft), with shining, bright foliage and a welcome succession of shapely, glowing, pale pink flowers from summer into autumn. Sun or shade.

'Noisette Carnée' ('Blush Noisette') is 3-4m (10-12ft) high with almost unarmed stems and a rather open, carefree habit. It may be grown as a shrub but is good against a wall, which helps to give it form and can be an effective background for the matt-green foliage. The summer to autumn succession of fully doubled, pale pink flowers are spicily scented and rather informal. The petals are often lobed at the outer margins. They measure some 4cm (1½in) across but seem more with their cupped form and feathery petals. Sun or part shade.

'Parkdirektor Riggers' is an outstanding, vigorous plant easily reaching 4m (12ft) high, with healthy stems and dark foliage. Flowers, of excellent form and 6cm (2½in) across, are borne in plentiful clusters from midsummer until autumn. They are deep scarlet-red. This is probably still the best red climber. Sun.

'Paul's Lemon Pillar' grows up to 6m (20ft) in erect pose with dark foliage and summer flowers of hybrid tea shape and each some 12cm (5in) across. They are lemon-coloured and lemon-scented but fade quickly to white. Not a repeat flowerer but still a popular choice for warmer walls. Sun.

'Paul's Scarlet Climber' is an old favourite, often thought of as a rambler, with muscular, arching stems and dark foliage making a mass at least 3m (10ft) high and wide. It has lots of summer bunches of rounded, rich red flowers, sometimes a few later as well. Sun or part shade.

'Pink Perpétué' is a stiffly upright rose with robust dark leaves and very pleasing, rounded, scented flowers of neatly graded petals, all rich deep pink, even deeper on the petal reverses. They are produced from midsummer until autumn. 3m (10ft). Sun or part shade.

'Scharlachglut' ('Scarlet Fire'), a climbing or arching shrub of extrovert habits up to 3m (10ft) high, is endowed with exemplary foliage and brilliant scarlet-crimson blooms, 12cm (5in) wide. Autumn brings red, pear-shaped fruits. Sun or partial shade and could even be planted in light woodland-type sites.

'Schoolgirl' is not encumbered with too much foliage and has splendid, scented, hybrid tea flowers in warm apricot shades with pinker reverses. The colour may fade in strong, hot sunshine but lasts well in half shade and in cooler areas. 'Schoolgirl' flowers from

The rose 'Paul's Scarlet Climber' has been relied upon for decades to provide luxuriant growth and an abundance of double flowers. It must be found on a thousand pergolas, this one being in the formal garden of Wolfson College, Oxford.

midsummer until autumn and is up to 4m (12ft) high. Probably best in light shade.

'Swan Lake' is a modern repeat climber that does not grow too high, perhaps 2.5m (8ft). It has large, neatly doubled, white flowers shaded pink in the centres.

RAMBLING HYBRIDS

'Adélaide d'Orléans' is over 150 years old but is still a very pleasing graceful rambler, growing to some 5m (15ft) and almost evergreen. It bears crowded clusters of small, double flowers of creamy-white, bright pink in bud. You will notice the primrose scent as you pass. Sun or semi-shade, airy conditions.

'Albéric Barbier' is another old variety that is almost evergreen with rich green leaves and arching growth up to 5m (15ft). Clusters of rather informal flowers, 8cm (3in) across, are creamy on opening but soon become white with golden stamens. A repeat bloomer which should be pruned in the winter. Sun.

'Albertine' was introduced in 1921 and is still one of the most popular ramblers. It is one of the earliest to bloom and is then prolific with masses of coppery buds opening to release a sweet scent and salmon-shaded, light pink blooms, each 8cm (3in) across. The foliage is dark. The plant produces a lot of thrusting shoots from low down. These can be given more room by cutting away older, flowered wood. 'Albertine' is exceptionally vigorous and is ideal for

The old rambler 'American Pillar' is featured here with clematis 'Mme Julia Correvon' and the tall Campanula lactiflora. 'American Pillar' is a vigorous plant with good foliage and is very free with its large bunches of blooms, a really enjoyable bit of exuberance.

disguising a garden shed or training to a rustic screen or pergola. It flowers once but is a fine sight for several weeks. (It can refuse to let go of its old flowers, especially if they get sodden when dying off.) Best given an airy position, not on a wall, as this will help to ward off some of its susceptibility to mildew.

'American Pillar', which was introduced in 1902, can be grown as a shrub in the open, when it makes a formidably large bush of hugely vigorous arching stems from low down and good rich green, polished foliage. These support a huge number of clusters of single, deepest pink flowers with startling white eyes. Not scented. It can also be grown on a screen, a pergola or pole where it can reach upwards of 5m (15ft); given the chance, it will also be as wide. Sun or light shade.

'Bobby James' is an exceptionally energetic rambler capable of growing 10m (30ft) high and having huge heavy heads of shining, creamy, semi-double flowers with a pervasive perfume. It can cover unsightly buildings or pergolas and is also suitable for growing into tall trees. Sun or light shade.

'Crimson Shower' naturally produces widespread stems, well-furnished with glossy foliage and, from summer until autumn, later than most, many clusters of semi-double, deep crimson flowers, opening to show the golden stamens; each bloom is 3cm (1¼in) across. Sun or light shade.

'Dr van Fleet' is a strong plant, to 4-7m (12-20ft) high, with healthy, lustrous leaves and large, fully double, pale pink flowers. Sun or light shade.

'Easlea's Golden Rambler', an oldie growing to 6m (20ft) and almost as wide, has tough leaves and summer blossom of informal, bright yellow, scented flowers, lightly splashed red. Sun or light shade.

'Félicité Perpétue' makes 5m (15ft) with slimline stems carrying plenty of foliage and lots of summer blossom. The flowers are well-doubled, rather fussy, wide-open and very pale pink fading to white; each is about 4cm (1½in) across. A very light pruning will suffice; it would not be a major disaster if some seasons it was left unpruned. Sun or light shade.

filipes 'Kiftsgate' is capable of at least 10m (30ft) into trees or over tall walls. Light green leaves consist of 5-7 narrow leaflets. Astonishing clusters of single, creamy-white flowers are borne in late summer, often a hundred or more to a bunch. Only for places where space can be allowed for its rampant nature. Happy in sun or shade.

'François Juranville' has 6m (20ft) high stems well clothed with shining dark foliage. These are decorated with copious summer bunches of many-petalled, salmon-pink flowers, 8cm (3in) wide. Best in an airy, not-too-dry position.

'Hiawatha' is a widespreading grower with rich foliage and a large summer crop of single flowers. These are rich crimson made more brilliant by the white eyes. Up to 5m (15ft). Sun or light shade.

'Minnehaha' is a strong plant, to 5m (15ft) high, with good-looking rich foliage and plenty of fully double, glowing pink blossom. Sun or light shade.

'Paul's Himalayan Musk' is another very vigorous plant that may be at its best thrusting through a tree to a height of 9m (28ft). It has a lot of very long, arching stems that give rise to many narrow-twigged bunches of double, very pale pink flowers for several weeks from early summer.

'**Paul Transom**' has lacquered foliage and produces lots of coppery buds that open to double, salmon-pink flowers with ruffled petals and a good perfume. The summer bonanza may be followed by lesser flushes when it is growing happily in warm spots. Somewhat loose habit. 3-5m (10-15ft) high. Sun or light shade.

'**Phyllis Bide**' does not ramble too far, perhaps a maximum of 3m (10ft) high, and has wand-like branches and smallish, mid-green leaves. Unusually for a rambler it is repeat-flowering; the wide sprays of yellow flowers are flushed salmon and have a nice perfume. Prune in winter. Sun.

'**Rambling Rector**', see box.

'**Sander's White Rambler**' is a contrast to 'Rambling Rector' in being almost unarmed, somewhat later in bloom, and with more doubled, scented, white flowers. Less mildew-prone than many. To 6m (20ft). Sun or part shade.

'**The Garland**' is strong-growing, 5m (15ft) high, with lots of flowers. These are salmon in bud but open cream and sweet citrus scented. Sun or light shade.

'**Veilchenblau**' grows up to 4m (12ft) high and wide and has large bunches of double, violet-red flowers in summer. Very few thorns. Earlier than many. Flower colour holds best in somewhat shaded area.

Rosa 'Rambling Rector'

This is a very vigorous, thorny rose ideal for growing up into trees or on tall supports. Its many arching branches can make a huge covering mass. For many weeks through summer, it is very free with its extraordinarily wide clusters of semi-double, fragrant, cream flowers that fade to white. Happy in sunny or partially shaded position. Deciduous, height 6m (20ft), Z6 H4. There are several similar cultivars such as 'Sanders' White Rambler', 'Wedding Day', 'The Garland', 'Thalia', or 'Seagull'.

❋ Very easy to cultivate

❋ Adaptability. A free-standing mass, through trees, up major screens, over pergolas

❋ Healthy and disease-free

❋ Very generous with flower

❋ Unlikely to need propagating, but this can be easily done by layers or cuttings

'**Wedding Day**' makes a monster plant for a sunny aspect where it has plenty of room – it is capable of making over 9m (28ft) in height. It produces huge clusters of scented, single, white flowers, 2.5cm (1in) wide, for several weeks in summer. The blossom takes on a pink blush with age.

A border is given extra height by the roses 'Fritz Noblis', to the left, and 'Bobby James', to the right, growing over an arch. Among the medley of herbaceous plants is the ever-popular Alchemillia mollis, hardiest of perennials and an excellent stand-by for flower arrangers.

Rubus Rosaceae

The large bramble genus has few species sufficiently well-behaved for garden use. The two chosen here are energetic growers enjoying healthy well-drained soils. They need space to show off; do not try them in very limited areas. Both have some minor prickles but are not as aggressive as most blackberries.

R. flagelliflorus

A handsome foliage plant with lots of long, slender, whipping stems rising each year from the rootstock. They are white-felted in youth. The 8-18cm (3-7in) leaves are marbled above and yellow-felted below. White flowers are carried in small clusters up the stems in their second year, blackberries follow. Train it up a post or trellis; the stems have the bramble vigour and may grow up to 2m (6ft) in their first season. Not completely hardy in colder areas. Evergreen, height 3-4m (10-12ft), Z7 H3-4.

R. henryi var. *bambusarum*

Growing very fast, this handsome foliage plant has arching, whipping stems, fleecy white in youth, with spiny prickles. The leaves are 3-lobed or divided into 3 leaflets. They are rich green above with contrasting white felt below. Undistinguished pink flowers are followed by many bunches of small blackberries. Best grown up a pergola if it is on a large scale; alternatively train it over an independent post with the taller stems tied in and lesser ones allowed to arch outwards – whichever, it needs plenty of room. Sun or shade. Evergreen, height 6m (20ft), Z7 H4.

Sabia Sabiaceae

A genus of deciduous climbers with inconspicuous flowers but attractive fruit. Rarely offered but hardy, they are not difficult and are pleasing in foliage and unusual with blue or purple fruits.

S. latifolia

This leaning, clambering climber has oval leaves, 5-13cm (2-5in) long and two-thirds as wide. Tiny, greenish-yellow flowers are followed by bright blue fruits, up to 1cm (½in) long. Deciduous, height 3m (10ft), Z6-7 H4.

S. schumanniana

Narrow leaves, 2.5-10cm (1-4in) long and pointed, are carried on clambering stems, as are small sprays of tiny green or purple-flushed flowers. Fruits, in two swollen halves, are blue and not much over 5mm (¼in) wide, but they are attractive when produced in quantity after a good spring. Deciduous, height 3m (10ft), Z6-7 H4.

Senecio scandens Asteraceae

From a genus which once numbered some 3,000 species, but that has lost many of these to other genera so is now only a modest 1,000, this species is an evergreen twiner and scrambler. It goes upwards but with middle-age spread becomes more bushy. The greyish to bright green leaves are ovate or an elongated triangle shape, 5-10cm (2-4in) long, usually toothed but sometimes entire. It will start to produce clusters of yellow daisies in the middle of summer and can still be going in late autumn. It can be made to climb up a wall, but may look more pleasing just playing about over other shrubs or through a hedge. In hard winters the growth can be killed back partially; in very cold areas right down to ground level. This is no great loss, as the rootstock will send forward strong new growth in the spring. Best in a sunny position in soils that are well drained and do not get sodden; the soil does not need to be highly fertile. Evergreen, height 5m (15ft), Z8-9 H2-3.

The pergola shown here positioned alongside the house helps marry house to garden in a very firm union. The rose is 'Paul's Himalayan Musk', a rambler capable of prodigious feats and, infact, sometimes difficult to restrain.

Solanum jasminoides 'Album', the very effective white form of the potato vine.

Solanum Solanaceae

There follow two of the most decorative species of this large deciduous genus, which includes the potato and the aubergine. *S. crispum* is hardy, *S. jasminoides* is less so, but with the shelter of a wall it can be very good indeed.

S. crispum, see box.

S. jasminoides

The potato vine is not quite as hardy as *S. crispum* but grows well in warmer areas such as the southern half of Britain, with only the help of a wall or fence. The potato flowers are a paler blue with yellow pointed centres, but it is the very fine white form **'Album'** that is more often planted. This is a wonderful scrambling, climbing plant with pointed, long, triangular leaves, some with basal lobes, the strongest having two smaller leaflets at the base. Very freely borne clusters of gold-centred, pure white flowers, each up to 2.5cm (1in) across and held clear of the foliage, are borne from early summer well into autumn. In my West Midlands home we can get some cold winters, but it is only the exceptionally hard ones that will bring this climber down to soil level again. As I write, in mid-October, there is one here full of flower and easily twenty feet high. Semi-evergreen, height 6m (20ft), Z9 H3.

Solanum crispum

One of the outstanding scramblers, this species is best against a sunny wall or fence, but will manage with a ration of sun and can be used to clamber over a shed or other structure which it can transform. It is usually offered as the fine form 'Glasnevin' which originated in the Dublin Botanic Garden. Growing strongly into a cloud-shaped shrub, it is dressed with pointed oval leaves 6-13cm (2½-5in) long. It starts producing clusters of potato flowers, that are bluish purple with pointed, yellow centres of fused anthers, early in summer and carries on into autumn; it even has the good nature to wink open a few in mild winter weather. It should have reasonably drained soil of any type but it is one of the best of plants on chalk. Only needs pruning to keep it within bounds; best put your gloves on as some may get a rash from the foliage. Evergreen/semi-evergreen, height 6m (20ft), Z9 H3.

* Energetic climbing-scrambling plant for walls or odd corners
* Evergreen effect
* Attractive, unusual 'potato' flowers
* Long season of bloom from summer well into autumn
* Hardy and easy to grow

Tripterygium regelii Celastraceae

A shrubby climber that has some twining habits. With long-stalked, bright, ovate leaves, 8-15cm (3-5in) long, each finished with a slender point, this makes a handsome foliage plant for clothing a wall or a pergola or draping over a tree. Small, ivory-white flowers are produced in summer as leafy panicles about 25cm (10in) across. The green fruit turns fawn and is an interesting 3-winged structure. Plant in a sunny or lightly shaded spot in normal well-drained soil. Deciduous, height 10m (30ft), Z5 H4.

WALL SHRUBS

Almost any shrub can be planted close to a wall and thrive. However, there are some that particularly benefit from the shelter of a wall and others that benefit from a wall to lean against – at least in their youth. These are reviewed here, along with a selection of those that are just too good to miss. Some of the shrubs included will eventually be quite large and may be best sited away from the house walls. They are here because they add to the concept of the vertical garden.

There is always going to be competition for the limited special places close to the walls, so gardeners have to make the choice between resisting the temptation to plant too many plants or to plant what they like and accept the extra work required to keep greater numbers under some spatial control. Shrubs that are free standing can be kept within limits by pruning top growth and, if necessary, giving the roots some gentle cutting back. Pruning of some shrubs may be little more than nipping out shoots by hand, while others can be tackled by secateurs, shears or even power tools.

A-Z Guide to Wall Shrubs

Abelia Caprifoliaceae

A genus of about 30 deciduous and evergreen species containing some fine border and wall shrubs of amenable habits. Best in sun with normal well-drained soil.

A. chinensis (syn. *A. rupestris*)
With pointed, oval, shining, dark green leaves 4cm (1½in) long, this forms a bush wider than it is tall. It has a plentiful supply of blush-pink flowers in terminal clusters from midsummer until autumn. They are the typical abelia funnel shape with open, 5-lobed mouths. Deciduous, height 1.5m (5ft), Z8 H4.

A. floribunda
Arching stems with shining dark leaves, 5cm (2in) long, carry lots of hanging clusters of very long-tubed slender flowers just opened at the 5-lobed mouth. The colour, a vibrant fuchsia or cerise-pink, is very striking in early summer. The quoted height can be well overtaken when grown against a wall, a position it will relish. Evergreen, height 3m (10ft), Z8 H3.

A. × grandiflora (syn. *A. rupestris*)
This is a strong grower with polished leaves 5cm (2in) long. A profusion of bunches of deep pink-budded flowers open to pale pink from midsummer until autumn. The flower colour is allied to the darker shade of the calyces. There are several named clones of which **'Francis Mason'** is one of the most distinct with yellow leaves marked dark green and similar flowers but on a half-sized bush. Evergreen or semi-evergreen, height 3m (10ft), Z5 H4.

A. schumannii
The leaves grow out of their early bronzing to become mid-green, pointed and oval to 3cm (1¼in) long. Many scattered or small bunches of mauve-pink buds open, in the second half of the summer into autumn, to show flowers with paler centres marked with orange. Lightly scented, the flowers are chubbier than the others listed. Deciduous, height 2m (6ft), Z7 H4.

Abeliophyllum distichum Oleaceae

A relative of the forsythias but much less vigorous, this has forsythia-shaped, 4-petalled flowers that are

Abelia grandiflora.

white or lightly flushed pink; they open before the winter is over and in earliest spring. The earliness of the blossom can mean some frost damage, so a sheltered place near a wall may help and it will certainly aid the all-important ripening of the wood. Ovate, matt-green leaves, up to 8cm (3in) long, follow the blossom; they may turn a deep purple in autumn before dropping. Deciduous, height 1-3m (3-10ft), Z4 H4.

Abutilon *Malvaceae*

A diverse genus of around 160 species, many from warm parts and normally grown with glass protection in Europe. The three below are frost hardy in climates such as Britain's, enjoying sunny or lightly shaded spots with freely draining soils.

A. megapotamicum

With thin, trailing or arching stems, this plant needs training to a wall to build up its branchwork. It carries bright, ovate or narrower leaves and exotic-looking, summer and autumn, hanging flowers. The flowers start as scarlet globes that split open to allow shorter lengths of yellow petals to push through around the central nob of purple stamens. At 4cm (1½in) long, they are smaller than those of the greenhouse species but the brilliance of the display makes up for this. Evergreen or semi-evergreen, height 2m (6ft), Z8 H3.

A. × suntense

A jack-in-the-box grower, but with the same tenderish status as the others listed. This produces strong, felted stems and greyish, 12cm (5in) leaves with 3 or 5 distinct lobes and serrated edges. Flowers, usually a deep violet, open to 6cm (2½in) across in late spring and early summer. The most popular cultivar is **'Jermyns'** with large, open flowers in very rich mauve. There are also white forms. Deciduous, height 4m (12ft), Z8 H3.

A. vitifolium

This rapidly makes an upright bush, having some of the vigour of a vine and vine-like leaves as much as 15cm (6in) long. Young shoots and foliage are covered with hair. In early summer lots of long-stalked, purple-blue flowers open to form 8cm (3in) saucers with projecting stamens. This is a strong shrub that can go twice as high as quoted below in very favoured spots. There is a good white form, **'Tennant's White'**, with silken, flat flowers. **'Veronica Tennant'** is another good form with paler flowers than the standard. They may be tidied up and pruned back after flowering to give fresh growth for next season's bloom. Deciduous, height 5m (15ft), Z8 H3.

Acacia *Mimosaceae*

An extraordinarily large genus of considerably more than 1,000 evergreen species. Most are tender in cooler climates but the two following are possible against a warm wall, particularly in milder districts. Hard winters may damage them, but if dead material is cleared away they normally soon recover. Newly planted specimens are best given some extra protection until they have become established. They are not good on chalky soils.

A. baileyana

Lovely, soft, ferny foliage is blue-green in colour and composed of 20-40 tiny leaflets. Each composite leaf is 5-8cm (2-3in) long. At the end of winter and

Above:
Abutilon × suntense.

Acacia baileyana.

can burn the young leaves. It is slow growing but even small specimens are pleasing, becoming more so as they grow to venerable old age. There are many different leaf forms and colours; all turn to brilliant reds in autumn. **f. atropurpureum** is one of the most widely grown forms. A fine kind, it has deeply indented, pointed leaves of a deep maroon-purple. Deciduous, height 8m (25ft), Z6 H4.

Acradenia frankliniae *Rutaceae*

A rarely seen but worthwhile wall shrub for milder areas, best with shelter and some shade. The opposite, paired leaves, 7cm (3in) long, are each made up of 3 narrow dark leaflets. They are dotted with pinpoint oil glands and are aromatic when crushed. Flat-topped clusters of small, white stars are borne in early spring, each posy is 5cm (2in) across. Evergreen, height 3m (10ft), Z8 H2-3.

Adenocarpus decorticans
Papilionaceae

This is a scrubland shrub of hedgehog stiffness, but not armed. It has grey, flaking bark and tiny leaves somewhat silvered with hair. At the end of spring and into early summer it is generously covered with terminal bunches of bright yellow, pea flowers. Will manage in a drier spot than many. Deciduous, height 2m (6ft), Z8 H4.

Aloysia triphylla, see Base of Wall Plants p.226.
Anagyris foetida, see Tender Plants p.243.
Aplopappus ericoides, see *Haplopappus ericoides*.

Ardesia crispa *Mysinaceae*

An upright shrub with very handsome foliage arranged spirally, but often giving the effect of whorls. The leaves are polished, dark green, long and elliptic with neat and gentle serration. In summer it produces terminal bunches of pink stars, each probably only 1cm (½in) wide. These are followed by highly decorative large, crowded bunches of round, deep red berries. One of a large tropical or subtropical genus, when grown outside this species will need the warmest, sunniest spot in reasonable soil with first-class drainage. Evergreen, height 1-1.5m (3-5ft), Z8-9 H1-2.

Aristotelia chinensis 'Variegata'
(syn. *A. macqui* 'Variegata') *Aristolochiaceae*

The variegated form of this species is normally grown. It has glowing, dark, ovate leaves, up to 12cm (5in)

beginning of spring it bears typical, golden, fluffy blossom, the small, rounded heads closely packed on racemes 5-10cm (2-4in) long. Evergreen, height 5-7m (15-22ft), Z8 H2.

A. dealbata
The mimosa sold in the florists, and possibly the hardiest species, this has silvery-green leaves, very much like a delicate fern, up to 13cm (5in) long and wide and composed of 40-80 little leaflets. The flowers are borne in rounded clusters 10cm (4in) wide and long. They are scented little bobbles in rich yellow. Evergreen, height 10m (30ft), Z8 H2.

Acer palmatum *Aceraceae*

Acers, such as this species, benefit from shelter from fierce winds and cold in early spring as bad weather

Acer palmatum.

long, heavily variegated with rich gold and clusters of insignificant small, greenish flowers. A hard winter may cut it back but it will usually quite quickly make good the loss. A wall shrub for a warm spot in normal soils. Evergreen, 5m (15ft), Z8 H3.

Aucuba japonica 'Variegata', *Cornaceae*, see box.

Azara *Flacourtiaceae*

Attractive evergreen, small-leaved shrubs and trees suitable for milder areas and growing near sunny walls, these can produce bloom in the first few months of the year. All the species featured bear flowers from the leaf axils of last year's wood.

A. integrifolia

The tough, oval leaves, up to 5cm (2in) long and polished on both sides, are not serrated. The plant produces lots of small posies of little flowers that are yellow in effect, this being the contribution of the stamens; the lost sepals are pale purple. The flowering can take place very early in the year and might already be in evidence at Christmas in Britain. Evergreen, height 10m (30ft), Z8 H3.

A. lanceolata

This shrub can be very prolific and attractive in bloom and is very respectable out of bloom being bright green with its dense cover of polished, oval or lance-shaped, serrated leaves on pleasing, arching stems. The spring flowers are abundant small clusters, rich yellow. Evergreen, height 5m (15ft), Z8 H3.

A. microphylla

This might be the hardiest species. Its small, round, deep green leaves are rarely more than 2.5cm (1in). Nicely scented clusters of yellow stamens appear early

Aucuba japonica 'Variegata'

This very well known evergreen shrub has polished oval leaves of bright green decorated by spots and variegation in gold, and always seems to look healthy. The spotted laurel is a real workhorse and is a pleasing rounded bush that will brighten wherever it is stationed. It is one of the few things that will manage well in poor soil, in deep shade as well as in the full sun and in moist or dry conditions. Often has some round red berries in auturmn. Several other good cultivars, such as 'Gold Dust' with dark green leaves dusted gold, are available. Evergreen, height 2m (6ft) Z7 H4.

* Mint-fresh foliage all year
* Equally happy in deep shade or full sun
* Grows well on very poor soil
* Shapely but can be pruned as required – can be kept moderately small
* Foliage can be cut to augment indoor floral work
* Can be grown in a large container
* Propagates easily from layers or cuttings

in the year. Will grow in drier situations than the others. Evergreen, height 6m (20ft), Z8 H3.

A. petiolaris (syn. A. *gilliesii*)

An arching, spreading shrub with holly-like leaves, up to 8cm (3in) long, and scented, primrose-yellow flowers borne in tight posies in late winter and early spring. Well worth planting. Evergreen, height 4m (12ft), Z8 H3.

A. serrata

This species has downy stems and serrated, dark oval leaves, 6cm (2½in) long, with polished upper surfaces. Stalked, rounded, tight clusters of deep yellow stamen-flowers appear later than the other species. Evergreen, height 4m (12ft), Z8 H3.

Berberis × stenophylla

A series of very vigorous shrubs with narrow, dark leaves, up to 2.5cm (1in) long, on arching stems. Every part of the bush is covered with tightly-clasped golden blossom in mid-spring, a quite splendid sight. It can be used as a specimen shrub, making a wide mass, or as a decorative hedging plant. There are many named clones of which **'Corallina Compacta'** is interesting. It only grows to 30cm (12in) high

Left: Azara serrata.

and wide and yet is very floriferous: orange in bud and golden when open. Evergreen, height 3m (10ft), Z7-8 H4.

Buddleja *Buddlejaceae*

A deciduous and evergreen genus of easy-going species, too often only represented by forms of *B. davidii* sold popularly as the butterfly bush. *B. auriculata* and *B. colvilei* are in the same league of almost weedy hardiness as *B. davidii*. They grow easily in full sun and in damp soils, provided there is free drainage.

B. alternifolia

This is a distinct species with very pendent or arching stems and narrowly spear-shaped leaves of sombre green or grey, up to 7cm (3in) long. In early summer tight, rounded posies of lilac flowers cluster all along the falling stems of last year's wood. Fragrance adds to the pretty picture. It can be trained up a wall but is good up a pergola post or an independent post, where it will eventually become a fine specimen plant. Prune back after blooming to encourage new wood for next year's flowering. Deciduous, height 4m (12ft), Z6 H4.

B. auriculata

An erect shrub with narrow ovate leaves of rich green, white underneath. Fragrant flowers are creamy-white but with a touch of yellow, orange or salmon in their centres. The tight panicles are produced late – in autumn and well into the winter. It is only worth trying in milder areas. Evergreen, height 3m (10ft), Z8 H2.

B. colvilei

A bulky shrub with rich green, elliptic leaves, 12cm (5in) long. It may hesitate to drop the leaves unless autumn and winter get really bleak. Nodding,

rounded panicles, up to 20cm (8in) long, of relatively large flowers in pinky-red, appear in early summer. Deciduous/semi-evergreen, height 6m (20ft), Z8 H3.

B. crispa

A very good wall shrub with lots of young upright branches, white with felt, and more arching older ones. The 5-7cm (2-3in) long, lance-shaped leaves are silvery-grey downy on both sides. It will not be fully hardy in cold areas and needs a warm wall spot. There it is one of the freest flowering of shrubs and covers itself with fat panicles of massed, small, white-eyed, lilac flowers from mid- until late summer. The terminal panicles are reinforced by auxiliary lateral ones so that the whole inflorescence can be cone-shaped. The flowers are scented. Deciduous, height 3m (10ft), Z8 H3.

B. davidii

The familiar buddleja in various colours – white, lilac, purple and pinky-red. It is very vigorous and perhaps too extrovert for any choice spot, but can be cut back hard each winter to encourage long, arching flowering stems. Good in cold climates or in open areas. Deciduous, height 3m (10ft), Z6 H4.

OTHER BERBERISES

Other berberises are very well worth considering for places in sun or with some shade. The various purple-red coloured *B. thunbergii* clones are all attractive but deciduous.

B. verruculosa is a tightly packed evergreen with arching branches and spine-tipped, dark leaves. Along the branches a series of relatively large, singly borne, golden flowers appear in late spring. *B. linearifolia* 'Orange King' and *B. x lologensis* 'Apricot Queen' are a couple of the most sumptuous in bloom being a mass of glowing tangerine in spring and often producing some later bloom in summer and autumn. 'Apricot Queen' is somewhat taller at 3m (10ft).

Left: Berberis ×
tenophylla.

Below left: Buddleja
davidii.

Shrubby Burpleurum
fruticosum *and*
Santolina pinnata subsp.
neapolitana *in the second
half of the summer with
seedheads of honesty and
the pint-sized* Kniphofia
'Little Maid'.

B. fallowiana

This grows as quick as an overdraft and has arching stems and grey foliage, the 12cm (5in) leaves being white-felted below. Panicles, 15cm (6in) long, of densely packed, lavender flowers with orange eyes and a good scent appear from late summer into the first part of autumn. Deciduous, height 3m (10ft), Z8 H4.

Bupleurum fruticosum *Apiaceae*

This species has lots of upright stems opulently furnished with a dense but tidy foliage mass, becoming wider than it is tall. The dark, blue-green, shiny leaves, 8cm (3in) long, look very tidy and respectable. They are then topped with rounded domes of lots of small, lime-coloured flowers from midsummer until autumn – a spurge (*Euphorbia*) type colour scheme. Good in coastal areas. Not the hardiest of all shrubs without wall protection, though our plants have lasted out in the open for several seasons without turning a hair. We have had it equally happy in partial shade as full sun in well-drained soils. Evergreen, height 2m (6ft), Z8 H4.

Bursaria spinosa *Pittosporaceae*

A shrub for near a sunny wall in milder areas. It has obovate leaves, about 3cm (1in) long, and many scented, little, white flowers in clusters in the second half of summer. Some stems have spines, others do not. It is at its best later when carrying a crop of rust-coloured seedheads, each capsule about 1cm (½in) wide. Evergreen, height 2-4m (6-12ft), Z8 H3-4.

Buxus sempervirens 'Suffruticosa'

This is the most popular of the boxes, being compact in growth and amenable to clipping. The topiarist's stand-by, it will grow in almost any situation including heavily shaded ones. Evergreen, height 1m (3ft), Z6 H4.

Caesalpina gilliesii *Caesalpiniaceae*

This plant has beautiful ferny foliage, each leaf 20cm (8in) long and doubly pinnate, the 9-11 leaflets being again divided into perhaps 9 pairs of little leaflets just over 1cm (½in) long. The blossom is spectacular: upright, pointed racemes, 30-40cm (12-16in) long,

have as many as 50 flowers each. These are golden bowls or cups each with up to 12 long, protruding, scarlet-red stamens perhaps 3-4cm (1¼-1½in) clear of the petals. One of the treats of high summer, usually to be seen close to the wall for the protection it needs and deserves. Sun and good drainage. Deciduous, height 3m (10ft), Z8 H3-4.

Calceolaria integrifolia, see Annuals p.236.

Callistemon Myrtaceae

The evergreen bottlebrushes are shrubs for warm spots and best in mild localities, such as south-west England. The 'brush' is formed by the stamens that protrude at right angles to the flower stem. Sun and dryish rather than wet conditions.

Camellia sasanqua 'Sparkling Burgundy'.

C. citrinus

This species has lance-shaped leaves, up 10cm (4in) long, that are dark green and have conspicuous oil glands: crushed leaves give off a lemony scent, the justification for the name. The 'flowers' are 5-15cm (2-6in) long and produced generously in spring and summer. This is probably the best species in the garden, though much more familiar as a greenhouse shrub. **'Splendens'** is the finest form, with broader leaves, shoots that are red in youth, and large, rich crimson flowers. Evergreen, height 3m (10ft), Z9 H3.

C. linearis

A spreading shrub with thick, hard, dark, narrow-pointed leaves and, from late spring until autumn, a succession of 12cm (5in), glowing red flowers. Evergreen, height 4m (12ft), Z9 H3.

Right: Camellia japonica 'Adolphe Audusson'.

C. pallidus

Elliptic leaves, 3-6cm (1¼-2½in) long, are silky and blushing pink when young before becoming a staid, sombre adult grey-green. From late spring until mid-summer the bush is lit up with lots of 10cm (4in) brushes in cream or pale greenish-primrose. Evergreen, height 2-3m (6-10ft), Z9 H3.

C. salignus

This species has slender, pale green leaves, up to 10cm (4in) long, suggesting the common name willow bottlebrush. The flowers are usually white, but they can be red, pink or mauve. Evergreen, height 4m (12ft), Z9 H3.

C. viridiflorus

A compact plant but with arching stems of sharp-pointed, hard, dark, small leaves packed closely around the stems. Lime or greenish-yellow brushes appear from early to late summer. Evergreen, height 1.5m (5ft), Z9 H3.

Camellia Theaceae

These are hardy, evergreen shrubs, but many have early flowers that can get frosted. They like shelter and soil full of humus and not too dry. They will not

grow on chalk or limy soils. Many will manage well on a shady wall, but sunnier ones will be first choice. If at all possible, pick your cultivars when you see them in bloom. The choice is wide in colour, form, degree of flower-doubling and habit.

C. japonica

A much-branched, rounded shrub or small tree with highly polished, dark green, tough leaves. The hardiest of the species and forms. Five petals form a single flower, from 6cm (2½in) to double this, with a showy boss of golden stamens in the centre. Very many cultivars are raised and offered for sale. Usually the most successful ones are the singles and semi-doubles, the very double ones sometimes have fewer buds, or greater numbers of buds that fail to open, and the ones that do tend to hang on the bush when finished, each a distressing brown mass. The following are among the choice cultivars: **'Adolphe Audusson'** makes a well-shaped bush with semi-double, red flowers. **'Berenice Boddy'** is a strong, arching bush with large, semi-double flowers in clear pink though darker on the outer petals. **'Doctor Tinsley'** makes a tight bush. Its pink buds open to white flowers, flushed pink, darker towards margins. **'Gloire de**

Nantes'** is compact and erect with semi-double, rose-red flowers from late autumn until late spring. **'Janet Whitehouse'** has beautifully formed, rounded, semi-double or fuller flowers. **'Lady Vansittart'** is white but irregularly striped pink. **'Lavinia Maggi'** produces perfect, round, white semi-double flowers, splashed irregularly with stripes of deep pink. Evergreen, height 10m (30ft), Z8 H4.

C. 'Leonard Messel'

This was raised from crossing the rich pink 'Mary Christian', a C. × williamsii cultivar, with C. reticulata. The result is an admirably hardy shrub of sensible rounded form with matt-green leaves, up to 15cm (6in) long, and large, rich clear pink blooms in semi-double form with a boss of golden stamens. These are freely produced from the beginning of spring right

through that season. With 'Donation' the most popular duo of the genus. Evergreen, height 4m (12ft), Z7-8 H4.

C. reticulata

This plant's broadly elliptic leaves have a network of veins that give it its name. Various cultivars were imported before the true wild plant, which has rosy-red, single blooms. It is a strong grower, although it will take quite a while to reach the height quoted. It starts flowering in early spring for a long season. The following are choice cultivars: **'Arch of Triumph'** has 17cm (7in) loose, peony-formed flowers, crimson-pink with some salmon suffusion. **'Captain Rawes'**, an early nineteenth-century introduction from China, has large, semi-double, deep carmine flowers, up to 17cm (7in) wide. **'Mandalay Queen'**

CAMELLIAS IN TROUBLE?

✳ Frost can brown flowers, especially if they are rapidly unthawed. Try to provide shelter from frost and early morning sun.

✳ Drought at root level in late summer onwards may result in promising flower buds aborting and falling off. Try to maintain even soil moisture.

✳ Camellias are shallow rooting. They will enjoy humus-rich mulches.

✳ Leaf scorch that spoils the even-polished shining green foliage can be caused by persistent cold winter winds. Try to position the plants with some shelter, natural or artificial.

✳ Leaves turning yellow could mean the presence of killing lime in soil.

Camellia japonica *'Gloire de Nantes'*.

bears semi-double, deep pink flowers up to 14cm (5½in) wide. Evergreen, height 12m (40ft), Z8 H4.

C. saluenensis

Not so widely grown, as it is a little less hardy than *C. japonica* and the hybrids between the two (see *C. × williamsii*), this is a bushy plant with polished, dark leaves noticeably narrower than those of *C. japonica*.

Camellia x williamsii 'Donation'

The most famous of all the cultivars, a shrub of good form with pleasing foliage and very freely produced semi-double, shapely, rich pink flowers that will be darker in partial shade where they may last longer.

✳ Good evergreen foliage

✳ Tidy, compact shape

✳ Prolific in bloom

✳ Good for cut flowers

✳ Adaptable. For wall sites, in the open, in large containers

✳ Propagate by semi-ripe cuttings in late summer or winter. Alternatively, layer or air-layer

It has neatly formed, 5-petalled flowers of pink or white, sometimes with deeper veining. Evergreen, height 1-4m (3-12ft), Z7 H4.

C. sasanqua

With dark, gleaming, elliptic leaves, this is another species with many named forms. It is almost as hardy as *C. japonica* but blooms very early, some cultivars beginning in late autumn. They are therefore vulnerable to frosts so need all the shelter they can get from cold and relish more sunshine than the other camellias. For growing outside this plant is perhaps best left to those with really mild winters. Here is a selection of the best: **'Crimson King'** has bright red single flowers. **'Jean May'** is pale pink, shading darker towards the base of the attractively doubled flowers. **'Narumigata'** is splendid with many smallish, single, bowl-shaped, white flowers with a light pink blush. **'Satan's Robe'** is a dark bush with splendid, deep red, semi-double flowers with golden stamens. **'Sparkling Burgundy'** makes a spreading shrub with dark, narrow leaves and rich red flowers of peony form.

Evergreen, height 6m (20ft), Z8 H4.

C. × williamsii (*C. japonica × C. saluenensis*)

This very useful hybrid range combines much of the hardiness of *C. japonica* with the good flower form of *C. saluenensis*. It has lustrous foliage of broadly elliptic leaves, similar to those of *C. japonica*. These strong hybrids are now most widely planted as they have a wide range of colour and form, and bloom from the end of winter through spring. The following are among the best. **'Debbie'** is a double in the form of a peony and rich pink. **'Francis Hanger'** has single, pure white flowers with a boss of golden stamens on a good upright shrub. **'J. C. Williams'** produces many single flowers of delightful pale pink with golden stamens. **'Water Lily'** is a very large double in rich pink. There are other good cultivars such as **'Bow Bells'**, single pink; **'Caerhays'**, peony-formed, crimson-pink; **'E. G. Waterhouse'**, double pink, paler leaves; **'St Ewe'**, single, reddish pink. Evergreen, height 3m (10ft), Z8 H4.

C. × williamsii 'Donation', see box.

Carpenteria californica *Hydrangeaceae*

This is a relative of *Philadelphus*, a relationship gardeners might guess from its open, pure-white flowers all properly fragrant and with a round boss of yellow stamens, but would wonder about the tough, dark, narrowly elliptic leaves. Individual flowers measure 4-8cm (1½-3in) across and are borne in bunches of 3-8 at the stem ends for weeks in midsummer. Makes a splendid wall shrub and deserving its protection, so long as it is not too close to the wall as it likes space for its roots; is equally good in the open. Provide well-drained soil. **'Ladham's Variety'** is a strong clone with larger flowers. Best in full sun with moist but freely draining soil. Evergreen, height 2m (6ft), Z8 H3.

Caryopteris *Verbenaceae*

Free-growing, erect, deciduous shrubs with aromatic, pointed foliage and blue, late summer and autumn blossom. Easy and attractive plants that can be pruned in the early spring to encourage a lot of new wood on which the flowers are borne. Try these in sunny spots in open-structured soils; they dislike heavy wet soils.

C. × clandonensis

This has lots of upward-pointing, slender stems with grey-green, pointed leaves, 5cm (2in) long, and terminal and auxiliary clusters of crowded, small, blue flowers, some clones being more purple than others.

Heavenly Blue' is a dark blue. **'Worcester Gold'** has lavender-blue flowers combined with light yellow-green foliage. Deciduous, height 1m (3ft), Z8 H4.

C. incana (syn. *C. mastacanthus*)

Making a thick bush of grey-green, aromatic, lance-shaped leaves, 7cm (3in) long, this species bears round clusters of purple-blue flowers from the upper leaf axils through the autumn months. There are white-flowered clones. Deciduous, height 1.2m (4ft), Z6 H4.

Ceanothus Rhamnaceae

There are many species and many hybrids of California lilacs; the number is growing season on season. While there are both deciduous and evergreen kinds, it is the later that are mainly grown in gardens. Unless otherwise stated, assume that leaves are a rich green and glossy. Some species are a little tender, but most of the kinds currently sold in such large numbers are relatively safe, especially as they are likely to be placed close to warm walls. Cuttings root readily and quickly make good plants. There are white-flowered

varieties but it is the traditional blues that find great favour for their very free-flowering habit. They can be easily trained up a wall and trimmed to tight, tailored shapes. If only one pruning is given, this will be most expedient as soon as the bush has finished blooming. Sun or light shade, normal soil conditions.

C. arboreus **'Trewithen Blue'**, see box p.198.

C. dentatus

This species has oval leaves only to 2cm (¾in) long. It is commonly grown, justifiably so, for its huge crops of densely packed, rounded clusters of bright rich blue. The branch ends can hold several of these stubby-finger-shaped clusters for weeks at the end of spring and early summer. Evergreen, height 1.5m (5ft), Z8 H3-4.

C. incanus

This spiny-twigged shrub has large grey-green leaves, 6cm (2½in) long. Its flowers are scented and creamy-white. They are borne in globose clusters from mid- until late spring. Evergreen, height 3m (10ft), Z8 H3-4.

C. papillosus var. *roweanus*

Spreading twice as wide as tall, this variety has dark leaves to 5cm (2in) long and stickier than many. A profusion of terminal and lateral racemes in purple-blue are borne through mid- and late spring. Evergreen, height 1.5m (5ft), Z8 H3-4.

C. purpureus

This is a very distinct species on account of its attractive, flat, polished leaves in the toothed shape of miniature holly. The leaves are up to 2cm (¾in) long and quite broad. In spring it is covered with lots of rather flat-headed, lateral clusters of flowers, reddish in bud but opening to a purple-blue. Evergreen, height 1.2m (4ft), Z8 H3-4.

C. rigidus

As its name suggests, this is a stiffly and intricately branched shrub with leaves only 5-12mm (¼-½in) long. Rich blue, densely packed, lateral umbels of flowers, 2cm (¾in) wide, are borne in late spring and early summer. Evergreen, height 1.2m (4ft), Z8 H3-4.

C. thyrsiflorus

Making a strong, upright shrub, with arching branches, this species produces lots of mid-powder-blue spring clusters, up to 8cm (3in) long, in the leaf axils. **var. repens** is more often planted. It is a wide-spreading shrub of many branches covered with rich blue blossom. It will make a dense groundcover up to 1m (3ft) high but 3m (10ft) wide and can be pushed up a wall. (See photograph, p.63.) Evergreen, height 6m (20ft), Z8 H3-4.

A CHOICE OF CEANOTHUS CULTIVARS

'Autumnal Blue', light powder-blue, height 3m (10ft), spread 2.5m (8ft), late spring until autumn.

'Blue Mound', deep blue, height 1.5m (5ft), spread 2m (6ft), late spring.

'Cascade', powder-blue, height and spread 4m (12ft), late spring-early summer.

'Gloire de Versailles', light blue, height and spread 1.5m (5ft), midsummer into autumn.

'Italian Skies', vivid rich blue, height 1.5m (5ft), spread 3m (10ft), late spring.

'Perle Rose', pink, height and spread 1.5m (5ft), midsummer-early autumn.

'Skylark', rich blue, height and spread 6m (20ft), late spring-early summer.

C. arboreus 'Trewithen Blue', rich blue, height 6m (18ft) spread 8m (25ft), spring-early summer.

There is an invasion of new cultivars, mostly bred in USA.

Left: Caryopteris × clandonensis *'Heavenly Blue'*.

Ceanothus arboreus 'Trewithen Blue'

Strong-growing, spreading evergreen with rich green foliage, covering itself in rich blue blossom in spring and early summer. Evergreen, height 6m (18ft), Z8 H3-4.

✻ Evergreen cover, bolder leaves than many

✻ Prolific bloom over long period and from a very young age

✻ Strong tall grower capable of covering wide, tall, wall spaces

✻ Amenable to wall culture and close pruning

✻ Very hardy in sun and drought resistant

✻ Propagates easily from cuttings or layers

C. × veitchianus

This hybrid is a stiff rigid shrub with leaves only up to 2cm (¾in) long. Dark blue, crowded, rounded lateral, rather flattened clusters appear from mid- to late spring. Evergreen, height 3m (10ft), Z8 H3-4.

Cestrum Solanaceae

An evergreen and deciduous genus of close to 200 species, most of which are of doubtful hardiness. The ones listed here are among the most reliable, but will still be best in a sheltered spot or near a warm wall; some show the beginning of a clambering habit. Well-drained soil.

C. aurantiacum

Left to its own devices, this will produce a series of scrambling, leaning stems that will reach over neighbouring shrubs or start up a wall. It can be pruned to an orthodox, tidy shrub shape. It has handsome, broadly ovate leaves of shining mid-green, each up to 12cm (5in) long. Lots of hanging clusters of tube-shaped flowers of old gold or tangerine appear in spring and early summer. The fruits that can follow are squelchy, round, white berries. For mild areas only, it is normally evergreen, but extreme weather can lessen its resolve to keep all its leaves. Evergreen or semi-evergreen, height (6ft), Z8 H2.

C. elegans

An outstanding species of obvious vigour with plenty of arching stems carrying lance-shaped, matt-green leaves of crisp, ovate outline. From summer until autumn it bears a succession of more or less pendent, closely packed bunches of showy tube-shaped flowers in crimson, maroon-red or rich pink. The individual flowers are about 2cm (¾in) long and are followed by purple-red berries. Mild areas. Evergreen, height 3m (10ft), Z8 H2.

C. parqui

And now a species that does drop its leaves – usually! It is an erect shrub commonly called the willow-leaved jessamine on account of its willow-shaped, mid-green leaves up to 12cm (5in) long. Its floral display is in fat, cone-shaped terminal clusters, up to 15cm (6in) across, and smaller lateral posies. All consist of narrow-tubed flowers, 2.5cm (1in) long, with mouths like 5-pointed stars, in a vivid, limy yellow and evening scented. Midsummer for some weeks is parade time; later come blackish or violet-mahogany berries. Perhaps not the showiest, but hardier than most and worth having for the perfume. Deciduous, height 2m (6ft), Z8 H3.

Chaenomeles *Rosaceae*

This deciduous genus only has three species but there are plenty of fine forms and a series of hybrids. They are valuable for their early blossom that can begin to open in early winter and still be opening when the leaves unfurl in spring. They are extraordinarily hardy but the warmth of a wall will encourage early blossom and the ripening of wood which ensures a very high proportion of flower buds. Flowers are followed by quince fruits, similar to those of its larger relative, the true quince, *Cydonia oblonga*. They grow easily in most soils in sun or part shade. The warty appearance of twigs is entirely natural.

C. × *californica* 'Enchantress'

This plant's parents are a form of C. × *superba* and C. *cathayensis* and so combines the genes of all three species. It is a sturdy shrub making a thicket of upright stems armed with plenty of spines. The large flowers, 4-5cm (1½-2in) wide, start opening early, well before the leaves unfurl. They are rich, glowing, pink clusters in such numbers as to make this a real picture. The leaves are rather narrow, serrated and up to 8cm (3in) long. Large yellow fruits. Needs plenty

Chaenomeles japonica, often simply known as 'japonica', is one of the hardiest of the early-flowering shrubs. It is particularly good against a wall when it may start blooming in midwinter and continue until spring.

Above right:
Chaenomeles speciosa
'Moerloosei'.

of room as it will probably end up wider than tall.
Deciduous, height 3m (10ft), Z6 H4.

C. cathayensis

This is a rather coarse, extrovert species making an erect, strong shrub or small tree with spear-shaped leaves up to 12cm (5in) long. Flowers like apple blossom are white, flushed pink, each 4cm (1½in) wide and opening in early to mid-spring. Limy-yellow fruits are spectacularly large – up to 15cm (6in) long. Deciduous, height 5m (15ft), Z6-7 H4.

C. japonica

This is a low, dark-stemmed, spiny species that spreads sideways twice its height. Clearly serrated leaves are oval and 2.5-5cm (1-2in) long. Flowers are bowls of deepest red or orange, 4cm (1½in) wide, in spring. Deciduous, height 1m (3ft), Z5 H4.

C. speciosa

Making a sprawling tangle of branches more or less armed with spines, this has oval leaves, 5-10cm (2-4in) long, with very fine teeth. Blooms are produced in early spring or late winter against a warm wall. Good on all walls, less happy in deep shade. **'Moerloosei'** ('Apple Blossom') is white, flushed pink. **'Geisha Girl'** has double, deep apricot-orange flowers. **'Nivalis'** makes a rangy shrub with pure white flowers. **'Phylis Moore'** produces flowers that are semi-double and light rose-pink. **'Simonii'** is a low, twiggy shrub bearing darkest scarlet-red, bowl-shaped

flowers. **'Snow'** has pure white flowers. Deciduous, height 2.5m (8ft), Z5 H4.

C. × superba (C. japonica × C. speciosa)

A fine series of hybrids that grow well and cover a wide spectrum of colours. They make rounded, spreading, twiggy shrubs with glossy, oval leaves up to 6cm (2½in) long and bloom from early spring until early summer, earlier against a wall. The fruits are similar to the others – hard green quinces that mellow to yellow and have the typical scent (see the list in the margin for choice). Deciduous, height 1-1.5m (3-5ft), Z5 H4.

C. × superba 'Knap Hill Scarlet', see box.

Chimonanthus praecox (syn. C. *fragrans*), *Calycanthaceae*, see box opposite.

Choisya ternata *Rutaceae*

Mexican orange blossom is almost a standard shrub for gardeners. The shining foliage, the shrub's neat rounded shape and the freedom with which it flowers, combined with its easy culture, make it a favourite. The long, oval leaves are 4-8cm (1½-3in) long and are arranged in dense whorls. It flowers in late spring and again in late summer well into autumn – and it is not unusual to find odd sprays through winter. These rounded clusters of upward-facing, white flowers are very fragrant.

Only very severe, prolonged cold winds can cause much damage, and such frost damage is quickly overgrown in spring. I cannot think of a hardier plant from Mexico. **'Aztec Pearl'** is a splendid form with larger leaves and showier flowers, these being pink in bud but opening white and semi-double. The clone **'Sundance'** is grown for its primrose-yellow young

Chaenomeles x superba 'Knap Hill Scarlet'

This is an old favourite in traditional rich orange-red with good-sized flowers. This shrub grows healthily, but there are no poor cultivars. Deciduous, height of 1.5m (5ft), Z5 H4.

✳ Blooms freely for a long period

✳ On a warm wall, will bloom in the second half of the winter

✳ Easily trained to a wall

✳ Reasonable polished foliage

✳ Does not need rich soil

✳ Can be propagated by layering

✳ Budded twigs can be brought inside for flower arrangements

Chimonanthus praecox

The wintersweet is one of nature's introverts – steadily building up to its height with relatively slender stems and twigs, making an upright, rather than spreading, shrub with shining, mid-green, spear-shaped leaves, up to some 20cm (8in) long – however, in midwinter, when devoid of any suggestion of foliage, it plays its unrivalled part as one of the sweetest scented of the many fragrant winter flowers. These blooms, about 2.5cm (1in) wide, are more or less hanging; the outer petals and the first row of inner ones are translucent limy-yellow and the smaller inner ones are deep maroon. The shrub can be grown in the open but is more likely to be trained up a wall close to a window through

which the perfume may drift. A number of clones have been propagated. 'Luteus' ('Concolor') has wide, saucer flowers of primrose. 'Grandiflorus' justifies its name with larger flowers of deeper yellow, up to 4.5cm (1¾in) long. Full sun, well-drained soil. Deciduous, height 4m (12ft), Z7 H4.

* Winter blossom

* Fragrance – 'wintersweet'

* Unusual flowers

* Good for sunny walls

* Not rapacious grower

* Hardy and long-lived

* Propagate by seed, or softwood cuttings

foliage; older, shaded leaves may be a little greener. It has only a few unspectacular flowers and can be reduced to a poorly thing in a bleak spot, which has caused some adverse publicity, but in sheltered spots its foliage lightens up the scene and proves very worthwhile. Enjoys good soil and is happy in various fertile soils; it can cope with a damp one if it is open structured and free draining. Evergreen, height 2-3m (6-10ft), Z8 H4.

Cistus *Cistaceae*

These evergreen shrubs are useful for drier, sunny areas and will manage well on poor soils. They can produce a large number of wide, saucer-shaped flowers in the summer, each bloom lasting only one day. Their foliage is usually rough textured and often sticky. (See margin list for a selection.) Evergreen, Z8 H4.

A CISTUS SELECTION

C. creticus, strong, mauve-pink flowers, 6cm (2½in) wide on plants 1m (3ft) high and wide.

C. x cyprius, dark leaves, round, white flowers, 8cm (3in) across, with crimson-maroon basal blotches, on plants 1.5m (5ft) high and wide.

C. 'Elma', shiny dark leaves and white flowers on shrubs 2m (6ft) high and wide.

C. impressus, deeply impressed leaves and dark blue flowers in mid- and late spring on plants 1.5m (5ft) high by 2.5 (8ft) wide.

C. ladanifer is 2m (6ft) high but less wide and has dark leaves and white flowers, 10cm (4in) across, sometimes with crimson marks at the base of the petals.

C. laurifolius, dark leaves and white flowers, 8cm (3in) across, with golden centres. Shrubs 2m (6ft) high and wide.

C. 'Peggy Sammons' is evergreen with oval, grey-green leaves, making a bush 1m (3ft) tall and wide. Lots of pale pink blossom in early summer.

C. pulverulentus 'Sunset' produces grey-green leaves, 5cm (2in) long and rich pink flowers, 5cm (2in) wide on plants 60cm (2ft) high by 1m (3ft) wide.

C. x purpureus, 1m (3ft) high and wide shrubs with narrow leaves and deep pink, 7cm (3in) flowers with a maroon spot at base of each petal.

Top: Choisya ternata 'Aztec Pearl'.

Left: Cistus 'Peggy Sammons'.

Right: Crinodendron hookerianum, *the lantern tree.*

Clerodendron trichotomum var. *fargesii* *Verbenaceae*

This upright, bushy shrub has shining, dark green leaves with clearly drawn, impressed veins. They are ovate with a tapering point and up to 20cm (8in) long. From late summer well into the autumn, lots of wide clusters of small, starry, white flowers make perfumed bunches up to 22cm (9in) wide. These are followed by bright blue berries that are quite persistent and make the bush look decorative and unusual. While enjoying full sun it is not averse to some light shading in midsummer; the soil is best a fertile humus-rich one with good drainage. Deciduous, height 5m (15ft), Z6 H4.

Colquhounia coccinea *Lamiaceae*

A sub-shrub with aspirations, this species is erect with large, aromatic, 15-20cm (6-8in) long leaves, textured like sage and woolly on the undersurface. Blunt-ended, terminal spikes bear crowded whorls of orange-yellow, lipped flowers in later summer. A severe winter may cut the top growth down to soil level, but it will usually sprout again. A thick mulch will help protect the rootstock through winter. Evergreen or semi-evergreen, height 2.5m (8ft), Z9 H3.

Clerodendron trichotomum *var.* fargesii.

Cotinus coggygria 'Royal Purple'

This form of the smoke bush has no need for wall protection but makes a useful contrast of foliage colour in all parts of the garden. Its circular, purple-maroon leaves clothe a shrub of cloudy form and turns scarlet in autumn. The flower inflorescences are of intricately divided filigree stems giving it its common name. Probably best in sun or partial shade in a not-too-rich soil with reasonable drainage. Deciduous, height 5m (15ft), Z5 H4.

Cotoneaster *Rosaceae*

A genus of over 200 deciduous or evergreen species, many of which are grown for their beauty in fruit. Some make small trees; the C. × *watereri* series are fine spreading kinds with huge crops of clustered red berries that can be carried from autumn through until spring. Other species are good groundcover plants but the three selected are excellent against walls.

C. horizontalis

The commonest grown and always pleasing with its stylized, herringbone branch pattern, neat, glossy, rounded, small leaves and masses of pink-flushed, white flowers, followed by shining, bead-like berries, strung along every twig. Fine on walls but also very good working its way up railings, which make a good contrast to its form, and worth allowing to sweep across the ground in more open areas. Deciduous, height 1m (3ft), Z5-6 H4.

C. linearifolius (syn. *C. microphyllus*)

A very compact, almost hunch-backed shrub with rigid branches well furnished with dark, shiny, small leaves. Pink buds open to white flowers followed by dark red berries. Can be trained up walls where it makes more than the height quoted. Evergreen, height 1m (3ft), Z6 H4.

C. sternianus
(syn. *C. franchetii* var. *sternianus*)
The dark, shiny, broadly ovate leaves of this species are around 4cm (1½in) long. It is very free with its tight clusters of pink-flushed, white flowers in summer. Heavy crops of tightly clasped, round, orange-red fruits make it brilliant in autumn and winter. Excellent trained tight to a wall or fence. Evergreen or semi-evergreen, height 3m (10ft), Z6 H4.

Crinodendron *Aristolochiaceae*

A genus of really handsome lustrous, deep green evergreen shrubs of cloudy form having lots of exotic-looking blossom. Shade or partial shade with moist but well-drained soil.

C. hookerianum (syn. *Tricuspidaria lanceolata*)
The lantern tree makes an upright bush, taller than wide, with a luxurious cover of narrow elliptic, pointed, dark green leaves, 10cm (4in) long, as a background for lots of nodding, almost succulent, globular or urn-shaped, deep crimson flowers, hung on long stalks from late spring until late summer. Best in a sheltered spot which gives some protection from the frost that may threaten young growth and buds. Evergreen, height 6m (20ft), Z8 H3.

C. patagua (syn. *Tricuspidaria dependens*)
This quickly makes a soldierly shrub with leathery, shining, dark, ovate leaves, 7cm (3in) long. Bell-shaped flowers, 2cm (¾in) long, are smaller than those of *C. hookerianum* and are white. The dark foliage and white blossom can make a pleasing late summer picture. It is quicker growing than the previous species, but is also somewhat more tender. Evergreen, height 8m (25ft), Z7 H2-3.

Cytisus battandieri, *Leguminosae/Papilionaceae*, see box.

Daphne odora *Thymelaeaceae*

A neat, rounded bush of narrow leaves, 8cm (3in) long and dark green. Its terminal tight posies of 4-petalled, purple-red flowers are deliciously fragrant from mid-winter in mild spots. Plant as a youngster and leave undisturbed. **'Aureomarginata'** is popular with leaves narrowly margined yellow. Sun or half shade, dry rather than wet soil but not desert-dry. Evergreen, height 1.5m (5ft), Z8 H3.

Cytisus battandieri

The pineapple broom is a fast growing plant that enjoys a wall to give its rangy branches support, to encourage the leaves to be evergreen and to produce plenty of distinctive flowers. It can quickly go up a suitable wall. The leaves, 8cm (3in) long, consist of 3 leaflets and are very attractive and light, silvered by the silky finish. Crowded bunches of bright yellow pea flowers decorate the shrub for some weeks early to midsummer. Their scent is of pineapples. Let it have plenty of room and prune only to encourage fresh growth to produce flowering wood for the following year. Full sun, good drainage; can cope with rather dry conditions. Deciduous or semi-evergreen, height 5m (15ft), Z7-8 H4.

* Bold silvery foliage
* Unusual character – quite unlike any other broom
* Long, bold flower display
* Fragrance
* Tallish wall shrub, foliage and flower from soil level to tip top
* Quick, easy culture
* Propagates easily from seed

Daphne odora 'Aureomarginata'.

Decaisnea fargesii *Lardizabalaceae*

An erect, sparingly branched shrub with impressive, flat, pinnate leaves, up to 1m (3ft) long, composed of 13-25 ovate, pointed leaflets. Hanging bunches, up to 45cm (18in) long, of greenish bells in summer are followed by 10cm (4in) long pods of dark purple-blue with a grey bloom, usually in hanging bunches of up to 12. Most unusual and certainly worth growing for its foliage and these amusing blue beans. Find it a sheltered sunny site with a healthy moist soil. Deciduous, height 6m (20ft), Z6 H4.

Dendromecon rigida *Papaveraceae*

The tree poppy has sturdy shoots and neat, oblong or spear-shaped, tough leaves, grey-green with a light bloom. This shrub is rarely out of bloom from spring until autumn and can have a generous offering of many open 4-petalled, scented, poppy flowers in bright yellow, the petal edges sometimes gently serrated or crimped. Full sun with extremely good drainage. Evergreen, height 3m (10ft), Z8 H2-3.

Desfontainia spinosa *Loganiaceae*

From the rainforests of the Andes, and not for dry areas, this is a dense shrub, grown as much for its fine, shining, holly-like foliage as for its flowers. The latter are long, narrow, tube-like, 4cm (1½in) long and in orange-red with touches of gold at the tips. Best in neutral to acid soil, rich in humus and in a sheltered spot; excellent in cool moist spots, such as parts of Scotland. Evergreen, height 2m (6ft), Z8 H3.

Dichotomanthes tristaniicarpa
Rosaceae

This shrub has privet-like leaves, but the upper leaf surface is bright green while the underneath is silky white. The young shoots are very downy. Tiny, white flowers in terminal bunches, 5cm (2in) across, appear in early summer, and later there may be interesting fruits. These are in 5mm (¼in) cases surrounded by expanding fleshy, woolly, persistent calyces. Rare and a curiosity that your neighbour will not have. Needs the warmth of a wall as it could be damaged in a severe winter. Normal soil, better dry than very wet. Evergreen, height 6m (20ft), Z8 H3-4.

Diospyros kaki *Ebenaceae*

This is the persimmon. It has broad, oval, clearly veined leaves, polished above and downy below, and 10-20cm (4-8in) long. Insignificant, creamy flowers

are surrounded by larger calyces that still remain when the tangerine-orange or deep gold, apple- or tomato-like fruits are produced, on female plants. These fruits need a good summer and a warm wall to ripen. **'Hachiya'** is female with large, conical fruits, up to 8cm (3in) long. Both sexes needed for fruiting. Fullest sun in well-drained soil. Deciduous, height 10m (30ft), Z6 H3.

Diplacus glutinosus, see *Mimulus aurantiacus*.

Discaria toumatou *Rhamnaceae*

Somewhat strangely called the wild Irishman, this New Zealand shrub is formidably armed with sharp, green spines, up to 5cm (2in) long, set at right angles to the slender stems. They take on some of the work of photosynthesis as the clusters of leaves are tiny and can be lost on established bushes. Tight clusters of small, ivory-white flowers appear in late spring. For lovers of the curious, and owners of stout gloves. Sunny site with free-draining soil. Deciduous, height 2.5m (8ft), Z8 H3-4.

Dregea sinensis
(syn. *Wattakaka sinensis*) *Asclepiadaceae*

Twining evergreen with 10cm (4in), heart-shaped leaves, bright green above, felty grey below. In summertime umbels, 7cm (3in) across, of perfumed flowers appear. Creamy or pale pink and dotted red, they are 1.5cm (½in) wide. Narrow seedpods, to 7cm (3in) long, follow. Will need tying to its support until it starts twining. Sun or part shade. Keep it from sodden winter conditions though it can cope with plenty of moisture in growing months. Evergreen, height 3m (10ft), Z8 H3.

Drimys winteri.

Drimys winteri *Winteraceae*

Known as winter's bark, this species has aromatic bark and foliage. It makes a strong, erect shrub or tree with tough, rich green leaves like those of laurel and up to 20cm (8in) long. In mid-spring it produces wide, rounded, loose umbels of up to 20 perfumed, ivory-white flowers, each 2.5cm (1in) wide with perhaps 12 petals. Best sheltered from cold winds and grown in full or partial shade but will cope with sun; it likes a moist but well-drained soil. Evergreen, height 12m (40ft), Z8 H3.

Elaeagnus pungens 'Maculata'
Elaeagnaceae

A dense, vigorous – sometimes almost rampant – bush that will grow in full sun or partial shade (the colour is better in sun) and is armed with a number of randomly placed, sharp spikes. The oval leaves are dark green but this is pushed to the edges by the central golden variegation, which can almost cover the whole leaf. Always bright and cheerful, this takes on a special glowing depth in winter, just when any colour is sorely needed. Note: cut out any branches that revert to all green before they get large. Evergreen, height 4m (12ft), Z7 H4.

Erica arborea var. alpina *Ericaceae*

A dark-leaved heather with very crowded, upright, pointed racemes of white heather flowers in the second half of the winter and in spring. The blossom is honey-scented and attracts any precocious bees. Evergreen, height 2m (6ft), Z8 H4.

Eriobotrya japonica *Rosaceae*

This species, commonly known as loquat, has strong shoots and makes a shrub or tree clothed with magnificent foliage. The wonderful, arching leaves are about 30cm (12in) long and have impressed, chevron veins along their length. They are pointed oval and richest green, almost blue-black. Through autumn until winter it bears panicles of fragrant, white flowers. The fruits follow but it is in spring when they eventually turn from green spheres or pear shapes to the edible orange-yellow loquats. Sunny spot, with fertile open-structured soil. Evergreen, height 8m (25ft), Z9 H2-3.

Escallonia *Escalloniaceae*

These are very easy shrubs for sun or part shade. They are useful as specimens, by walls, for screening or for

hedges, being amenable to pruning. All have rich dark, polished foliage. See margin list (left) for some of the best. Evergreen, height to 3m (10ft), Z9 H4.

Eucalyptus nicholii *Myrtaceae*

One of the most graceful of the eucalyptus, this is best in the open where it makes an erect, rather narrow tree with slender branches, thin stems and very slim, grey leaves, 7-15cm (3-6in) long. The hanging leaves are rarely completely still, producing a graceful and lively effect. Normal soil, it can cope with fairly dry conditions better than excessively wet. Evergreen, height 12m (40ft), Z8 H3-4.

Escallonia 'Iveyi' is a popular shrub with very dark polished leaves contrasting with snow-white blossom.

Eucalyptus nicholli.

205

THE PLANTS

Eucryphia Eucryphiaceae

Eucryphias grow into heavily clothed trees or shrubs, the trees making strong statements. They are free-flowering during the second half of summer, bearing squarish, 4-petalled, white flowers, with attractive stamens. Best in spots that are not too exposed or windy: use near a garden wall as they are too big against most house walls. Sun or partial shade; moist soil.

E. glutinosa

This is the hardiest of the eucryphias. It is an erect shrub or tree with pinnate leaves, 6cm (2½in) long, with 3 or 5 leaflets. They are dark, glossy green and turn to orange-red in autumn before dropping. Plentiful bowl-shaped blooms, sometimes somewhat doubled, are about 6cm (2½in) across and have a central boss of stamens. Deciduous, height 10m (30ft), Z9 H4.

E. × intermedia

These are upright, robust trees usually furnished to the ground with oblong, tough, dark leaves up to 7cm (3in) long. Lots of saucer-shaped, white flowers, 5cm (2in) wide, appear from late summer into autumn. Evergreen, height 10m (30ft), Z9 H3-4.

E. × nymansensis 'Nymansay'

This tree is very vigorous, growing quickly upwards in soldierly manner. Elliptic, tough, dark evergreen leaves are up to 6cm (2½in) long and composed of 3 leaflets. It has lots of cup-shaped, white flowers with a boss of yellow stamens. Evergreen, height 15m (50ft), Z9 H3.

Euonymus Celastraceae

A large and varied evergreen genus. The following are two very utilitarian species. The many forms of *E. fortunei* can be used as groundcover or specimen plants (see pp.142-143); they are also successful as low interior hedges and trained up walls or pillars. Sun or shade, dryish or dampish.

E. alatus

Winged spindle is a thick, bushy shrub that can spread twice or thrice wide as high. It is noted for its corky, flanged or winged stems. The foliage is an orthodox deep green through the growing months but it gets into party mode in the autumn dressing up in shades of brilliant crimson-red. Deciduous, height 2m (6ft), Z3 H4.

Fabiana imbricata Solanaceae

This is a heather-type shrub pretending to be a porcupine with stiff branches thickly packed with sharp needle-like leaves that are rather sticky and downy. At the end of spring, lots of narrow, bell-shaped flowers are arranged along the branches between the leaves. The type is white or pale mauve but there is a fine richer lavender form **f. *violacea***, which is perhaps more erect, with horizontal branching. Well worth trying near a sunny wall. Can be tidied up with gentle pruning after flowering. Fertile, well-drained soil. Evergreen, height 2.5m (8ft), Z9 H3.

Left:
Eucryphia glutinosa.

Autumn colours come from many quarters; the Euonymus alatus *var* apterus *is always brilliant before dropping leaves. Here it is accompanied by the ornamental apple,* Malus *'Butterball'.*

× *Fatshedera lizei* *Araliaceae*
(*Hedera helix* 'Hibernica' × *Fatsia japonica*)

One of the rare intergeneric hybrids, a useful, very hardy foliage plant bearing highly polished leaves with 5 or 7 clearly defined, pointed lobes. Needs support as a young plant, and then will form a loose limbed spreading shrub, or it can be trained against a wall or up a post. It produces ivory umbels in autumn, halfway between those of the parents. The flowers are sterile. Evergreen, height 1-2m (3-6ft), Z7-8 H3-4.

Fendlera rupicola, see Tender Plants p.247.

Ficus carica *Moraceae*

Where there is plenty of space the fig can be a splendid foliage plant with its large, rounded leaves with 3 or 5 lobes like clumsy fingers, 10-24cm (4-10in) long and wide. Small, green fruits form during one year and then mature in size and to darker colours the next one. Sun. More prolific of fruit on lighter, well-drained, not over-rich soils. Good drainage almost essential. Deciduous, height 3m (10ft), Z9 H3-4.

Forsythia suspensa *Oleaceae*

Because the free-standing forsythia cultivars are so much better known and are such show-offs with their spring displays, the charm of this arching, stumbling shrub, with its somewhat paler flowers, gets overlooked. Trained up a wall to give it backbone, it can make a display that will please many who find the acres of 'Lynwood' and others just a little bit too much of a good thing. Slender stems will arch away from the main secured branches, making a pleasing stage for the flowers, early in spring on a warm wall and just a little later on a cooler one. With the display over, these arching stems can be pruned back to two buds, making all tidy and encouraging lots of fresh growth for next spring's entertainment. Will grow reasonably in most soils, moist or dryish. Deciduous, height on support 8m (25ft), Z5-6 H4.

Fremontodendron *Sterculiaceae*

There are two species of fremontodendron that can be recommended for growing against a wall in milder areas. They both grow strongly with relatively few stout branches. There are no proper petals, so the large, brilliant golden calyces make the flower. Plant as young, potted specimens at the beginning of spring. Do not expect many decades from one plant as they are not long-lived. Have a seedling or so ready

Fremontodendron 'California Glory'

If you only have room for one fremontodendron, this must be it. It is hardier than *F. mexicanum* with rather similar, rounded, 5-lobed, dark leaves, and produces a succession of brilliant shining yellow flowers, 4-6cm (1½-2½in) wide, either singly or in small clusters, from late spring well into autumn. Evergreen or semi-evergreen, height 6m (20ft), Z9 H3.

✳ Spectacular flowers from spring until autumn

✳ Trains well against a sunny wall

✳ Bold dark foliage. Evergreen or semi-evergreen

✳ Strong rapid growth

✳ Does not require rich soil

✳ Propagates from semi-ripe summer cuttings

for replacement, or, with the hybrid, try tip cuttings in the summer. Best in full sun, with restricted diet, and dryish rather than wet.

F. californicum
Slightly furry stems are clothed with alternate, 3-lobed leaves up to 10cm (4in) long. Upper surfaces

HAMAMELIS CULTIVARS

There is now a long list of hybrid forms, bred between *H. japonica* and *H. mollis*, all of which are worthy garden plants. Those with red and mahogany-coloured flowers should be planted where they can be inspected or seen closely; the yellows will show up well at greater distances.

'Arnold Promise', free-flowering, mid-yellow.

'Diane' has dark red flowers and foliage that turns beautiful shades of orange and dark red in autumn.

'Jelena', coppery-orange petals shading to yellow tips; good autumn foliage colours.

'Pallida', one of the oldest cultivars, is free with its lemon-yellow blossom.

'Vezna' dark orange-red flowers with darker reddish bases.

Below:
Hamamelis mollis.

are matt-green, below there is a brown fuzz. Saucer-shaped flowers, usually not less than 6cm (2½in) wide, are carried singly and a plant is rarely without a show from late spring until the end of summer. Evergreen or semi-evergreen, height 6m (20ft), Z9 H3.

F. 'California Glory' (*F. californicum* × *F. mexicanum*), see box.

F. mexicanum

Less grown as it is slightly more tender, this has rounded, deep green leaves with up to 7 lobes. The flowers are rather more starry and gold with a flush of red, especially as they age and towards the flower stalk. Evergreen or semi-evergreen, height 6m (20ft), Z10 H3.

Garrya elliptica

This is often grown as a wall shrub as it can do with support in its early years and, in colder areas, is certainly happier with this extra cosseting. Plants are either male or female; it is the male that you want as this has much the longer catkins. The rather sombre-leaved bush begins to produce tight little silvery catkins in autumn. These gradually elongate and end up being 15-20cm (6-8in) long: those of the clone 'James Roof' are 20-30cm (8-12in) long. The rounded or broadly oval leaves are tough, dark and often waved at the margin; the surface may be polished or matt, depending on the clone you buy. Sun or shade. Dry or damp soil. Evergreen, height 4-5m (12-15ft), Z9 H4.

✳ Blooms for months through the winter

✳ Evergreen of distinct character

✳ Excellent wall shrub

✳ Not fussy about soil conditions

✳ Very good for shady spots

✳ Healthy and easy to keep under control

✳ Twigs can be cut for indoor decoration

✳ Propagate by semi-ripe summer cuttings or by layering

Fuchsia magellanica Onagraceae

The winter-hardy fuchsia of which **'Riccartonii'** is usually thought to be the most useful and popular form. However, there is a delightful pale form *F. m.* 'Alba' with graceful slender flowers of a light whispered pink, a real contrast to the usual crimson and purple of the type.

F. 'Riccartonii' is possibly the hardiest of the fuchsias, an old favourite, with upright and arching stems and dark, pointed leaves. It produces a mass of blossom from summer until autumn. The flowers have dark red sepals and neat central purple corollas. Can be used for informal, decorative hedging in frost-free areas. Sun or partial shade; if possible moist, well-drained soil. Deciduous, height 2-3m (6-10ft), Z9 H3.

Garrya elliptica, Garryaceae, see box.

Grevillea Crassulaceae

Most of the 250 evergreen grevilleas prefer Australia to other, cooler parts. The two below are those most often found in cooler gardens but here they will need to be given all the warmth and shelter available. Best in acid soils that are not too sodden in winter; in growing months will cope with plenty of moisture provided there is reasonable drainage.

G. juniperina f. sulphurea (syn. G. *sulphurea*)
With narrow leaves, like pine needles, on lots of stems from low in the plant's framework, this has tight bunches of narrow, lemon-yellow flowers, with long, protruding styles from late spring until midsummer. The contracted racemes are in contrast to the longer, almost bottlebrush efforts of some species. Possibly the hardiest but still needs looking after. Evergreen, height 2m (6ft), Z9 H3.

G. rosmarinifolia
The dense foliage of this multi-branched species is close to rosemary in form and colour. The stems can

Hamamelis 'Diane', the witch-hazel, as an autumn foliage shrub.

be erect, spreading or arching and may sometimes look loose-limbed. Rosy-red flowers, some 2.5cm (1in) long, are grouped in tight clusters and have protruding rosy styles; in bloom from early to midsummer. Evergreen, height 3m (10ft), Z9 H3.

Hamamelis mollis Hamamelidaceae

Chinese witch-hazel is perhaps the finest of winter-flowering shrubs. It has large, rough-textured leaves, like those of hazels, but stronger, and is a steady rather than rapid grower, making a broadly branched, erect shrub. By the end of the year, it is ready to unfurl lots of golden petals, like tiny paper streamers, to decorate itself. The flowers are persistent and can stand a lot of frost. Long-lived and well worth the initial investment. (See the margin, far left, for a selection of cultivars.) Deciduous, height 5m (15ft), Z6 H4.

Below right:
Hoheria sexstylosa.

Below:
Hibiscus *'Pink Giant'*.

Haplopappus ericoides Compositae

This small shrub is best in warm districts in a sunny spot; in other parts it should be treated as tender. As its name suggests, it looks like a heath and grows perhaps at most to 45cm (18in) high, but is more often less than half this. It has small, dark, heather-like leaves, thicker at the axils. Late summer, bright yellow flowers are clustered in panicles well clear of the foliage. Best increased by midsummer cuttings – plants do not live a huge number of years. Not too wet. Evergreen, height 15-45cm (6-18in), Z9 H2-3.

Hedysarum coronarium Leguminosae

French honeysuckle is a shrubby perennial that is notably short-lived, occasionally biennial. Its pinnate leaves have 3 to 7 pairs of pea-like leaflets, and it bears brilliant red, pea flowers in crowded spikes above the foliage in summer. Grows as wide as it is tall. Evergreen, height 1m (3ft), Z5 H4.

Hibiscus syriacus Malvaceae

Once thought to have come from Syria but native to India and China, this is the best of the species that are hardy enough to grow outside in cooler climes.

Making a sturdy, upright shrub, it has irregularly se[rated, 3-lobed leaves from dark to palish green. Exo[ically showy, rounded, trumpet flowers, 6-10c[(2½-4in) wide, are borne from the second half o[summer until autumn. Blooms most freely whe[planted in fertile, well-drained soil that does not dr[out and where it can enjoy plenty of sun. Will b[happy with some lime in soil. (See margin fo[choices.) Deciduous, height 3m (10ft), Z5-6 H4.

Hippophaë rhamnoides Elaeagnaceae

Sea buckthorn is a most useful coastal shrub, fo[windbreaks or to help stabilize dunes. It forms a[intricate bush armed with vicious spines and clothe[in narrow, silvery-green leaves, 6cm (2½in) long[scaly on both surfaces. Insignificant limy flowers ar[followed by bright orange, round fruits that cling o[well into winter, long after the leaves have fallen[and they do not fall early. Deciduous, height 6n[(20ft), Z3 H4.

Hoheria Malvaceae

Elegant, evergreen or deciduous shrubs with clean-cu[foliage and sprays of white flowers. Grow in borders o[near walls. Neutral to alkaline soil, in sun or part shade[
H. angustifolia (syn. *H. microphylla*)
This is a tall, narrowly pyramidical shrub or tree wit[dark, 3cm (1½in) leaves. White summer flowers ar[2cm (¾in) across. Best in a sheltered place. Ever[green, height 6m (18ft), Z9 H3.

Illicium floridanum.

H. glabrata

A spreading shrub or tree with many branches and clean, bright foliage. The leaves are broadly ovate, coming to a point, and 10cm (4in) long. Midsummer brings lots of small, rounded, loose sprays of fine-spun white flowers, 4cm (1½in) wide, a little like May blossom. Probably the best to try, for hardiness and display; certainly a class turn. Deciduous, height 6m (20ft), Z9 H4.

H. sexstylosa (syn. H. populnea var. lanceolata)

A rapid grower, and the best of the evergreens to try (the evergreens are somewhat less hardy than the deciduous ones). It is erect with pointed glossy leaves, up to 10cm (4in) long but usually a little less. Hanging sprays of flowers, 2cm (¾in) across, are arranged like those of a flowering currant, but each more starry and widely spaced. They appear in mid- and late summer. It will also have solitary flowers. Hard winters can cause some leaf fall. Evergreen, height 6m (20ft), Z9 H3.

Illicium Illiciaceae

Aromatic, evergreen shrubs with tough, simple leaves similar to magnolias, to which they are related. Best out of persistent winds. Shade or semi-shade. Neutral to somewhat acid soils that are moist rather than dry.

I. anisatum

This species has clean, tough, narrowly oval, dark leaves, 5-10cm (2-4in) long, and makes a handsome mass. The leaves have an aniseed scent. The flowers have up to 12 narrow, pointed petals making ivory stars, 2.5cm (1in) wide, and are produced in spring. Evergreen, height 8m (25ft), Z7-8 H4.

I. floridanum

A touch less hardy than the previous species, this is commonly called the aniseed tree. Rather narrow,

Itea ilicifolia

This classy evergreen grows erectly but has some arching branches. It is neatly dressed with wide, oval, dark, tough leaves, spiny-margined in a slight imitation of holly. It is very decorative from midsummer until autumn with its very long, narrow 'catkins' of scented, ivory flowers. Although the flowers are individually only 8mm (¼in) wide, the inflorescences can be up to 30cm (12in) long, and they are produced over a long period. A fine plant near a sunny wall. Fertile soil that does not dry out. *Itea virginica* is a similar character with rather wider white catkins, a newer garden introduction. Evergreen, height 4m (12ft), Z9 H3.

✱ Handsome dark foliage

✱ Distinct, classy flowers; long catkins

✱ Late summer- and autumn-flowering

✱ Hardy and long-lived

✱ Sun or semi-shade

✱ Propagates from semi-ripe summer cuttings

tough leaves are 7.5-12cm (3-5in) long. Starry, nodding, solitary, scented, red-purple blooms appear in late spring and early summer and are 5cm (2in) wide. Evergreen, height 2.5m (8ft), Z7-8 H4.

Itea ilicifolia, *Escalloniaceae*, see box.

Kerria japonica *Rosaceae*

This species forms a suckering thicket of upright branches with lesser lateral ones; the stems are green in youth. The bright green, ovate, pointed leaves have impressed veins. The single-flowered species is scarcely worth growing; however, **'Pleniflora'** has lots of rounded, fully double, golden blossom from mid- to late spring, each button flower about 3cm (1¼in) wide. There is also an improved clone **'Golden Guinea'** with single flowers up to 6cm (2½in) wide. Very easy in sun or partial shade in moist soils provided they are reasonably drained. Deciduous, height 3m (10ft), Z5 H4.

Lagerstroemia indica *Lythraceae*

Crepe myrtle is an upright shrub-cum-tree with peeling bark making patterns of grey and brown. Bronze when young, the leaves are up to 6cm (2½in) long and become dark green. Broad, crowded panicles of red, purple, pink or white flowers are borne at the end of each growing shoot. Individual flowers are 2-2.5cm (¾-1in) across and consist of 6 crumpled petals and lots of stamens. Can be colourful in the autumn before the leaves fall. Grows quickly near a warm wall where it can feel the sun and tuck roots into well-drained soil. Deciduous, height 8m (25ft), Z10 H3-4.

Leptospermum scoparium *Myrtaceae*

A relative of myrtle, the Manuka is one of the sights of New Zealand and has proved popular in Europe, where it has been grown for over 200 years; over 30

Kerria japonica.

cultivars are currently on offer in Britain. It makes a rounded bush of erect and arching branches, well furnished with deep green, narrow leaves only around 1cm (½in) long and aromatic when crushed. The stems and leaves may be silvered with fine hairs in youth. During the late spring and early summer flowering season, the whole plant can become smothered with closely held, white blossom. Individual flowers are saucer-shaped, 1.5cm (½in) across with 5 very rounded petals that do not overlap. **'Gaiety Girl'** is semi-double, deep pink in bud but paler pink when open. **'Keatleyi'** has flowers double the size and pale pink to accompany foliage that is crimson-flushed in youth but then a silvery-green. **'Kiwi'** has purple foliage and flowers of glowing cerise-crimson. **'Nicholsii'** has purple or bronze foliage and crimson flowers with darker centres. **'Red Damask'** is impressive with dark foliage and double, dark red flowers. Excellent in milder, sheltered gardens; good coastal plants. They like sun and well-drained soil that veers to the acid side of neutral. Evergreen, height 3-4m (10-12ft), Z9 H3.

Lippia citriodora, see *Aloysia triphylla*, p.226.

Lonicera *Caprifoliaceae*

There are one or two non-climbing, shrubby honeysuckles, useful for winter bloom and scent.
L. fragrantissima
This makes a very twiggy bush, twice as wide as high, with oval leaves in pairs, each about 7cm (3in) long. Creamy-white, highly scented honeysuckle flowers are each compressed into 1cm (½in). Can be very free of flower in winter if grown near a wall or with a somewhat restricted rootrun in a warmish spot. Deciduous or semi-evergreen, height 2m (6ft), Z6 H4.

Right: Lonicera fragrantissima.

Far right: Magnolia grandiflora 'Goliath'.

Left: Leptospermum scoparium.

L. standishii

This is similar to the last species with slightly larger leaves and it may come into bloom a little earlier. The flowers are of similar size, scented, and creamy, but sometimes with a touch of pink. Deciduous or semi-evergreen, height 2m (6ft), Z6 H4.

L. × purpusii 'Winter Beauty'

A useful hybrid between the two foregoing species, this has leaves that are 8cm (3in) long and large, white flowers, 2cm (¾in) long, with somewhat protruding yellow anthers and a rich scent. Free-flowering and a useful winter and very early spring shrub. Deciduous or semi-evergreen, height 2m (6ft), Z6 H4.

Magnolia Magnoliaceae

These upper-class, deciduous and evergreen shrubs and trees are all quite splendid – all the species and the increasing numbers of hybrids. Here are two species that can be trained against a wall very satis-factorily, and make fine foliage plants, but you can also do this with some of the deciduous M. × *soulangeana* cultivars. They will cope well with wall sites that are somewhat dry and alkaline.

M. delavayi

This species has fine, oval or oblong, dark leaves with impressed, chevron veins and looks very impressive. Flowers appear in late summer. They are fleeting, cup or bowl arrangements, up to 20cm (8in) wide, with 6 or so spoon-shaped, cream or pale yellow petals. Ever-green, height 10m (30ft), Z9 H3.

M. grandiflora, see box.

Magnolia grandiflora

This plant has very polished leaves, 20cm (8in) long, of a brighter green than *M. delavayi*. The upper surfaces are smooth, resembling a broad-leaved laurel. The popular clone 'Exmouth' has fractionally narrower leaves but they are still opulent and a shining mid-green. It is favoured for its hardiness, quickness into flowering maturity, and for the fine large pure white flowers, up to 25cm (10in) wide, which appear at intervals from summer until autumn. 'Goliath' has huge flowers 20-30cm (8-12in) across, and broad foliage just slightly twisted. Evergreen, height 6-15m (20-50ft), Z6-7 H4.

* Bold and classy

* Grows well against a wall to almost any height with comfortable spread

* Very large impressive flowers

* Perfume

* Not fussy about soil

* Sun or part shade

Mahonia Berberidaceae

A series of tough, evergreen shrubs. Some, such as M. *aquifolium*, M. × *wagneri*, M. *japonica* and the M. × *media* hybrids, are of undoubted hardiness; others, such as M. *lomariifolia* from Western China, may be just a touch tender in bleak gardens. All are excellent foliage plants. Sun or partial shade. Soils may range from rather dry to rather wet.

M. × *media*, see box.

M. × *wagneri*

As the status of M. *pinnata*, one of the parents of this hybrid, is uncertain, the derivation of these fine hybrids is in some doubt. They have the hardiness of the common M. *aquifolium*, but do not normally spread by its suckering habit, being discrete, tidy shrubs, slightly wider than tall. The leaves are 20cm (8in) long and may have up to 11 leaflets, which are broad and toothed, but more modestly than the M. × *media* hybrids. My favourite clone is **'Moseri'**. This has tidy foliage that is pale green strongly flushed pink and red, making the plant a focal point around the year. Its bunched yellow flowers are close to those of M. *aquifolium* and appear in early spring, a striking contrast to the foliage colour. Plenty of seed is set in the purple berries. Seedings raised from these give a wide range of plants; most of ours have had foliage that is all green but there are one or two whose leaves are soft salmon or apricot for at least the first few months of their life. Evergreen, height 1m (3ft), Z7-8 H4.

Melia azedarach Melianthaceae

The bead tree is an elegant plant for stationing near a warm wall. Its leaves are bipinnate and 30-60cm (12-24in) long and give it a pleasing appearance. Loose, falling clusters of lilac, perfumed flowers appear from spring until midsummer. The 5 petals are narrow strips but the flowers are made more distinctive by the rich violet stamens fused into a central pointing tube. In autumn the plant can look its most distinguished as it is furnished with bright yellow, round fruits 1cm (½in) or more long. These are used as beads in Asia. Normal, well-drained soil. Deciduous, height 10m (30ft), Z9 H1-2.

Michelia Magnoliaceae

A genus related to *Magnolia* with the same tough leaves and fleshy, cup-shaped flowers. The main botanical distinction is that the flowers are borne from leaf axils rather than the stem ends – not a

Mahonia x media

These are stout-stemmed, sturdy, upward-reaching shrubs. The leaves, up to 45cm (18in) long, are composed of 15-21 leaflets that are basically lance-shaped but are spiny and may be likened to flattened holly leaves. They are a good rich green and quite shiny. The lemon-yellow flowers are little globes arranged in racemes up to 40cm (16in) long, but more often closer to 25cm (10in). They are produced terminally and freely – 12 or more is normal – from late autumn through winter. 'Charity' has widespreading, downward-facing racemes (see below). 'Lionel Fortesque' keeps its racemes pointing upwards. 'Buckland' has long racemes that tend to arch outwards, as do the bright, crowded ones of 'Winter Sun'.

A young plant will tend to grow steadily upwards and may look as if it is doing an imitation of a palm tree. Do not be afraid to cut it down to a stump of perhaps 15cm (6in) and force it to make several 'trunks'. The resulting regrowth will look better and give a more pleasing floral and foliar display. The 5m (15ft) height is achieved after some years, but, if this seems excessive, the plants can be kept to a height of around 2m (6ft) relatively easily. Evergreen, height 5m (15ft), Z9 H4.

* Elegant, distinct pinnate foliage

* Plenty of well-displayed blossom for months from early winter

* Fragrant blossom

* Long-lived

* Can be cut back

* Good in open or near walls

* Propagate by leaf bud cuttings or semi-ripe summer cuttings

world-shattering difference as far as gardeners are concerned. Neutral to acid, humus-rich soils not subject to drought conditions but preferably not too wet in winter. Sun or part shade.

M. *doltsopa*

This species, which makes an upright bush that spreads with age, has oval leaves of polished, bright green, 7.5-18cm (3-7in) long. Flower buds are formed in autumn and the rounded, many-petalled white, ivory or palest yellow blooms open from spring until early summer. They are 7-10cm (3-4in) across, with a delicious scent and suffused green at the base. A splendid plant, but for milder areas only. Semi-evergreen, height 8-12m (25-40ft), Z9 H3.

M. figo (syn. M. *fuscata*)
Known as the banana shrub because of the unusual scent of the flowers, this plant has leaves that are like those of the laurel. The flowers are globe-shaped and greenish-ivory, cream or pale limy-yellow with 'petal' margins pencilled maroon, the pigment sometimes slightly suffusing other parts of the flower. They are borne from mid-spring until early summer. Again, you need to garden in a mild area to be able to grow it. Evergreen, height 1.5-3m (5-10ft), Z9 H3.

Mimulus aurantiacus Scrophulariaceae

This makes an airily upright or arching shrub with sticky, pointed, rich green leaves 7cm (3in) long. Widely open, long, 2-lipped and 6-lobed, trumpet flowers have wavy-margined petals and are rich gold, tangerine or red. They appear from late summer until autumn. Best in full sun in somewhat moist rather than dry soil, but wanting free drainage. Evergreen, height 1m (3ft), Z9 H2-3.

Myrtus communis Myrtaceae

Common myrtle has probably been cultivated in Britain for 500 years and is a very familiar plant generally in gardens of Europe, especially around the Mediterranean. It is a much-branched, upright shrub, spreading with age, bearing dark, polished, deep green foliage on the privet pattern but emitting an attractive fragrance when crushed. From midsummer until the frosts, rounded, pink buds open to 5-petalled, hawthorn-like, white flowers with lots of stamens. Later it has purple-black berries. **'Variegata'** has cream leaf margins. **subsp.** *tarentina* is a

Myrtus communis.

Right: Philadelphus
'Belle Etoile'.

respected plant of tidy, compact form with neat smaller leaves only up to 2cm (¾in) long, cream flowers, with a hint of pink, and white fruits. All forms are more floriferous and fruitful in hot or warm spots and good summers. Evergreen, height 3m (10ft), Z8 H3.

Olearia *Asteraceae*

A large, evergreen genus from Australia and New Zealand with some members that have proved very useful and attractive in European gardens. In Britain O. × *haastii*, O. *macrodonta* and others have been used as hedge plants and, in coastal areas, for wind breaks. They are amenable to pruning severely if the need arises. Cannot get too much sunshine; most soil conditions apart from excessively wet.

O. *erubescens*

Olearia macrodonta.

This is an upright shrub with tough, spear-shaped leaves, shiny and dark toned and up to 4cm (1½in)

long. From late spring into the first half of summer it bears daisies, 2.5cm (1in) wide. They are white with yellow disc centres and are either alone or in small sprigs of 3-6, the latter forming large, leafy panicles some 45cm (18in) long and looking impressive. Evergreen, height 1.5m (5ft), Z9 H3.

O. × *haastii*

This well-known hybrid is grown for its prolific cover of blossom from mid- to late summer. A rounded, tight bush, it has neat, shining, dark, oval leaves 2.5cm (1in) long. Individual flowers are tiny, white and yellow daisies, but these are crowded in large number in wide, slightly domed clusters, 8cm (3in) wide and touching and overlapping each other. Evergreen, height 2.5m (8ft), Z9 H3-4.

O. *ilicifolia*

True to its common name, mountain holly is a holly look-alike with wavy-edged, spiny leaves up to 10cm (4in) long but more grey-green than real holly. It has summertime white and yellow daisy flowers, each 1.5cm (½in) wide in clusters 10cm (4in) wide. A comfortable, properly clothed and spreading shrub that looks good as a specimen. Evergreen, height 5m (15ft), Z9 H3-4.

O. *macrodonta*

This is a strong-growing, upright but bushy plant with holly-like leaves, up to 10cm (4in) long. The leaves are shiny above, but on the underside they are almost white. Scented daisies are arranged in wide, almost flat sprays, some 15cm (6in) or so across. White ray petals surround the small, rusty-brown centres, each individual flower being perhaps 1cm (½in) wide. Evergreen, height 6m (20ft), Z9 H3.

Osmanthus *Oleaceae*

Osmanthus are evergreen shrubs and small trees that are very respectable in growth, pleasing in bloom and useful in a variety of ways, in the open, by walls or as hedge plants. Happy in sun or shade, healthy well-drained soil.

O. × *burkwoodii*

This is a well-bred, rounded shrub with a thick cover of pointed, oval, tough, dark green leaves, up to 5cm (2in) long and with a slight attempt at teeth. Highly scented, very tubular flowers are borne in many spring clusters. The narrow tubes open to 4 outward-pointing lobes at the mouth, their pure white contrasting well with the dark foliage. Evergreen, height 3m (10ft), Z-9 H4.

O. *decorus*

Glossy, dark, narrow elliptic leaves, up to 12cm (5in) long, are characteristic of this shrub, as are lots of closely clasped clusters of tiny, white, tubular flowers in mid-spring, followed by blue-black fruits as large as peas. Evergreen, height 3m (10ft), Z-9 H4.

O. *delavayi*

A small-leaved, dense, rounded bush of arching stems and foliage, making a glossy, dark green background for the many nodding clusters of fragrant, small, tubular, white flowers in mid- and late spring, the largest clusters being at the stem ends. Evergreen, height 3-5m (10-15ft), Z-9 H4.

Osteomeles schweriniae *Rosaceae*

This is a rare and classy shrub with willowy stems and beautiful pinnate foliage. Each 5-10cm (2-4in) long leaf is composed of 15 to 31 oval-oblong leaflets precisely placed as opposite pairs. They are bright green above, lightly grey-felted below. White summer flowers with 5 long petals, pointing outwards or somewhat reflexed, and prominent stamens are produced in loosely arranged 8cm (3in) sprays of 12-24. Blossom may be followed by egg-shaped fruits, up to 1cm (½in) long. These are chestnut coloured to start with, but end up a sombre, near jet-black. An unusual item, give it a place near a sunny wall. Evergreen/semi-deciduous, height 3m (10ft), Z9 H3.

Philadelphus *Hydrangeaceae*

The heady-scented mock oranges are worth growing near a wall if you have the space, although they are mainly very hardy, easy shrubs. If you decide to squeeze one in, you might consider the following, all of which are less demanding of space than the popular 'Virginal', which can easily go 3m (10ft) high and nearly as wide. All enjoy sun and well-drained, fertile soils. Would prefer dryish to wet conditions.

P. 'Beauclerk'

One of the best hybrids, this has ovate leaves up to 6cm (2½in) long, and bowl-shaped, white flowers, usually at least 5cm (2in) across, heavily perfumed and with a pink flush behind the boss of yellow stamens. Solitary blooms or sprays of up to 6 are borne for some weeks starting early summer. Deciduous, height 2.5m (8ft), Z6 H4.

P. 'Belle Etoile'

Arching stems, pointed, oval leaves, up to 10cm (4in) long, and lots of single, very fragrant flowers, 5cm (2in) across, from late spring into summer, are the hallmarks of this plant. The flowers are standard snow-white but with pale purple shading in their centres. Deciduous, height 1.5m (5ft), Z6 H4.

In this assemblage of herbs are lavender, Symphytum uplandicum (Russian comfrey), Phlomis fruticosa (Jerusalem sage), chives and golden marjoram – all sun lovers.

P. microphyllus

Making a tight, erect shrub with brown, peeling bark and small, glossy, elliptic leaves, this species produces a plethora of wide-open, 4-petalled flowers, white with golden stamen bosses, in a cloud of perfume in early summer. Deciduous, height 1m (3ft), Z6 H4.

Phlomis fruticosa *Lamiaceae*

Jerusalem sage forms a wide, rounded mound of grey-green leaves that justify the 'sage' tag in form and wrinkly texture. The undersides, and often the margins, are paler, adding to their distinctiveness. Early to midsummer sees the flowers hoisted comfortably above the foliage as rather flat-headed whorls of deep golden flowers of the unusual nettle type of the Lamiaceae. Sun and moist, open-structured soil. Evergreen, height 1m (3ft), Z9 H3.

Photinia × fraseri 'Red Robin'
Rosaceae

This energetic shrub certainly does not need wall protection but can be useful for the contrasting foliage mass, for which it is valued. It is particularly grown for its young foliage which is painted in gleaming tones of bright red, a colour range that is kept up for a long time, much longer than most young foliar colouring. It makes a reasonably compact, rounded bush and the leaves are shining, tough, elliptic and 10-15cm (4-6in) long. It can be pruned to shape. Happy in sun or partial shade. Normal soils with slight preference for acid. Evergreen, height 4m (12ft), Z9 H4.

Phygelius capensis, see Base of Wall Plants, p.233.

Piptanthus nepalensis
(syn. *P. laburnifolius*) *Leguminosae/Papilioniaceae*

Known as the evergreen laburnum, this is not necessarily evergreen, as a hard winter can cause some leaf fall. Usually, however, it can be depended upon to be formally attired through the year, a mass of many dark branches and 3-part leaves, each a rich blue-toned green, paler below and 15cm (6in) long. Lots of terminal racemes of flowers start to open in late spring and last for several weeks. They are bright golden, pea-shaped blooms and are in upward posies, not hanging like laburnums. The green seed pods do hang and are 20cm (8in) long. Sun and well-drained fertile soil. Deciduous or semi-evergreen, height 2.5m (8ft), Z9 H3-4.

Pittosporum tobira *Pittosporaceae*

A tidy, densely leaved shrub that can eventually grow into a modest tree. Tough, rich, glowing green leaves are smooth with margins that tend to recurve, not unlike some rhododendron foliage, and 4-10cm (1½-4in) long. In late spring and early summer each stem produces a rounded cluster, up to 7cm (3in) wide, of highly scented, creamy-white flowers rather like those of daphnes but 5-lobed and 2.5cm (1in) across. The cream becomes yellow with age and the blossom is eventually followed by round or pear-shaped seed capsules of tawny-yellow, the seeds being red. Often pittosporum forms are grown for their foliage alone:

Photinia × fraseri 'Red Robin'.

Prunus x subhirtella 'Autumnalis'

Especially valued for its blossom from the very end of the autumn until the spring, this tree has foliage that is narrower than most cherries and turns pleasing orange shades in autumn. Smallish, semi-double flowers open in mild weather and look like a flurry of snow; very severe weather kills off open blossom, but new buds open when it abates. In warmer weather the flowers take on a pink flush; this is often the case when the last lot of flowers open at the end of the winter. Deciduous, height 7m (21ft), Z5-6 H4.

✳ Small to medium size for all gardens, including small ones

✳ Blooms late autumn to spring, especially in milder weather

✳ Easy to cultivate in normal soils

✳ Good autumn leaf colour

✳ Relatively long lived

✳ Propagate by grafting

this species makes a good erect foliage shrub but the flower fragrance, bringing to mind orange-blossom, is a worthwhile bonus. Good drainage and preferably in sun. Evergreen, height 2-3m (6-10ft), Z9 H3.

Prostanthera rotundifolia *Lamiaceae*

One of the mint bushes, this plant is beautiful and worth a try by a warm wall in not-so-mild areas. Thin, grey-white, downy shoots are clothed with dark green, oval or round, shiny leaves around 5mm (¼in) long and wide. When crushed the foliage is highly and pleasantly aromatic. Bell-shaped outward-facing flowers in lavender or purplish-blue from late spring into summer. Sun and good drainage. Evergreen, height 2-3m (6-10ft), Z9 H2.

Prunus *Rosaceae*

This is a large genus of evergreen or deciduous trees and shrubs. Most of the flowering cherry types are perfectly suited to growing in the open but there are a couple that will be happy and look appropriate close to a wall: *P. ilicifolia*, an evergreen oddity, and the hard-worked *P. triloba* for jolly, early blossom, and *P. × subhirtella* 'Autumnalis', the winter-flowering cherry, is one of the most useful of small trees for the modern garden. In any normal, fertile soil in sun or light shade.

P. ilicifolia

Often best against a wall where any vulnerability to frost will be minimized, this scrunchy, spreading, corsetted shrub pretends to be a holly with leaves as leathery and highly lacquered as well as spiny and richly coloured. They are up to 7cm (3in) long. The white blossom comes later than most of the genus, in summer, and is then displayed in arching racemes of bowl-shaped single blooms just under 1cm (½in) across. Cuddle or otherwise protect young plants in severe weather; they become less subject to damage as they mature. Evergreen, height 8m (25ft), Z9 H3-4.

P. × subhirtella 'Autumnalis', see box.

THE PLANTS

PYRACANTHAS

P. rogersiana orange-red berries

P. rogersiana f. *flava* yellow berries

P. coccinea 'Red Column' rich red berries

P. 'Golden Charmer' orange-red berries

P. 'Orange Glow' (see box)

P. 'Soleil d'Or' heavy crops of large golden berries

P. 'Teton' small berries but huge crops, golden-orange

Punica granatum.

P. triloba 'Multiplex'

To enjoy its early blossom, this plant is best either trained against a wall or planted nearby. The warmth encourages the formation of lots of flower buds by the end of the year; after blooming the normal plan is to severely cut back all growth to a few buds to force strong, fresh growth to form next spring's enwreathed wands. For the first season or so against the wall it may be best to concentrate on forming a framework of branches from which this new growth can arch outwards. In the open the plants are cut back as to a stool that will provide an erect fountain of branches. To maximize the effect, three specimens are often planted as a close triangle. Foliage is mid-green, serrated and often 3-lobed, 2.5-5cm (1-2in) long. Flowers are very doubled and form rounded buttons of rich pink, 4cm (1½in) wide. They are closely packed and clasped the whole length of the stems. Deciduous, height 3m (10ft), Z3 H4.

Punica granatum Punicaceae

Although this is the shrub that bears the pomegranate, do not expect to ripen fruits in British-type climates. It can be trained against a wall or grown in a sunny spot nearby and will clothe itself with slender clean-cut leaves, 8cm (3in) long, in polished rich green, but often very attractively coppery-red in unfurling youth. For most of the summer, it will decorate itself with orange-red, rather creased, trumpet-shaped and 5-petalled flowers with coloured stamens. The blooms are either produced alone or in small sprays of up to 6. In good summers tawny-yellow fruits follow. There is a compact version **var. nana** which is often preferred as it has all the interesting good qualities, being very free of flower and fruit, and is a more manageable size, often less than 1m (3ft) high and wide. Best dryish in winter, but well watered in growth. Deciduous, height 6m (20ft), Z9 H3.

Pyracantha Rosaceae

The firethorns are deservedly among the most popular of wall shrubs, often being used for hedges, too. Little wonder, for their evergreen foliage is dominated from early autumn until spring with extraordinary, heavy crops of fruits in large bunches, either gold, orange or red, in various shades according to the cultivars chosen. In late spring, blossom covers all in wide clusters of small, white flowers, similar to those of hawthorn. Pyracanthas can be grown in the open, especially if given a stout stake for initial support. Sun or semi-shade. Any normal soils. See margin for a short list. Evergreen, height to 3m (10ft), Z6-8 H4. **P. 'Orange Glow'**, see box.

Pyrus salicifolia 'Pendula' Rosaceae

This is not a wall plant but a small tree that is useful as a specimen, or among other shrubs and trees, because of its silvery foliage and dense pendent habit. The leaves are narrowly willow-like. This is a spreading animal and its plentiful white pear blossom is almost lost in the pale silvery ensemble. Sunny spot, good drainage. Deciduous, height 5m (15ft), Z5 H4.

Rhaphithamnus spinosus

(syn. *R. cyanocarpus*) Verbenaceae

This thickly branched and leaved shrub has all the bristly attitude of a hedgehog, with rough stems and spines up to 2.5 (1in) long. Leaves, less than 2cm (¾in) long, are usually in threes. They are oval and wickedly toothed. One can almost overlook the small, lilac flowers in spring and early summer, but the same cannot be said of the fruit, which is a vivid blue when mature and remains for many weeks. More successful in mild areas. From Chile, it needs a warm, sheltered, sunny spot in fertile, well-drained soil. Evergreen, height 7m (22ft), Z9 H3-4.

Ribes speciosum *Grossulariaceae*

...ad winters can strip the shiny gooseberry-like shrubs ...f the fuchsia-flowered currant of leaves. The ...ranches are spiny and bristly with clean mid-green ...- or 5-lobed leaves, similar to those of the goose-...erry. Lots of small, red, narrow flowers with protrud-...ng red stamens that can be almost 2cm (¾in) proud ...f the main flower, hang from the spreading branches ...n spring. Round, red berries 1cm (½in) across follow ...nd are bristly. Enjoys some warmth and is easily ...ropagated from layers. Normal soils, best neither ...xcessively dry or wet. Deciduous/semi-evergreen, ...eight 3-4m (10-12ft), Z7 H4.

Robinia hispida *Papilionaceae*

...Commonly known as the bristly locust or rose acacia, ...his is indeed a tough, bristly shrub of suckering and ...rect form. It has attractive pinnate leaves, 30cm ...12in) long, with 7-13 oval, rich green leaflets. ...hrough late spring and early summer it opens plenty ...f rosy-pink, pea flowers in hanging bunches perhaps ...0-15cm (4-6in) long. It looks well in a sunny spot ...with its back to a wall. Not fussy about soil, but not a ...og plant. Deciduous, height 3m (10ft), Z5 H4.

Pyracantha '**Soleil d'Or**'

This is one of the popular pyracantha cultivars, a dense, erect evergreen getting to about 3m (10ft) wide and with dark foliage. Clusters of white flowers in spring are followed by an abundance of golden-yellow fruits. The berries may remain decorative for months; on the other hand, birds may decide it is party time and descend for a quick gorge. Evergreen, 5m (15ft), Z6 H4.

✳ Heavy crops of berries held for several months

✳ Dense evergreen cover

✳ Responds well to discipline of clippers

✳ Adaptable. Fine on walls or fences. Makes an impressive hedge. Can be an open garden shrub

Ribes speciosum *trained on a brick wall.*

Sambucus racemosa 'Plumosa Aurea' *Caprifoliaceae*

The red-berried elder makes an erect and arching bush with pinnate, bright golden-yellow leaves, up to 25cm (10in) long, composed of finely cut, pointed leaflets. Foliage colour is more limy in the shade, and the young leaves are tawny-orange. The foliage is best if the plant is a little out of the fiercest sun, which could cause some scorching. To make the most of the foliage it is best to severely cut back the bush every second year. This encourages fresh growth with optimum-size leaves. Push the prunings into the ground in the winter for an easy method of propagation. By growing two specimens one can cut back in alternate years so there is always a major display, though the bush cut back to stumps will be lively through the year as it grows rapidly upward. This shrub has no need of wall protection but is a useful contrast in colour. Not fussy about soils but more exuberant in

Sambucus racemosa 'Plumosa Aurea'.

moist ones. The cultivar **'Sutherland Gold'** is very similar but not so prone to sun scorch. Deciduous, height 3m (10ft), Z6 H4.

Santolina pinnata subsp. neapolitana *Asteraceae*

This is a rounded, silver bush with stems and narrowly divided leaves covered with fine, silken hairs. Bunches of bright yellow daisy flowers are produced in midsummer. Tidy at the end of autumn or the end of winter. Cannot have too much sun or too much drainage; best in poorer soils. Evergreen, height 75cm (30in), Z6 H4.

Sophora *Leguminosae/Papilionaceae*

The best-known of this evergreen and deciduous genus are the New Zealand shrubs which are worth trying for their foliage and rather exotic flowering displays. They are certainly easier in milder districts and spots where the wood can be well ripened. Plant young and do not disturb roots. Likes sun and healthy, well-drained soil.

S. davidii (syn. S. *viciifolia*)

Deciduous and smaller than the other species, this spreads wider than it is high, with plenty of branches very decently clothed with pinnate leaves up to 8cm (3in) long and having up to 10 pairs of oval leaflets less than 1cm (½in) long, grey-green above and silken below. A pleasing foliar arrangement is established before the late spring to early summer show of freely produced blossom. This consists of terminal racemes, up to 8cm (3in) long, of pea flowers in shades of white to lavender-blue with darker calyces. Deciduous, height 2.5m (8ft), Z5 H4.

S. microphylla

This spreading bush or small tree has a rigid parade-ground stance. The pinnate leaves, 15cm (6in) long, are composed of many dark, oval. small leaflets – perhaps as many as 40 pairs. Spring brings lots of hanging, 5cm (2in) long racemes of deep golden flowers. They are pea-like but with the petals projecting forwards. Evergreen, height 8m (25ft), Z9 H4.

S. tetraptera

Kowhai is a spreading shrub or small tree with branches tending to arch down with age. The dark green leaves have bronzy silk on both surfaces, more below, and are 18cm (7in) long and composed of 10-20 oval leaflets. Hanging bunches of 5-10 golden flowers appear in late spring, not pea-like this time, but with petals all forward to make neat bells. Evergreen, height 5m (15ft), Z9 H3-4.

Styrax *Styracaceae*

This genus contains both deciduous and evergreen shrubs and small trees. Here are a couple of pleasing characters, but not for those with limy soils. Equally happy in sun or semi-shade; enjoys moist soil, neutral or acid.

S. officinalis

A spreading shrub or little tree, styrax has broadly and bluntly ovate leaves, 5-10cm (2-4in) long, in dark green, but paler with white hair below. The foliage is completely in place before the early summer blossom opens. This is a plentiful series of pendent clusters towards the ends of the growing tips, 3-8 flowers to each cluster and each individually 2.5cm (1in) long, globose and with 6-8 pointed lobes. They are pure white and perfumed. Deciduous, height 5m (15ft), Z9 H3.

S. wilsonii

This twiggy, rounded bush has hairy stems and leaves 1-2.5cm (½-1in) long, indented at their tips. White bells, hanging singly or in groups of up to 4, are borne at intervals along the new growth in early summer. Deciduous, height 2.5m (8ft), Z9 H4.

Teucrium fruticans *Lamiaceae*

Known also as shrubby germander, this is an attractive plant of rather undisciplined growth and is somewhere betwixt an herbaceous plant and a proper shrub. The leaves are bluntly oval and measure from next to nothing up to 4cm (1½in) long. In freely drained soil, preferably light, and with a warm aspect, it will grow well until its late summer- and autumn-flowering. Flowering is a matter of terminal, loose racemes, each leaf apportioned a little pale blue flower, but as there are plenty of small leaves and a plethora of upward-reaching stems, this means a long succession of many flowers. Leaf colour is grey-green above and woolly white below; the stems are very white with close wool. When flowering has finally

Viburnum x bodnantense 'Dawn'

A series of hybrids between the somewhat tender but impressive *V. grandiflorum* and the very hardy *V. farreri*, raised at the North Wales garden Bodnant, were christened *bodnantense*. All clones in commerce are worthwhile plants. Being winter-flowering and very hardy, they are especially valuable. 'Dawn' was the first to capture the interest of gardeners and is the most widespread. It starts to flower as the leaves begin to drop and is then rarely out of bloom through the winter. Perfumed flowers are offered as tight posies all over the bush. The flowers are rich pink in bud and when open have their basic white suffused with this pink. Other cultivars include 'Deben', a rather more gaunt, upright shrub with pale pink flowers, and 'Charles Lamont', which is a good shrub with whiter blossom. Deciduous, height 3m (10ft), Z6 H4.

* Long season of winter blossom
* Strong upright and spreading habit
* Rich green foliage, bronzed in youth
* Unfussy about soil
* Happy in the open or by a wall
* Hardy
* Propagates easily from layers

finished, the plant's rather lax habit can be gently tidied with secateurs or shears. Evergreen, height 1m (3ft), Z6 H3.

Tricuspidaria dependens, see *Crinodendron patagua*.

Viburnum *Caprifoliaceae*

A good-natured, comfortable, deciduous and evergreen genus with lots of good things for the garden in most seasons and positions. The evergreen *V. tinus* was a favourite Victorian plant and is still one of the most useful viburnums for windproof screens or hedges; and it is in bloom from autumn until spring. The evergreen hybrid *V. × burkwoodii* has a series of cultivars, such as 'Anne Russell' and 'Park Farm Hybrid', with fragrant flowers, and there are good deciduous choices, including *V. × carlcephalum* and *V. juddii* with pink-budded, white blossom. The various forms of the deciduous *V. carlesii* are all good – particularly 'Aurora' – all have properly perfumed, wide posies of spring flowers. While these can be grown near walls they certainly do not need them as they are excellent in the open. However, the species listed below are some that benefit from the extra warmth of a wall. Will grow in most normal conditions from rather dry to moist.

V. × bodnantense 'Dawn', see box.

V. grandiflorum

This is a splendid, stout-stemmed, healthy-looking, erect plant producing wide oval leaves, up to 10cm (4in) long, with impressed veins. From late autumn through winter it bears many tight posies of fragrant, white flowers blushing pink. Deciduous, height 2m (6ft), Z6 H3-4.

Vitex agnus-castus.

Viburnum plicatum 'Lanarth'.

V. macrocephalum

Commonly called the snowball bush, this is a rounded shrub that is likely to be evergreen near a wall and in mild winters. It has rich green, ovate, pointed leaves, up to 10cm (4in) long, and is one of the more extrovert of the genus with its massive, rounded heads of sterile flowers, aping those of hydrangeas, from late spring into early summer. The flowerheads are greenish or ivory when developing but milk-white when mature, 'snowballs' up to 15cm (6in) across. Semi-evergreen, height 5m (15ft), Z6 H4.

V. odoratissimum

A strong plant with tough, oval leaves, 8-20cm (3-8in) long, this species is later flowering than many. It produces lots of 8-16cm (3-6in) wide clusters of very fragrant, little, white flowers in late spring and early summer. Egg-shaped fruits follow. They are 1cm (½in) long and turn from green to red, ending black. With the autumn and winter, much of the foliage can take on a definite red or copper sheen. Needs a sunny aspect in all but the mildest areas. Evergreen, height 5m (15ft), Z6 H4.

V. plicatum 'Lanarth'

Bright green, embossed leaves, up to 10cm (4in) long, and rather layered, horizontal branching like its relative 'Mariesii' are characteristics of this plant. ('Mariesii' has the more pronounced layering.) In late spring it produces wide, flat bunches of creamy-white flowers, ringed with large, sterile ones that are up to an impressive 5cm (2in) wide. **'Pink Beauty'** is similar but white flowers age to pink. Perfectly hardy. Deciduous, height 3m (10ft), Z5-6 H4.

V. rhytidophyllum

This species is hardy but can be impressive close to a wall where it will make a formidable, rounded, upright shrub bearing large, dark, oval leaves with impressed veining and up to 20cm (8in) long. I eventually got rid of my first plant as it seemed to me that the leaves hung from the plant with all the grace of so many wet socks. A second attempt was more successful with a more pleasing, dark green, lively appearance. There seem to be various clones in commerce so it is as well to be careful which you get. The late spring and early summer flowerheads are wide, flattish, some 10-20cm (4-8in) across and a matt pinky-red in bud and opening creamy. After a warm summer they can be followed by autumn fruit – bunches of shining red and surprisingly gay berries on this respectable but rather staid bush; later the red gives way to black. Evergreen, height 5m (15ft), Z6 H4.

Vitex agnus-castus *Verbenaceae*

This is an airy, spreading shrub with splendid foliage of palmate leaves formed of 5 or 7 clean-cut, slimline, pointed, lance-shaped leaflets up to 10cm (4in) long and a good rich colour. The leaves and stems are aromatic when bruised. Worth finding space for the foliage alone, this shrub also has scented blossom arranged as dense whorls of tiny flowers in racemes, 7.5-15cm (3-6in) long and pointing upwards at the ends of current growth for weeks in autumn. The colour may be from lilac to blue. **var.** *latifolia* is stronger and larger in all its parts. Deciduous, height 3-8m (10-25ft), Z7 H4.

Wattakaka sinensis, see *Dregea sinensis*, p.204.

Xanthoceras sorbifolium *Sapindaceae*

An unusual, upright shrub for training on a wall or growing without support in a warm, sheltered spot. It has attractive pinnate foliage up to 30cm (12in) long and made up of 13 to 17 pairs of narrow, elliptic leaflets in polished bright green. The new foliage appears late in spring and at the same time come the upright, columnar panicles of flowers. These are up to 20cm (8in) long and composed of many wide-open, 5-petalled flowers with lime-green centres ageing tawny. Deciduous, height 4m (12ft), Z5 H3-4.

Xanthoceras sorbifolium.

BASE OF WALL PLANTS

While much space by the walls and fences may be taken up with shrubs and climbers, there will be places where a series of herbaceous and bulbous plants can be grown. And these can be chosen from among those that like a wall or fenced site better than the open. The following is a selection of plants that are worth growing. They belong to sector one as described on pp.112-119.

A-Z Guide to
Base of Wall Plants

Agapanthus *Alliaceae*

These plants form bold clumps of arching, strap-shaped, bright green leaves and send up leafless stems with rounded heads of many trumpet- or bell-shaped flowers, perhaps over a hundred in a 22cm (9in) wide head. There are evergreen kinds, but the most popular ones, both species and hybrids, die down for the winter months. They all enjoy a moist but open-structured soil in a good state of fertility. Here they will bloom more freely after they have settled down; these plants are not happy with disturbance. They are splendid in large containers as well as in a sunny spot in the garden. While all are attractive, it pays to pick named cultivars because there are some lesser forms among those often marketed as Headbourne Hybrids.

A. campanulatus

This is a strong species making clumps of narrow foliage that is less bright green than some and 15-45cm (6-18in) long. It has bell-shaped flowers that can be dark blue, mid-sky-blue or sometimes white (var. *albidus*). Flower stem height varies according to the clone, how long it has been established, and the growing conditions. A good hardy species, but will be better for some winter protection (extra thick mulch of compost, shredded bark or bracken) in very cold districts. Herbaceous, height 60-120cm (24-48in) in flower, Z7 H4.

AGAPANTHUS HYBRIDS

'Bressingham White' has good heads of white bells held on stems up to 1m (3ft) high. Individual flowers are trumpet-shaped and point outwards and down to make a rounded ensemble. Late summer into autumn. 'Lilliput' is one of the dwarfer cultivars, the stems only reaching around 75cm (15in) but carrying good heads of deep blue bells from mid- until late summer. 'Loch Hope' is a favourite, proven kind of extra vigour and stature. It will stand 1-1.5m (3-5ft) high towards the end of the summer and into the autumn when it displays its large heads of trumpet-shaped, dark blue flowers.
'Snowy Owl' has very many flowers in graceful heads of rather narrow-petalled bells. The stems reach 1.2m (4ft) high by late summer.

Aloysia triphylla
(syn. *Lippia citriodora*) *Verbenaceae*

Lemon verbena is not absolutely hardy, and in most areas is best planted in a safe, warm spot by the base of a wall where it will thrive; should it be damaged by severe weather it can be cut back to sprout afresh. It makes an erect shrub with whorls of rough, narrowly elliptic leaves that readily emit the lemon scent when bruised. Used in cooking and pot-pourri. The tiny, pale lilac flowers in late summer are of no real account. Deciduous, height 3m (10ft), Z8 H3.

Amaryllis belladonna
Amaryllidaceae

This is the true amaryllis (unlike the large-flowered indoor hippeastrums, which are commonly called amaryllis) and the only species in the genus. It is

BREEDING COUNTS

Gardens are full of gift-horses that need looking in the mouth. It is often the quickest, most invasive of plants that are passed around most freely. Do you really need another plant that you will be throwing away by the barrow load in a short while? An outstanding cultivar will take just as much room and work as an indifferent one. Choose those that please you most; do not put up with second or third best.

Amaryllis belladonna.

Far right:
Crinum × powellii.

hardy in mild ares, such as southern England, given the warmth of a nearby wall. Large bulbs are best planted with a covering of up to 10cm (4in) soil, in a sunny well-drained spot. The arching, strap-shaped leaves of glossy rich green appear, after flowering, as winter approaches or early in the year and are best given some frost protection, perhaps merely by the shelter of nearby plants. Foliage usually dies away around midsummer, after which, in autumn, dark maroon stems rise rapidly from the bare ground and each open 1-6 large, funnel-shaped, 6-petalled blooms, each 6-10cm (2½-4in) long. The usual bright candy-floss pink colour shades down to a white base. There are variously coloured clones: **'Johannesburg'** is pale pink. **'Kimberley'** is very much darker with a white throat. **'Hathor'** is pink in bud but white when open. **Galaxy Hybrids** are brightly coloured, some noticeably deeper veined towards the throats. Bulbs increase steadily if left alone; a group can be a spell-binding sight. Herbaceous, height 40-60cm (16-24in), Z8-9 H4.

Coronilla valentina *subsp.* glauca.

Anthemis tinctoria Asteraceae

The golden marguerite dies back to basal growth for the winter. It has attractive, intricately divided, fresh green, ferny, aromatic foliage and tall stems carrying bright daisy flowers with prominent golden central discs in summer. There are many cultivars suitable for sunny spots to fill in areas between shrubs or in mixed borders. The colour range is from cream to old gold. One of the best is **'E. C. Buxton'** which stands about 45-60cm (18-24in) high with a dense cover of lemon-yellow daisies, 4-5cm (1½-2in) wide. Cut back in the middle of autumn to allow time for new basal growth to be made before the winter; doing this will help this otherwise short-lived perennial to see another year. Herbaceous, height 50cm-90cm (20-36in), Z7 H4.

Coronilla valentina subsp. *glauca*
Papilionaceae

A dense little shrub with pinnate, blue-green leaves of up to 7 leaflets. It produces light bunches of bright yellow pea flowers in early spring and again at the end of the summer. Evergreen, height 75cm (30in), Z9 H2-3.

Crinum × *powellii* Amaryllidaceae

The massive crinum bulbs should be planted with their necks just at soil level in a well-drained spot in a sunny position. They produce huge arching leaves which can be 1.2-1.5m (4-5ft) long. From later summer well into the autumn, stout spikes carry impressive umbels of up to 12 wide trumpet blooms in fluorescent pink. There are paler-flowered clones and pure whites gathered under the 'Album' standard. This bulb needs planting where the rather copious

amount of foliage is an asset rather than an excessive nuisance, and where the bulbs can be left alone for a decade or so – they bloom more freely with little disturbance. Herbaceous, height 1-1.5m (3-5ft), Z7-8 H4.

Diascia Scophulariaceae

Diascias are useful spreading plants with small, dark leaves and a long succession of flowers in spikes from the beginning of summer often until well into the autumn. Sun and humus-enriched soil that does not become parched.

D. rigescens

A trailing plant, reaching at least 30cm (12in) wide, with wiry erect stems carrying the flowers well clear of the heart-shaped leaves. Blooms through summer into autumn with tightly packed, neatly pointed spikes of rich pink flowers. Semi-evergreen, height 15-30cm (6-12in), Z8 H3-4.

DIASCIA HYBRIDS

The newer hybrids are excellent and come in a range of pinks and pastel shades, they should certainly be tried. **'Blackthorn Apricot'** and **'Ruby Field'** are two well established kinds. **'Coral Belle'** and **'Appleby Apricot'** are almost as widely grown. The pink **'Appleby Appleblossom'** and **'Lilac Mist'** are excellent but each season sees more cultivars of these useful, adaptable plants being introduced.

Dicentra scandens Fumariaceae

This relative of the Dutchman's breeches, *D. spectabilis*, is perhaps the most unusual member of the genus. It is a climbing perennial with slender stems growing up any support, natural or artificial, to create a cover of deeply cut, bright green leaves that look almost ferny. Tight clusters of hanging flowers are held forward on arching stems well clear of the foliage. The individual blooms, 2-2.5cm (¾-1in) long, are tubular and swell at the mouth rather like a snapdragon bud. The usual colour is a creamy-yellow, but they can be white and tipped with purple, pink or orange. It is a summer flower and well worth trying up a wall or allowing to grow over a strong shrub. Best in sun or light shade, in moist rather than dry soil. Herbaceous, height 1m (3ft), Z8 H4.

Dictamnus albus Rutaceae

This perennial, often called burning bush, has a woody base and pinnate leaves of some 3-6 pairs of clean-cut leaflets. White flowers have 5 petals that are arranged as if there were originally 6 and the bot-

tom one had been pulled out. Stigmas and stamens poke out. The narrow, pointed spikes of flowers are 25-30cm (10-12in) long and appear in early summer. **var. purpureus** has flowers suffused pinky-mauve. In warm, calm weather the plant exudes oil that vaporizes and can be ignited to make the bush burn. Semi-evergreen, height 40-80cm (16-32in), Z7 H4.

Erythrina crista-galli Papilionaceae

This species is usually known as the common coral tree and is armed with a dangerous number of sharp spines. It makes a fine specimen shrub or tree in warm areas but is reduced to an herbaceous perennial with a woody base in cool localities. It is, however, worth growing whatever its status and produces very clean-cut oval or triangular leaflets in threes, each 7-10cm (3-4in) long. The blossom is very showy. It consists of narrow, terminal racemes of deep vermilion pea flowers from summer into autumn. Find a spot that has fertile, open-structured, moist soil in full sun and as warm as can be, and then enjoy a touch of the exotic. Plants can be heavily mulched for the winter for their better protection, and if they can be kept rather dry during this period it will help their general well-being. Herbaceous, height 5m (15ft), Z9 H2.

Eucomis Hyacinthaceae

This is a genus of unusual herbaceous bulbs that are hardier than is normally thought, provided that they are given a warm, freely draining site.

Right: Eucomis bicolor

The burning bush, Dictamnus albus, is attractive without its pyrotechnical abilities exploited. Once planted it is best left undisturbed. Here it is partnered by Penstemon glaber.

E. bicolor

Also known as pineapple flower, this has wavy-margined, quite broad, strap-shaped, somewhat fleshy leaves, 30-45cm (12-18in) long. Stout, erect green flower stems are heavily flecked or scrolled with maroon. The 'pineapple' is formed by the 30-60cm (12-24in) column of maroon-edged, limy-green flowers which is topped by leafy bracts. It flowers in late summer and early autumn. Herbaceous, height 30-60cm (12-24in), Z8 H4.

E. comosa (syn. E. punctata)

Like *E. bicolor* but larger, this plant has leaves up to 75cm (30in) long with their undersides spotted maroon-purple. Narrow, 30-60cm (12-24in) columns of creamy-white flowers, with margins pencilled maroon, are topped with a knot of green leafy bracts. Herbaceous, height 60-75 cm (24-30in), Z8 H4.

Fritillaria pallidiflora Liliaceae

There is a temptation to list several of the fascinating fritillaries, but for a near wall site this is a good choice as it can be planted and then, hopefully, will get better and better for the next decade or two. It grows strongly through the spring, producing lance-shaped, pale grey-green leaves up to 15cm (6in) long. In late spring it opens a number of square-shouldered, nodding, pale creamy flowers, 4cm (2½in) long or a little more. A very pleasing cool-coloured ensemble. Once established each stem will carry 6 large flowers, sometimes more. Plants die down a few weeks after blooming. Ensure good drainage and after planting the bulbs 7cm (3in) deep in gritty soil, leave alone until they are very crowded. Herbaceous, height 30-40cm (12-16in), Z7 H4.

Gladiolus Iridaceae

The large hybrids have tended to overshadow the species and smaller hybrids. This is a shame as these smaller-scale gladioli are much easier to work into garden schemes; the large cultivars tend to be top-heavy and somewhat awkward in borders. G. *communis* subsp. *byzantinus* has quite often been found naturalized in Britain.

G. communis subsp. byzantinus

This is a freely increasing, small-cormed form with erect, narrow leaves and late spring and early summer spikes of flowers, as many as 20 to a stem. These are funnel shaped, 5cm (2in) wide, and rich crimson-magenta. There are usually paler marks on the lip petals. Completely hardy in most areas. Herbaceous, height 1m (3ft), Z7 H4.

G. × colvillei (syn. G. nanus)

These small-flowered hybrids are not as hardy as G. *communis* subsp. *byzantinus* but are much hardier than

The hardy gladiolus, G. communis *subsp.* byzantinus.

the large-flowered hybrids. A few may be tried in a particularly warm, sunny spot near a wall. They have narrow, grassy leaves and dainty flowers in early summer spikes. **'The Bride'** has neat, pointed, pure white flowers with greenish throats. **'Charm'** has triangular, open flowers of rich, pink-mauve with white throats. **'Comet'** is deep cerise. **'Elvira'**, one of a number of bicolours, is pale pink with deep red-painted badges towards the centre of each petal base. Herbaceous, height 30-50cm (12-20in), Z8-9 H3-4.

G. tristis

This species has very slender, grassy leaves and wiry stems with up to 20 wide-open flowers, up to 6cm (2½in) wide, arching away from the stem. They are creamy-white and can be suffused with some green towards the centre, and may have mauve or purplish spotting. Best in a frost-free, warm, sheltered spot. Herbaceous, height 45cm-120cm (18in-48in), Z8-9 H3-4.

Helianthemum hybrids *Cistaceae*

This genus, also known as rock rose and sun rose, consists of some very hardy plants: there are wild specimens growing on the Malvern Hills, which we can see out of our windows. The garden plants are low-growing, sprawling sub-shrubs with thin wiry branches, stocky, grey-green, narrow leaves and wide, single-rose-type flowers. They can spread 1m (3ft) wide. It is best to choose from among the variously coloured hybrid cultivars which are available in white, yellow, orange, pink and red. They are useful to drape over small walls or for the front of sunny borders. Cut back after flowering to try to maintain a tidy appearance; cuttings will root easily and provide fresh stock to replace worn-out oldies. A few of the many cultivars are listed below. Evergreen or semi-evergreen, height 20-30cm (8-12in), Z5 H4.

'Ben More', vibrant orange-red.

'Fire Dragon', scarlet.

'Golden Queen', another free-flowering kind.

'Raspberry Ripple', white with a crimson centre flaring outwards.

'Wisley Pink', pale pink.

'Wisley Primrose', vigorous with soft yellow blossom.

'Wisley White', white with creamy centre and usual golden boss of stamens.

Hordeum jubatum *Gramineae*

The squirrel tail grass is just one of a number of popular grasses that should be considered as fillers, or

Helianthemum *'Wisley Primrose'*.

indeed as character plants in sunny borders. They withstand drought better than many. This one may behave as an annual or perennial, it hardly matters as the plentiful supply of viable seed will ensure a permanent presence. It has erect and arching, narrow, light green leaves and from early until quite late summer, nodding heads, up to 15cm (6in) long, of long-bristled spikelets starting green but becoming flushed red or mauve before taking on the fawn shades of maturity. Herbaceous, height 40-50cm (16-20in), Z7 H4.

ORNAMENTAL GRASSES AND SEDGES

More and more kinds of grasses and sedges are appearing in nurseries and garden centres as gardeners realise their usefulness, their ease of cultivation and the many ways in which they can be grown either as collections or to give borders more form and variety. If used freely they can give a sense of unity, a cohesiveness to any otherwise very mixed border. In continental Europe they are being used very extensively as they can withstand long periods of drought and cold; even their dead foliage can remain looking impressive through the winter. They are useful plants for the more difficult climates of parts of the USA and Australia.

Most grasses and sedges grow very easily; be careful of the very rampant ones. This includes the well-known gardeners' garters, *Phalaris arundinacea* 'Picta', but I would not be without this very bright variegated couch grass as it is really not that difficult to curb, even the most exuberant of kinds. Most will grow in a wide variety of soils and conditions, and although they usually prefer sunny sites, some do well in shade and most of the sun-lovers will manage well enough in partial shade. Wide range of sizes and forms.

Briza media has bright green spiky leaves, pale taller flowerheads 'quaking' and rustling in the slightest breeze. Height 45cm (18in).

Carex buchananii has somewhat arching, narrow, copper-coloured leaves turning more rusty with winter. Various clones, tallest about 60cm (2ft), but some only a quarter this.

Cortaderia selloana Pampas grass is best on its own. 'Sunningdale Silver' is a good clone with narrow, sharp-edged, arching leaves and tall persistent plumes. Height 1.5-2.1m (5-7ft).

Festuca glauca 'Eliza Blue' is one of several clones of dwarf porcupine grass with a mass of stiff, wiry leaves in steel blue. Height 22cm (9in).

Hakonechloa macra 'Aurea Variegata' is a dwarf arching grass with rich gold-variegated leaves. Height 22cm (9in).

Imperata cylindric 'Rubra' ('Red Baron'). Japanese blood grass has dark red, rusty-mahogany leaves getting richer through the summer months. They are very upright and sword-like. Best in moist soil and partial shade. Height 40cm (15in).

Millium effusum 'Aureum' is known as Bowles golden grass. It has lime-yellow, relatively broad, arching leaves. Good in sun, very good in partial shade. Height 40cm (15in).

Miscanthus sinensis 'Zebrinus' is an impressive, tall waterside plant with a mass of erect, narrow foliage unusually banded horizontally in yellow every hand's width. Can be grown in somewhat moist, ordinary soils.

Stipa splendens produces arching narrow rich green leaves and summer plumes 1-2m (3-4ft) high. Any soil.

Iris unguicularis (syn. *I. stylosa*)
Iridaceae

Algerian iris is invaluable for its generous succession of beautiful flowers in the depths of winter. The narrow, tough, grassy leaves can be 60cm (24in) long or more but arch over to form an evergreen mass. Old clumps can become 90cm (3ft) wide. Planted at the base of a wall in a sunny spot, the narrow, hidden, foreshortened rhizomes are encouraged to throw up lots of scented flowers. The flowers consist of wide spreading petals and are about 7cm (3in) across. They are deep lavender-blue with darker veining and a yellow central flash on the three falls (the outward turned petals). There are other shades. **'Mary** **Barnard'** has deeper coloured, violet-blue flowers. **'Walter Butt'** has even wider-petalled flowers of pale lavender-blue. There are white forms, some much better than others, in form and purity of colour.

Newly planted specimens may need a little attention to make sure they do not completely dry out before the roots have got properly settled in; thereafter they will look after themselves. Old dead foliage is best removed. As it is tough, it is best cut away. Some gardeners cut the leaves back by half in the summer to allow the narrow, creeping rhizomes to get better ripened and so encourage flowering. This may be needed in less sunny areas but I do not find the need to do this and we certainly get lots of blossom from around Christmas for several weeks. Evergreen, 40cm (16in), Z5 H4.

Lilium candidum *Liliaceae*

The Madonna lily is an unusual lily in two respects: its bulbs should be planted shallowly, that is with the noses just under the soil surface, the exact opposite advice given for other lilies, which should normally have at least 10cm (4in) over their noses; and after flowering it produces a rosette of leaves that overwinter and make the plant evergreen, unlike all its kin. All lilies enjoy sun around their tops: this one is happy to feel it near its toes, again unlike almost all other lilies. The flowering stems can have up to 20 outward-facing, sparkling white, perfumed flowers in midsummer, though a more modest 6 may be more likely. If plants seem to be failing this is likely to be due to viruses that sap their energy, the foliage becomes marked with pale stripes and there can be

Iris unguicularis.

some distortion of both foliage and flowers. Flower numbers can dwindle, or the stems can become blind. Any bulbs with virus should be destroyed – there is no cure in the gardener's hands. Evergreen, height 1-1.5m (3-5ft), Z8 H4.

Nerine bowdenii Amaryllidaceae

Nerine bowdenii is the only hardy nerine, though N. *sarniensis* and N. *undulata* might be tried in mild areas with little frost. It is a real stand-by in the autumn when its bright pink heads bring a freshness and excitement to gardens that can be beginning to look a touch tired.

The long bulbs are planted in early spring with their noses level with or just under the soil surface (some of our clumps have bulbs exposed to all weathers). A sunny spot below a warm wall is ideal but they can be grown in the open in well-drained soils, especially if they slope towards the sun. The bulbs dislike being disturbed so newly planted ones may take a little while to get into top gear and produce the masses of bloom that make them so exciting. Once planted they can be left for decades and only taken up when the bulbs have become hopelessly overcrowded.

Nerine bowdenii.

Sometimes leaves remain on the plants around the year, but usually they die away in the second half of the summer and the flowering spikes appear from the bare ground in the autumn. Usually there are 6-7 flowers to a spike but occasionally 10-12. Individual flowers, 7cm (3in) wide, are composed of 6 strap-shaped petals, with waved margins, that recurve to describe a half circle. The usual colour is bright shining pink, but there are a number of somewhat darker clones, such as **'Mark Fenwick'**, and some whites called **'Alba'** but usually still with a touch of pink. The darker the flower, the darker the stem. Herbaceous, height 50-70cm (20-28in), Z8 H4.

Narcissus tazetta Amaryllidaceae

The multi-headed N. *tazetta* forms come from around the Mediterranean and some may find the open garden too cool in colder climates such as Britain; the tenderer forms can be killed by hard winters, but nestling close to a wall, clumps can get to feel at home and provide early spring flowers for decades. If you try the golden and tangerine **'Soleil d'Or'** you will have a very much better display from bulbs that are accredited as virus-free – the florets are much larger and look very much more jolly. **'Avalanche'** is an outstanding white with neat cups of pale lemon, perhaps more than 12 on a stem. Herbaceous, height 38-45cm (15-18in), Z8 H3-4.

Phygelius Scrophulariaceae

A genus of two species, P. *aequalis* and P. *capensis*, both somewhat variable, and a series of intermediate hybrids. They are sub-shrubs that in very cold areas are best treated as herbaceous perennials as they can be cut back to the ground by repeated frosts. However, near a wall in warm areas, they not only grow upwards, at times to 2m (6ft), but when happy will sucker and spread as much or wider. They are all very well worth growing as they flower freely over a very long time through the summer into autumn, a longevity that can be increased by some judicious deadheading.

P. aequalis
This species has dark green, ovate leaves, up to 10cm (4in) long, on leaning stems that carry 25-30cm (10-12in) panicles of hanging, narrow-tubed flowers in a dusky rose-pink, each bloom being up to 6cm (2½in) long and only slightly opened at the mouth with its 5 pointed lobes. The flowers are usually painted dark crimson red above the inner throat of gold, and the lobes may be suffused with gold. **'Yellow Trumpet'**

differs from the type in having very much paler foliage and flowers of pale cream, not really yellow. Evergreen, height 1m (3ft), Z8-9 H3-4.

P. capensis

Cape figwort is the better known of the two species. It has rich green leaves, up to 8cm (3in) long, of pointed, oval form, and distinguishes itself in summer with lots of spikes of hanging flowers. The panicles often measure at least 60cm (24in) and are held clear of the leaves, along dark maroon stems. The dominant colour is a glowing rich orange, but the 5 flower lobes can be darker and the inner throats yellow. **'Coccineus'** is a stronger scarlet. Evergreen, height 1-1.5m (2-5ft), Z8-9 H3-4.

P. × rectus (P. aequalis × P. capensis)

This hybrid has produced a range of intermediate forms between the two above species, all of which are worth growing. **'African Queen'** has long, erect panicles of vertically hanging flowers in pinky-red with orange lobes and golden mouths. Up to 1m (3ft). **'Devil's Tears'** bears rich pink-red flowers that tend to curve back towards the stem, the lobes are more vermilion-orange and throats are gold. **'Moonraker'** produces erect, long panicles of pale cream flowers held close to the stem. **'Salmon Leap'** grows extraordinarily long flower spikes, up to 50cm (20in) long, with orange flowers that have lobes that are more recurved than most cultivars. To 1.2m (4ft).

Phygelius *'Salmon Leap'*.

'Winchester Fanfare' is popular with flowers of a red that appears to shine out of a pink bloom. Evergreen, height 1-1.5m (3-5ft), Z8-9 H3-4.

Sternbergia lutea *Amaryllidaceae*

In autumn the bulbs of this species produce a good number of rounded, crocus-like flowers accompanied by quite fleshy, dark green, strap-shaped leaves that might pass muster as those of a small daffodil. Plant in full sun in well-drained soil where they can be left undisturbed until they have formed very overcrowded clumps, when they can be lifted and replanted immediately with more room. **S. candida** is similar, rarer in cultivation and has snow-white blooms. Herbaceous, height 15cm (6in), Z7-8 H3-4.

Triteleia *Alliaceae*

The species of this cormous genus grow well in sunny, warm spots in well-drained soils. In very cold localities they are safer under glass. Upright, very narrow leaves tend to have wasted away by the time the leafless stems begin to open their upward-staring clusters of 6-petalled, starry flowers. Corms increase very quickly when happy and soon form useful clumps.

T. hyacintha (syn. Brodiaea lactea)

This species has very thin, erect leaves 10-45cm (4-18in) long. Crowded, shallowly domed clusters of up to 24 white or occasionally pale blue flowers, with green centres, open in late spring or early summer. Individual flowers are 1.5cm (½in) wide. Flowering time can be varied by planting corms late, that is, in spring; established clumps will bloom much earlier. Herbaceous, height 60cm (24in), Z8-9 H3-4.

T. laxa (syn. Brodiaea laxa)

This is another freely increasing corm with very slender, upright leaves, 20-45cm (8-18in) long, and early summer umbels of as many as 24 flowers. The flowers vary from pale to deep purple-blue and normally have a darker central line up each petal. They are often shaded to paler centres. The better clones in commerce have flowers 5cm (2in) long and 3-4cm (1-1½in) wide. **'Koningin Fabiola'** ('Queen Fabiola') is a particularly deep purple-blue. Herbaceous, height 60cm (24in), Z8-9 H3-4.

Zauchneria californica

(syn. *Epilobium californicum*) *Onagraceae*

This woody-based plant has a rhizomatous rootstock and small, narrowly lance-shaped, green leaves, greyed with hairs. It bears racemes of outward- or downward-pointing, tubular flowers, 2.5-4cm

Right: Sternbergia lutea.

(1-1½in) long, that widen a little at the lobed mouth from which the stamens and stigma protrude. The colour is a fiery orange-red. Grow in a sunny, sheltered spot where it will delight with its brilliant colour through the second half of the summer and into the autumn – a really long season of blossom. The plant usually grown is **subsp. *cana***, which has particularly silky leaves and very rich orange-red flowers, and is about twice as tall as the species, around 60cm (20in). **'Dublin'** is a brilliant, glossy-flowered cultivar growing to 30cm (12in). Evergreen or semi-evergreen, height 30cm (12in), Z8 H3.

Zephyranthes candida *Amaryllidaceae*

The hardiest of some 70 species, this is often used in rock gardens. It has narrow, dark green leaves, 20-40cm (8-18in) long. A series of sparkling white, crocus-like, upright flowers open in the second half of summer into autumn. Provide it with well-drained soil in a sunny spot at the front of a border and it will do well. **Z. *grandiflora*** is similar but with rich rosy-pink flowers, and needs more warmth and shelter. **Z. *citrina*** is also more tender and has lemon-yellow flowers. Herbaceous, height 15cm (6in), Z7-8 H3-4.

Zauchneria californica *subsp.* mexicana.

ANNUALS

Annuals can do much to enliven the garden scene. The exciting growing miracles of our childhood – cornflowers, marigolds, love-in-the-mist, clarkia and nasturtiums – they deserve to be considered afresh for their generous colour, rapid growth and huge crop of seed. Annuals can be selected for their summer and autumn colour, for planting in places where the display of the more permanent members is in spring. They can also be used as stopgaps. There is a range of climbing ones that are interesting and beautiful – morning glories, sweet peas, black-eyed Susans and others. They can clamber over trellis and wires put up for more permanent climbers that are slower off the mark, and they can run up and over shrubs, fencing and screens, as well as sometimes falling down from terrace and other walls.

Of all the annuals, it is the nasturtiums I remember best from my childhood, and still enjoy: their big wrinkly seeds and curious foliage, circles on stems like the juggler's whirling plates on canes and tasting of mustard, and the sudden eruption of bright flowers to make a posy for mother. Then came the arrival, from nowhere, of fascinating armies of caterpillars to share the leaves. What an exciting world!

There is a shortage of absolutes in horticulture: 'annual' is not a completely clear-cut term. While a true annual is a plant that grows from seed, flowers and sets its own seed in a single growing season, there are many plants that survive several years in their native lands but in temperate climates will usually die after one year's cycle of growth, although they can sometimes manage two or even three years. This chapter includes the genuine annuals, and other plants that, in temperate climates, are best treated as annuals, such as some of the morning glories (*Ipomoea*).

The vast majority of annuals to be found in the serried ranks of temptingly illustrated seed packets in the garden centres are of very easy culture. They can either be raised under glass and grown on in modules ready for planting out, post-frosts, or the seed can be sown *in situ* to germinate and grow quickly as soil and air temperatures rise. Annuals are hell-bent on growing to flowering size and producing seed for the next generation. Almost all will want plenty of sun, and a well-worked, weed-free soil.

OVERFEEDING?

Distributing fertilizers around is only going to help if they are worked into the soil and there is water to provide the dissolved food to the roots. In their youth, shrubs and other plants may be worth encouraging to grow into strong, larger specimens; later many will flower much more freely if somewhat starved of feed – certainly kept shorter of nitrogenous feed. This will apply particularly to shrubs such as *Buddleja, Ceanothus, Cytisus, Lavandula, Rosmarinus,* and *Viburnums* such as *V. tinus.*

Annuals may benefit more from feeding supplements, but overall there is a tendency to overfeed rather than underfeed. Over generous feeding may produce an embarrassment of growth that will be using up precious space; better to have healthy slim-line shrubs when space is at a premium. Overfeeding may only mean extra work pruning!

Eccremocarpus scaber.

A-Z Guide to Annuals

Calceolaria integrifolia Fruticohybrida Group

Scrophulariaceae

In the wild one of the parents of this group, *C. integrifolia*, is a sub-shrubby plant, but in gardens the hybrid cultivars are grown as annuals. These are the calceolarias used widely in hanging baskets, containers and for bedding, and available as named and unnamed strains. They have mainly bright yellow, slipper flowers. Height 30cm (12in), Z8 H3.

Cobaea scandens, *Cobaeaceae*, see box.

Cucurbita *Cucurbitaceae*

This genus includes the annual gourds and pumpkins (*C. maxima*), and they are a varied lot. They are best grown from a packet of mixed seed sown under glass and planted out in sites where they can rampage and climb when frosts are over. Take care where you site them – we had branches broken off a winter-flowering cherry by some – grown up firm support, they can be very decorative and entertaining from summer until the frosts.

C. **maxima** includes the giant pumpkins: they are very large-leaved and have rounded fruit stalks, **C. moschata** covers the varied squashes with 5-lobed leaves and ribbed and channelled fruit stems, **C. pepo** is the vegetable marrow but also covers interesting types such as the custards, crook-necks and orange gourds. The forms of this last species have bristly leaves and stems, leaves with roughly 5 lobes and deeply corrugated fruit stems. (See also *Lagenaria siceraria*.) They will all be killed by frost. Normally reaching across the ground, they can climb by means of tendrils up suitable natural or artificial 'climbing frames'. Height 1m (3ft), Z6 H4.

Eccremocarpus scaber *Bignoniaceae*

Chilean glory flower is one of the fastest-growing plants and is useful for clothing pillars, pergolas, arches or just to grow over a strong shrub or tree. It has distinct, 4-sided, angled stems and pinnate foliage consisting of pointed leaflets with impressed veins; each leaf has a branched tendril. From the time it really gets going in late spring until the first frost, it produces a succession of long, tubular flowers, opened at the mouth, in many-flowered racemes. The usual

Cobaea scandens

Called the cup and saucer plant or cathedral bell, this is grown as an annual, but its roots can be kept over winter under glass or may survive outside in very mild areas or in particularly sheltered corners. It has richly coloured leaves, up to nearly 12cm (5in) long, in 4 leaflets, accompanied by branched tendrils with lots of little hooks. These help it to climb, but a little extra help with ties early on can be rewarding. In fertile soil, in warm spots, the plants can grow for considerable distances. The bold, bell-shaped flowers, 5cm (2in) long, sit on a pale, creamy-green 'saucer'. The young buds and opening flowers are the same creamy-green but mature to strong purple. There is a white form, f. *alba*, which opens white and becomes creamier with age. I have seen profusely flowered specimens of this growing up to 6m (18ft) high in the Midlands, obviously plants that had overwintered. Evergreen, height 4-5m (12-15ft), Z8 H3.

✳ Unusual flowers

✳ Grows easily and quickly

✳ Sun or shade

✳ In less severe climates will adopt a perennial lifestyle

✳ Grows up wall supports or through and over shrubs and small trees

✳ Mauve, purplish, cream or greenish-white flowers

colour is flaming orange-red but there are golden and crimson forms, as well as a range of hybrids in reds, oranges, pinks and yellows. It may survive overwinter in milder areas. Evergreen, height 3-5m (10-15ft), Z8 H3.

Helianthus annus *Asteraceae*

Annual sunflowers are fun plants that delight children and adults alike. The smaller the child the taller he/she will want the sunflower to grow. Adults may pretend indifference to height, but they are not afraid of showing delight in some of the interesting new strains now being offered. These are often dwarf enough to fit into any reasonable garden border and may be grown in the open or near a wall. Traditional, deep golden colours have been joined by a range from cream to orange and deep mahogany or chocolate shades. They are best sown under cover in late winter and grown singly in pots until they can be planted out when frosts no longer threaten. Seedheads can be saved for the birds. Height 1-5m (3-15ft), killed by frost.

Ipomoea *Convolvulaceae*

This genus consists of both deciduous and evergreen, annual and perennial plants, many of which are grown as annuals in temperate climates. The plants are raised from seed, one or two seeds to a pot, scarified and soaked overnight before sowing. Once the seedlings have germinated and have grown sufficiently to handle easily, repot into a bigger pot without disturbing the ball of soil and then provide the growing plant with a twig to grow up before being planted out, which should be done after they are thoroughly hardened off. They need a sunny position and will then clamber energetically up trellis, poles or shrubs. The soil should be in good heart and the roots kept reasonably moist. Seed is available in packets of mixed colours – whites, pale lavenders, mauves and pinks ranging to dark near reds and purples. All are annuals or very short-lived perennials, killed by frost.

I. coccinea (syn. *Quamoclit coccinea*)

The star morning glory is perennial but, being tender, is grown as an annual twiner. With long, pointed leaves in arrow or heart form, it produces a large crop of brilliant scarlet flowers in the second half of summer and into autumn. The narrow flower tubes are golden-throated and expand widely at the mouth. The flowers open wide in the sunshine but are rather fleeting – no great worry as plants produce such quantities. Evergreen, height 3m (10ft), killed by frost.

I. indica

A very vigorous, twining plant that should only be planted if there is plenty of room to spare. It has heart-shaped leaves and large, funnel-shaped flowers of rich purple or purple-blue from late summer into autumn. They are 6-8cm (2½-3½in) across and are very plentiful. It will not survive winter outside; in a conservatory an established plant will start blooming in late spring. Evergreen, height to 6m (20ft), killed by frost.

I. lobata (syn. *Quamoclit lobata*)

This annual is hairless. The rich green leaves are pointed ovals, characterized by opposite pairs of deep cuts, nearly to the midrib resulting in 3 bold pointed lobes. The flowers are much smaller, at 2cm (¾in) across, than most kinds and either strong scarlet or, less commonly, white; the scarlet ones mature to cream and then white. They are more distinctly 5-lobed than most species and come in bunches of 2-5. Height up to 2-6m (6-20ft), half hardy.

I. purpurea

This is the common morning glory, a short-lived perennial, grown as a half hardy annual. It is a rapid twister with stems that are both hairy and bristly. The leaves are heart-shaped or sketchily 3-lobed. From summer into autumn it has wide trumpets usually dark purple or purplish-blue, with white throats, but there is a range of colour forms including white, pink or mauve and sometimes white with stripes of colour radiating from the centre. Flowers measure up to 6cm (2½in) across. Height 2-5m (6-15ft), killed by frost.

I. tricolor, see also box.

An annual or short-lived perennial, this is probably the best-known species and is commonly thought of as *the* morning glory. It grows very rapidly and furnishes itself with plenty of heart-shaped, shining, light green leaves, up to 10cm (4in) long. Very many flowers, each about 8-9cm (3-3½in) across, open

Ipomoea lobata.

Ipomoea tricolor 'Heavenly Blue'

Probably the most popular *I. tricolor* form, the brilliant 'Heavenly Blue', which can be readily grown from seed sown early under glass and planted out after the frosts. It has large trumpet flowers of an extraordinarily fresh sky-blue.

✱ Almost unparalleled flower colour

✱ Rapid, easy growth

✱ Will climb up wall supports, trellis, screens, in and over shrubs, up poles and pergolas

✱ Blooms over a long period

✱ Not fussy about soil

annual climber in the wild is pleasing enough in its various colour shades, but it really gives no idea of the inherent possibilities that have resulted in today's races of magnificent flowers. Gardeners have been known to become fanatics about this flower, undertaking extensive digging and excavating to allow the interring of copious quantities of humus to ensure maximum growth and cutting away flower sprays as soon as they fade so that no energy is wasted in producing seeds. To achieve their ends these enthusiasts will allow plants to flower up to their tops and will then disengage them from their supports and lay them on the ground. The growing stem is then reattached to another support a metre or so away and the plant starts its climbing and flowering process all over again.

Most of us do not feel the need to go to such lengths but most would feel deprived without some of the perfume of the flowers, and the summery atmosphere they engender. One or two narrow pyramids of canes are sufficient to grow some mixed colours to enjoy and to pick. They can also be run up trellis where there seems a chance of them making headway among the established perennial climbers. Here they add colour and scent when earlier spring blossom has

through summer and into the beginning of autumn. Their usual colours are vivid sky-blues and purples, with white centres and honey-gold narrow tubes. Various coloured forms have been named: **'Flying Saucers'** has white flowers with lesser or greater amounts of lavender striping from the centre to the rim of the trumpets; **'Crimson Rambler'** is red with a white throat. Height 4m (12ft), killed by frost.

Lagenaria siceraria

(syn. *L. vulgaris*) *Cucurbitaceae*

Known as bottle gourd, this annual plant is very vigorous with stems capable of travelling several metres when the plants have been put into their quarters in early summer, after all fear of frost has passed. It clambers and climbs by supporting itself with tendrils and has bristly heart-shaped leaves. It needs space and, like its brethren, it enjoys moist soil full of humus. It is grown for the variously shaped and sized fruits that have long been used in the tropics as containers for liquids. Pale yellow and usually long with crocked necks, the fruit can range from a modest 7cm (2½in) long to a staggering 90cm (3ft) or even more. Height up to 3-4m (10-12ft), killed by frost.

Lathyrus odoratus

Leguminosae/Papilionaceae

Plants grown under this name are one of the triumphs of the breeders' art. The original sweet-scented

DEADHEADING

While this may be thought a tedious job, with many shrubs and herbaceous plants it will encourage them to produce fresh flowers. This certainly applies with sweet peas. Setting seed consumes energy supplies and makes flowering a redundant exercise. Clip off pieces down to a strong bud.

Pueraria lobata

Often called Japanese arrowroot or the kudzu vine, this is an astonishingly vigorous, twining climber growing from a tuber. Even as an annual it will make huge headway with magnificent, large, wide, rich green leaves formed of 3-lobed leaflets. It is a fine foliage plant and in autumn it has scented pea flowers in upright racemes 25cm (10in) long. The individual magenta or reddish-purple flowers are 2cm (¾in) long. These are followed by slender, hairy seedpods up to 8cm (3in) long. You need plenty of room to allow this rumbustious climber its head; it will grow on a wall of any aspect. In colder areas it will be grown as an annual. Deciduous, height 20m (70ft), Z8 H3-4.

✱ Outstanding bold leaves

✱ Rapid growth produces very large plants in milder areas

✱ Long flower racemes. Scented

✱ Impressive wall plant, best in full or part sun

✱ Propagated easily from seed

Right: Lathyrus odoratus 'Beaujolais'.

Versatile sweet peas being acrobatic on a wigwam of sticks arranged in a pot. They are accompanied by the rose 'Frensham' and a smoke bush, Cotinus coggygria, one of the Rubrifolius Group.

faded. The more that are picked, the greater the number of flowers that are produced. Do not let any set seed unless you are saving seed for another year. However, this may be false economy, as the results can be poorer than buying good strains from a reliable source.

Basically there are three races of sweet peas, the familiar Spencer and Grandifloras strains, which are strong growing climbers, plus the dwarfs, some of which are without tendrils and more suited to containers. The Grandifloras, despite their name, are smaller than the Spencers; they have an old-fashioned

look and the genuine strong sweet pea scent. The Spencers are showier and are more commonly grown. They are usually scented but not always as strongly as one would wish. All colours seem to be represented, 'Beaujolais' with fragrant, deep wine-coloured flowers being one of the darkest.

Pharbitis, see *Ipomoea*.
Pueraria lobata (syn. *P. thunbergiana*), *Leguminosae/Papilionaceae*, see box.
Quamoclit, see *Ipomoea*.

Rhodochiton atrosanguineus
Scrophulariaceae

Usually grown as an annual in temperate zones, this species will scramble over the ground or up trellis or other plants, securing its slender branches by clasping leaf stalks. The foliage is pleasing being rich green,

MAKING ANNUAL NASTURTIUMS INTO PERENNIALS

The first frost will kill annual nasturtiums. However, if there are particular individuals that have a colour or combination of colours you would like to preserve, cuttings can be taken in late summer or in autumn and the small plants can be kept safe under glass away from frost over the winter. Cuttings are most successful if they are taken of short-jointed pieces with leaves as small as possible. If there are only big leaves on the cutting these can be cut down in size before being inserted in a gritty cutting compost. They will root readily and will be ready to plant out the following year when frosts are over.

Nasturtiums (Tropaeolum majus) making a dash for the heights up the wall behind a border of mixed herbaceous plants including dahlias and the sword-like leaves of phormiums.

broad, neatly toothed and heart-shaped with a terminal point, but it is grown for its curious and beautiful flowers. Borne on long, hanging stalks, these have 5-pointed calyces that sit elf-cap-like atop the long, tubular flower proper. Flower colour is a muted black or dark reddish-purple, the calyces are somewhat lighter and brighter, but the whole ensemble aims to charm rather than dazzle. It blooms from late spring until autumn. Deciduous, height 3m (10ft), Z8 H3-4.

Thunbergia alata *Acanthaceae*

In nature a perennial, twining climber, black-eyed Susan has become popular in gardens as an interesting annual for a sunny spot. The leaves are triangular or arrow-shaped and up to 8cm (3in) long. The flowers of bright gold are flat as discs, the 5 petals almost making a circle around the dark chocolate centre. This colouring is somewhat variable, the gold veering sometimes to tangerine and a small proportion of seedlings may be creamy-white. The distinctive dark centre can be missing in some. One of the most effective of annual climbers, this will quickly go up trellis and may even reach over rustic arches or pergolas. Ends with frosts. Evergreen, height to 1-2m (3-6ft), Z8-9 H3.

Tropaeolum *Tropaeolaceae*

Although there are nearly 100 species in this genus only a few are commonly grown. There are the very useful perennials that die back to fat rootstocks (see p.163), and, of the annuals, by far the best-known after the common nasturtium (*T. majus*), is the Canary creeper (*T. peregrinum*). *T. majus* types can be sown where they are to grow, but most of the other annuals or perennials that are treated as annuals are best started under glass and planted out when fear of frosts is over.

T. majus

Annual nasturtiums that have derived from this species are available in a range of flower shapes and plant sizes. There are the traditional long-spurred kinds or spurless ones, plain or bicoloured, double or single, with bushy dwarf habits, semi-trailing or full-blown rampaging spreaders and climbers. Colours range from pale creams through to deep golds and some pinky-salmon shades, and every orange, red and crimson. They bloom best on a poor diet. Dwarf strains may have as limited spread as 30cm (12in), while some climbers can reach several metres (yards). They will be killed by frost.

Thunbergia alata.

T. peregrinum (syn. *T. canariensis*)

As yellow as a canary, this species grows with extraordinary speed providing a cover of light green leaves, sometimes with a light greyish cast, with 5 bold lobes. From summer until the frosty death-knell the bright yellow flowers are scattered overall. They have curved spurs to the rear but their faces look almost orchid-like with 3 narrow petals pointing downwards and 2 large ones upwards, these being rather irregularly, but boldly, cut, perhaps to give 5 or so points. A frost-tender perennial normally grown as an annual. Height 2.5-4m (8-12ft), Z8-9 H3.

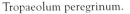

Tropaeolum peregrinum.

TENDER PLANTS

A tender plant is one that dies if subjected to frost. The difficulty arises in deciding just how much frost is needed to kill a particular plant. This may be measured by the number of degrees and the length of time that the plant is subjected to temperatures below 0°C (32°F). Even perfectly hardy plants can be damaged by the cold if they have just made new sappy growth when a severe late frost arrives.

Tender plants have a much better chance of a trouble-free life on or near walls or fences that face the sun, especially if they are open, and not over-shadowed by buildings or large trees. The patio with its stone or brick floor will reflect and store heat to make it an even more favoured spot. Built-up beds will be likely to have extra-free drainage and soils that warm up quickly in the spring and remain warmer than elsewhere thereafter. (See pp.98-109 gives information about frosts and microclimates.)

DEFEATING JACK FROST

If really cold, frosty conditions threaten, some more vulnerable shrubs and plants can be given temporary protection. How temporary will depend on the individual plant and the weather that threatens. In the spring, when late frosts are forecast, it may be sufficient to drape a piece of horticultural fleece over the plant; even newspapers will do a lot to protect new growth.

It is often a help to make sure that the bases of plants and shrubs are well covered. This could mean top dressing with shredded bark or raking up a mound of soil around them. In extremely cold conditions this protection could be augmented by a layer of straw, bracken or surplus conifer branches (if you are near a commercially farmed coniferous woodland). An individual shrub that needs special protection can be swathed in fleece or wrapped round with dry hessian and the whole then kept from wind and wet by a top layer of plastic. This plastic layer should be positioned to allow any warm air from the ground to make its way upwards through the protected bush. It is also helpful if the bush is not so tightly bound that there is little room for air, as any prolonged period spent wrapped in plastic, with its consequent lack of air circulation, may encourage fungus spores to get to work. The idea is to maintain an even temperature level without the repeated freezing and thawing that is so damaging.

Smaller plants that may have dashed into precocious growth can be protected by cloches with glass to close the open ends. Sudden frosts can be defeated by an upturned bucket, large pot or even cardboard box. It may not look decorative but it works. This is a temporary measure, and the plants will be happy when the cover is removed and the weather outlook returns to normal.

Annuals, pp.236-241, also contains a number of tender climbers.

A-Z Guide to Tender Plants

Acca sellowiana
(syn. *Feijoa sellowiana*) Myrtaceae

From scrub in subtropical South America to our gardens is quite a leap but this much-branched shrub will manage well enough in a sunny, protected spot. It is not something to try in very cold areas. Its elliptic leaves, up to 7cm (3in) long, are mid-green with a

Acca sellowiana.

grey cast emphasized by the grey underleaf. Midsummer flowers appear towards the ends of twigs; they are white in bud but open their 4 petals to reveal red – nearly maroon – inner surfaces and a bunch of protruding red stamens. They are have a rather square outline, as petals do not overlap. Overall size of the flower will be 4cm (1½in). Berries may develop; they are green and egg-shaped tinged with red. **'Variegata'** has cream-margined leaves. Sun. Evergreen, height to about 2m (6ft), Z8 H3-4.

Agave americana 'Marginata'
Agavaceae

Few plants have more sculptural appeal than agaves. In Britain they are kept safe through the winter by wheeling them into a conservatory or greenhouse; only in the mildest south-west can they be risked outside; there they are given protection in times of threatened frost. The huge rosettes of fleshy, long, pointed leaves spread more wide than high. They have spiny margins and are sharply pointed. The colour is rich grey-green but with cleanly painted creamy-yellow margins, these becoming whiter on the older leaves. Sunny site; well-drained soil. Evergreen, height 2m (6ft), Z8 H3-4.

Anagyris foetida Leguminosae

The word *foetida* applies to this plant when the leaves

Agave americana
'Marginata'.

are ground or crushed; the foliage and flowers is otherwise without smell, foetid or otherwise. Leaves consist of 3 leaflets each about 6cm (2in) long and grey-felted beneath. Bunches of 12 or more yellow pea flowers are produced late spring or early summer. Though a pleasing enough extra, this is not one for a starring role. A Mediterranean bush best in sunny, well-drained soil where, with time, it may eventually become a small tree. Deciduous, height 2-3m (6-10ft), Z8 H3-4.

Araujia sericifera Asclepiadaceae

An energetic, clockwise-twiner with long lance-shaped, pale green leaves, up to about 10cm (4in) long, the so-called cruel plant bears flowers from late summer into autumn. Held in racemes, the 2.5cm (1in) flowers are white (sometimes pale pink) and bell-shaped as they open but then widen somewhat to a more 5-petalled, star form, centred by sticky pollen masses that can trap moths lured by the scent, thus justifying its common name. It will stand only a very short burst of light frost and really needs a warm climate or the shelter of a conservatory; in these favoured spots it will grow rampantly. Normal, well-drained soil. Evergreen, height 8m (25ft), Z9-10 H3-4.

Aristolochia Aristolochiaceae

And now for something spectacularly different! The climbers in this genus are good wall plants, needing the warmth as most come from warm climes. The curious flowers are fashioned out of extended inflated calyces which make bent tubes. Those of the tropical species produce an obnoxious smell that encourages insects to enter the tube. The reverse pointing hairs that line it stop the insects getting out and their struggles within help to achieve pollination. A gruesome bit of nature. Well-drained soil.

A. chrysops
This is one of the best for growing outside: it makes a spreading, scrambling shrub with matt-green leaves, downy in youth. The flowers are about 5cm (2in) long, and consist of a slightly furry, yellow tube with a shining yellow throat and with dark maroon widespread lobes, so dark on occasion to look almost black. Sometimes grown under the name *A. heterophylla*. Deciduous, height 5m (15ft), Z8 H3-4.

A. littoralis
This species has attractive longish heart-shaped, bright green, pointed leaves and flowers that unfurl to a rounded bowl of deep purple-brown with white or pale yellow intricate patterns as detailed as the

243

Berberidopsis corallina

The coral plant needs some shelter from severe wind and will do well on a shaded wall; in milder localities it could be sent up the trunk of a tree. The tough, oval pointed leaves have margins that are armed with a series of short spines. The plant is at its most interesting and alluring from midsummer into autumn when it is decorated with long hangings of bead-like, bright, shiny, deep red flowers. These are arranged as a series of 3-flowered clusters, each with a long stalk as red as the flower. The tough, rounded, thick-textured blooms are persistent. Young plants want encouraging to their support and will do best in lime-free soils. Introduced from Chile over 100 years ago, it is now thought to be extinct in the wild. Shade, neutral or acid, well-drained soil. Evergreen, height 4-5m (12-15ft), Z8 H3-4.

✳ Good, tidy foliage

✳ Excellent by shady walls

✳ Long summer and autumn season of flower

✳ Striking floral appearance

✳ Not difficult to propagate from layers or semi-ripe summer cuttings

lines of a shattered windscreen. This is only recommended for the warmest of areas or for a large conservatory. Evergreen, height 4-8m (12-25ft), Z9 H3.

A. macrophylla

Dutchman's pipe is the best-known species in gardens, having been cultivated for 200 years. It is one of those fortunate plants that can be grown for its foliage alone: the broad, heart-shaped leaves are rich green above, paler below, and can be a formidable 10-30cm (4-12in) long. The interesting summer flowers are limy-green tubes that expand at the mouth into 3 lobes of yellow but much worked with brown and purple mottling, the purple usually more evident around the margins. These exotic offerings are borne in ones or twos, often partially hidden by the foliage. It will quickly clothe a wall, post or pergola and can make a substantial plant, with massive stems, the bark of which, if rubbed, will emit a pleasant smell. Deciduous, height 8-10m (25-30ft), Z6 H4.

Berberidopsis corallina, *Flacourtiaceae*, see box.

Billardiera longiflora Pittosporaceae

This is a quality twiner for more climate-favoured gardens; elsewhere it is best treated as half hardy. It is best in wall sites or growing through a strong shrub, with some shade from full sun and sheltered from cold winds. It will not overwhelm a host shrub as it has good manners, and it will create additional interest on its bed-fellow in a new season. The stems are wiry and the leaves are very narrow, strip-like and deep green. Summer sees the production of a series of singly borne, hanging bells in lime-green – a floral design of subdued elegance. It is the fruits that we await. These are rounded, papery, bubbly, egg shapes, 2cm (¾in) long, usually in shiny rich violet-blue, although they can be a purer purple, pink, red or white. Well-drained soil. Evergreen, height 2-3m (6-10ft), Z8 H2-3.

Bougainvillea hybrids Nyctaginaceae

These colourful climbers have become almost too common and prolific in warmer climates; in Britain

Brugmansia × candida.

they have been grown in frostproof conservatories and greenhouses for many years; in mild areas they could be tried up warm walls in sheltered corners, or perhaps over pergolas. Although they are not going to survive proper frosts, a little ingenuity would enable one planted within a conservatory to have some branches outside, where, in the summer months, lucky owners will be rewarded with clusters of the tiny flowers surrounded by their conspicuous bracts. The colour range is wide – rich mauves, purples, pinks, reds and more pastel shades as well as white. Fertile, well-drained soil. Evergreen, height 4-5m (12-15ft), Z9 H2-3.

Brugmansia × candida

(syn. *Datura × candida*) *Solanaceae*

This plant has impressive foliage of tough, textured, broadly elliptic leaves often with wavy margins and sometimes toothed. They can be up to 60cm (24in) long but range down to half this. From summer into autumn it can bear huge, hanging trumpets, 30cm (12in) long, particularly perfumed in the evening and of various colours from white to creamy-yellow and sometimes pink. The widely flanged mouth of the trumpet is made more decorative by the pointed lobes. Apart from virtually frost-free areas, these are shrubs to grow in large movable containers that can be brought out in late spring and wheeled back under glass in late autumn. Their summer-time position may be between other shrubs with the container lowered halfway or completely into the soil to encourage an equable root temperature and moisture content. Often they are used on patios among other potted favourites. Sun and fertile, well-drained soil. Evergreen, height 4m (12ft), Z9 H2.

Cantua buxifolia (syn. *C. dependens*)
Polemoniaceae

Growing higher than wide, though often of a dependent leaning character, this species has lightly lobed, lance-shaped, bright green leaves. In spring it decorates itself very effectively with lots of hanging, long-tubed flowers up to 7cm (3in) long and neatly flanged open at the mouth. The colour is a pinky-red. This plant, said to be the sacred flower of the Incas, needs a warm spot to help it combat the effects of frost: short spells may not spoil it, but prolonged periods of hard frost will cause damage unless it is given extra protection. Fertile, well-drained soil. Evergreen, height 2-5m (6-15ft), Z9 H2-3.

Bougainvillea × buttiana 'Lady Mary Baring'.

245

Cissus striata *Vitaceae*

This is the only species of this genus that is worth trying outside in temperate climates. A rapid, tendril
climber, it has irregularly serrated, palmate leaves
composed of 3 or 5 leaflets. These are tough and polished mid-green. Like its relative, *Parthenocissus* (see
p.148), the flowers are small, inconspicuous, greenish
efforts followed by small, black berries like currants.
Best in a warm, sunny spot. Can cope with plenty of
moisture in the growing season. Evergreen, height 5m
(16ft), Z8 H3-4.

Clematis *Ranunculaceae*

Both these interesting and attractive species are rare
in cultivation, but are interesting, and seed may be
available from specialist societies or botanical collections. (See p.167 for cultivation details.)

C. meyeriana

This species has tough leaflets arranged 3 to a leaf-
stalk, as in many clematis, and hairless stems. It
blooms very early in the year, somewhere between
mid-winter and early spring, and produces arching
bunches of white flowers each about 2-2.5cm (¼-1in)
across. Because it is somewhat tender and blooms so
precociously, it can be safer under glass but might be
worth trying in a warm corner in a mild district. Evergreen, height up to 6m (18ft), Z8 H3-4.

C. quinquefoliolata

Related to the last, and just as rarely seen, this has
slightly fluffy stems and pinnate leaves, each leaflet
being up to 10cm (3in) long. It blooms in late summer with clusters of white flowers, these having 4-6
straight-sided narrow petals. Silky, yellowish seedheads follow. Evergreen, height 4-5m (12-15ft), Z8
H3-4.

Cordyline australis 'Purpurea'
Agavaceae

Cordylines are sculptural plants, so perhaps it makes
sense to grow them in large movable containers so
that they can be placed in strategic positions on the
patio or elsewhere to help create an atmosphere and
make focal points. Plants grow steadily in height
rather than spectacularly, and a newly purchased
specimen will take a few seasons to make a really dis-
cernable trunk. It will be a decade or two before it
begins to look somewhat like a palm tree with the
rounded mass of outward-pointing foliage hoisted up
on top of a clean trunk. If cut down when the trunk
has got beyond the height required, the plant will

normally start again from the base probably with one
or more rosettes of leaves and stems. Not far from our
garden in the West Midlands there is a cordyline that
stands over 6m (20ft) high: it must have seen some
severe winters and has lived to tell the tale. We have
had them out in the open in our garden for over 15
years without any real bother. They are obviously
tougher than once thought. Sun, neither too wet or
too dry. Evergreen, height 3-8m (10-25ft), Z8 H3-4.

Distictis buccinatoria *Bignoniaceae*

This is an energetic climber that can get to the
quoted heights in frost-free areas, but is likely to be

*Plants as sculpture –
an eye-catching example
of* Cordyline australis
'Purpurea'.

much less in most British conditions outside. It will not manage in more than short bursts of temperatures around freezing point. It has plenty of ovate, deep green leaflets, up to a maximum of 12cm (5in) long. From summer into autumn it can make an attempt to partially cover these with large, long-tubed flowers that have a wide-open, 5-lobed, spreading saucer-form mouth, each 'petal' being gently centrally incised. The colour is purple-red at the mouth but may be yellowish at the base and along the tube. A really warm, sunny spot will encourage flowering; in poor seasons the display can be heroic rather than a blanket covering. Should be dryish through winter but moist in growth. Evergreen, height 10m (30ft), Z9 H3-4.

Euryops pectinatus *Asteraceae*

This plant grows strongly with precisely divided ferny foliage, grey with hairs and 7cm (3in) long. It makes a mound as high as wide and, well above this attractive foliage mass, bears upward-facing, narrow-petalled, starry, golden flowers, 5cm (2in) across, with small, central discs, from early summer until autumn is well advanced. The flowers are often borne singly but may be in small sprays. Sun, moist well-drained soil. Evergreen, height 1m (3ft), Z9 H2-3.

Feijoa sellowiana, see *Acca sellowiana*.

Fendlera rupicola *Hydrangeaceae*

This is a spreading, almost straggling shrub needing a really sunny spot. It has ribbed, striped stems and small, narrow leaves marked clearly with 3 veins and bristly rough to the touch; the undersides are hairy. White or palest pink, scented flowers, 2-3cm (¾-1¼in) across, appear in late spring and early summer. Plants can be given a light pruning after flowering to tidy their form. A rather tricky, rather tender shrub wanting well-drained soil that does not dry out and no root disturbance once settled. Deciduous, height 1.5m (5ft), Z7 H3-4.

Gladiolus, see Base of Wall Plants, p.229.

Grindelia chiloensis *Asteraceae*

This sub-shrub looks fairly robust with grey-green leaves up to 13cm (5in) long. Above the foliage, on long stalks, is borne a succession of large, deep-golden daisies, many-petalled and measuring 7cm (3in) wide. A cheerful addition to a sunny border where it will not be subjected to very rigorous winter conditions.

Grindelia chiloensis.

Best in humus-rich, well-drained soils that are neither too wet nor too dry. Evergreen, height 1m (3ft), Z9 H3.

Hebe hulkeana *Scrophulariaceae*

Long a favourite shrub, this tenderish species is very attractive in blossom. It has leaves 4cm (1½in) long, that are pointed and mid-green, margined purple-red. Flowers are borne in very many terminal panicles. They are usually lavender-blue or lilac but sometimes white. These panicles can be up to 30cm (12in) long and smother the bush in late spring and early summer. **'Lilac Hint'** is a pale-coloured form with noticeably paler leaves without red margins. There are 100 other species and many hybrids to try. After a series of mild winters all the hebes are gaining a reputation for hardiness that they do not fully deserve. Hard winters will kill all the large-leaved kinds, including *H. hulkeana*, but some wall protection may well help them through some cold weather and, even if some top growth gets killed, the base will probably produce fresh shoots to quickly regain its size. Sun or semi-shade, well-drained soil. Evergreen, height 1m (3ft), Z9 H3.

Helichrysum petiolare *Asteraceae*

This trailing, lax sub-shrub has oval or heart-shaped leaves, felty with woolly grey hair above, and is much used in containers. Killed by frost but easily kept over winter under glass in dryish soil. Sun and well-drained soil. Evergreen, height 50cm (20in), Z9 H1-3.

Kadsura, see Twiners, p.156.

Keckiella cordifolia

(syn. *Penstemon cordifolius*) *Scrophulariaceae*

This is a loose-limbed, scrambling, shrub which, on a sunny wall, will be colourful all summer with a succession of scarlet blossom in terminal panicles. The individual, tube-like flowers are up to 4cm (1½in) long. Needs little attention if given a sunny position; a light pruning in the spring is simply to clear weak and straggly growth. Well-drained healthy soil. Evergreen, height 1-2m (3-6ft), Z8 H3-4.

Lapageria rosea, see Twiners, p.156.

Lardizabala biternata *Lardizabalaceae*

This is a vigorous, twisting climber with either 3 leaves to a stalk or with each leaf divided into 3 to make 9 leaflets. They are thick-textured and dark green. The flowers are either male or female and are borne from late autumn into winter. They have 6 reflexed petals, more correctly tepals, of rich chocolate-brown with green on the reverses and contrasting white stamens and stigma. The males are borne as hanging columns of perhaps 12 or more. The singly borne female ones are rather longer – up to nearly 2cm (¾in) long. This is an interesting plant

Below left: A summer-time focal point created by the grey-leaved spreading Helichrysum petiolare *together with variegated myrtle,* Myrtus communis 'Variegata' *and daisy-flowered* Argyranthemum frutescens 'Chelsea Girl'.

for the mildest areas on a warm wall. It can be grown easily in a conservatory. Sun or partial shade, well-drained soil. Evergreen, height to 3-4m (10-12ft), Z9 H3-4.

Lippia citriodora, see *Aloysia triphylla*, p.226.

Mitraria coccinea *Gesneriaceae*

This very pleasant, classy plant shuns hot, dry spots, though if its roots are in shade, it can manage some sunshine. It is very useful by a shady wall where it can do well; it could be planted by a pillar or a tree trunk, and will also do well in woodland conditions or a

The plumbagos get into rapid growth with the warmer weather and then bloom freely. Here Plumbago auriculata looks very much at ease sheltering by a wall in Oxford.

sheltered shrubbery. It will not withstand really severe frosts unprotected and its rootrun should be moist and acid with plenty of humus. It makes a spreading shrub with lots of twiggy growth, well clothed with pairs of ovate, thick leaves, neatly saw-edged and 2.5cm (1in) long, with some short hairs on both surfaces. It will start to bloom at the end of spring and carry on into autumn producing single, drooping or semi-pendent, tubular flowers clear of the leaves on long stalks. They are a strong orange with golden stamens just pushed forward of the lobed mouth; the tube is slightly waisted three-quarters of the way towards the mouth which is just a touch wider but not really flared. Moist, well-drained, humus-rich, acid soil. Evergreen, height 2m (6ft), Z7 H3.

Penstemon cordifolius, see *Keckiella cordifolia*, p.248.

Plumbago auriculata

(syn. *P. capensis*) *Plumbaginaceae*

By no means hardy, Cape leadwort is well worth a try in milder areas, where it can be trained up an arch, pergola or wall supports. It is a scrambling, leaning shrub of quick growth once underway. It will be helpful to tie it to support as it grows upwards. By the summer it will be ready to start blooming and then there is no stopping it until the cold of winter starts. The leaves are healthy bright green, 4-7cm (1½-3in) long, and spoon-shaped. The racemes of flowers are 15cm (6in) across and very bright blue and pleasing. There is also a white form **var. *alba*** which would look effective alongside. Sun or semi-shade, any fertile, well-drained soil. Evergreen, height 3m (10ft) or more, Z10 H1-2.

Pueraria lobata, see Annuals, p.238.

Semele androgyna *Ruscaceae*

Known as climbing butcher's broom, this is a curious woody climber with glossy and handsome 'foliage'. Its leaves are reduced to scale-like bits and the stems look like leaves and have taken on the job of photosynthesis. Along these unusual stems appear clusters of tiny, cream stars in late spring and early summer. The plant is half hardy and needs to be in a mild district if it is to stay alive through winter, which will more likely prove successful if it is kept from being sodden. Plants also need some support. Butcher's broom enjoys a site in rich soil. Evergreen, height 6m (20ft), Z8-9 H3-4.

USEFUL INFORMATION

GARDEN CENTRES AND BUILDERS MERCHANTS

Most good garden centres and builders merchants will be able to offer a wide variety of garden landscaping materials and plants supports as well as arches, arbours, pergolas and so on. Manufacturers of good quality products are listed below.

Paving and other hard-landscaping

Bradstone Landscaping
Camas Building Materials, PO Box 193
Nottingham NG3 2HA

Stonemarket
Old Gravel Quarry, Oxford Road
Ryton-on-Dunsmore
Warwickshire CV8 3EJ

Fencing, trellis and other garden products

Agriframes Ltd
Charlwoods Road, East Grinstead
Sussex RH19 2HP
Metal arches, supports, gazebos, screens, walkways

Cannock Gates Ltd
Garden Factory Division,
Hawks Green
Cannock, Staffordshire WS11 2XT
Wide range of metal and wooden arches, arbours, obelisks, and so on

English Hurdle
Curload, Stoke St Gregory, Taunton
Somerset TA3 6JD
Willow hurdles, plant climbers, arches, arbours

Forest Fencing Ltd
Stanford Court, Stanford Bridge
Worcestershire WR6 6SR
A wide range of reliable products

J.E. Homewood & Son
20 Wey Hill, Haslemere,
Surrey GU27 1BX
Various fence styles and sizes

Jackson's Fine Fencing
61 Stowting Common, Ashford
Kent TN24 6BN
Wooden and metal products including arches, arbours, obelisks

Stuart Garden Architecture
Burrow Hill Farm, Wiveliscombe
Somerset TA4 2RN
Wide range of quality garden artifacts

Iron railings

Singer & James Ltd
Roebuck Road,
Hainault, Ilford
Essex IG6 3TZ

Watering systems

In Britain there are two main systems of automatic watering on offer to the gardening public. Both pipe the water to where it is needed and dispense it, either from 'micro-drip' nozzles or through spray heads. Automatic timing devices are available. They are the most expensive item of any installation, but they do ensure that time and effort are saved. A complete system provides an efficient service that should be eliminate water wastage. The manufacturers are Hozelock and Gardena and their systems are available, with detailed instruction booklets, from most good garden centres.

GARDENING GROUPS AND SOCIETIES

Britain

Royal Horticultural Society
80 Vincent Square, London SW1P 2PE
The headquarters are at the two exhibition halls where regular flower shows are held through the year. There are many benefits to membership, including the following:
Free entry to RHS flower shows and cheaper entry to some other important ones.
Free entry to RHS gardens at Wisley, Surrey and Rosemoor, Devon, as well as other affiliated gardens throughout Britain.
A high class monthly magazine.
Advice from RHS experts in person, by letter or by phone.
Lectures in London and countrywide.
Access to the leading horticultural Lindley Library at headquarters. Educational opportunities at increasing number of horticultural colleges.

Royal National Rose Society
Chiswell Green Lane, St Albans
Hertfordshire AL2 3NR
Publications on all aspects of rose growing with annual journal. The gardens at St Albans are a Mecca for all interested in roses.

National Council for the Conservation of Plants and Gardens (NCCPG)
The Pines, RHS Gardens, Wisley, Woking
Surrey GU23 6QB

Australia

Association of Societies for Growing Australian Plants
PO Box 38, Woodford, NSW 2778

Austalian Garden History Society
c/o Royal Botanic Gardens
Birdwood Avenue, South Yarraa
Victoria 3141

National Rose Society of Australia
271b, Balmore Road, North Nalwyn
Victoria 3104

The Organisation of Plant Collections in Australia
c/o Royal Botanic Garden
Birdwood Avenue, South Yarra
Victoria 3141

Eire

Irish Garden Plant Society
c/o National Botanical Garden
Glasnevin, Dublin 9

RHS of Ireland
Swanbrook House, Bloomfield Avenue
Morehampton Road, Dublin 4

New Zealand

National Rose Society of New Zealand
PO Box 66, Bunnythorpe

North America

American Horticultural Society
7931 East Boulevard Drive, Alexandria
VA 22308

Hardy Plant Society
Mid-Atlantic Group
49 Green Valley Road, Wallingford
PA 19086

North American Plant Collections Consortium
c/o AABGA, 786 Church Road, Wayne PA 19087
Botanical-led organization similar to Britain's NCCPG

North American Plant Preservation Council
c/o Sunshine Nursery, Renick West Virginia 24966
Also similar to NCCPG

South Africa

Botanical Society of South Africa Kirstenbosch, Claremont, Cape Town 7735

NATIONAL PLANT COLLECTIONS

In Britain the NCCPG (see opposite) has been responsible for the setting up of a number of National Plant Collections, which are open to the public. The collections are created and managed by volunteers and enthusiasts and give ordinary gardeners the opportunity to see a wide range of plants from the same genus in one location.

A directory of all present collections is published at a modest price. Some of the collections that are relevant to this book include the following:

Ampelopsis

National Trust for Scotland
Arduaine Garden, Arduaine, By Oban Argyll PA34 4XQ

Camellia

Mount Edgcumbe House and Country Park
Cremyll, Nr Torpoint, Cornwall PL10 1HZ

Ceanothus

P. Schofield
Gardens Manager, South Devon Healthcare
Torquay, Devon TQ2 7AD

R. Phillips
15A Eccleston Square, London SW1

Dudley Metropolitan Borough Council
Planning and Leisure Services
Stevens Park, Wollescote Road, Wollescote
Stourbridge, West Midlands DY9 7JG

Clematis

Treasures of Tenbury Ltd
Burford House Gardens
Burford House, Tenbury Wells
Worcestershire WR15 8HQ
230 species and cultivars

The Guernsey Clematis Nursery Ltd
Domarie Vineries, Les Sauvagées
St Sampson, Guernsey CI
320 kinds

Clematis montana types

D. Bradshaw
Busheyfield Nursery, Herne
Herne Bay
Kent CT6 7LJ

Hamamelis

Pat Edwards
Swallow Hayes, Rectory Road
Albrighton
Nr Wolverhampton
West Midlands WV7 3EP
50 species and cultivars

Hedera

Fibrex Nurseries Ltd
Honeybourne Road, Pebworth
Stratford upon Avon CV37 8XT
240 species and cultivars

Glyn Smith
National Trust Erddig Hall Gardens
Wrexham, Clwyd LL13 0YT
170 species and cultivars

Lathyrus

Miss S. Norton
Weavers Cottage, 35 Streetly End
West Wickham, Cambridge CB1 6RP
84 species, 26 cultivars

R. Parsons
Arum District Council, Civic Centre
Maltravers Road, Littlehampton
West Sussex BN17 6RT

Lonicera

D. Bradshaw
Busheyfield Nursery, Herne
Herne Bay, Kent CT6 7LJ
30 species, 50 cultivars

T.M. Upson
University Botanic Garden
Cory Lodge
Bateman Street, Cambridge CB2 1JE
91 species, 15 cultivars

Parthenocissus

National Trust for Scotland
Arduaine Garden, Arduaine, By Oban
Argyll PA34 4XQ

Pyracantha

M. Stimson
University College, Writtle, Chelmsford
Essex CM1 3RR
6 species, 29 cultivars

Rosa

Royal National Rose Society
The Gardens of the Rose, Chiswell Green
St Albans, Hertfordshire AL2 3NR
1800 species and cultivars

National Trust
Mottisfont Abbey, Nr Romsey
Hampshire SO51 0LP
(pre-1900 shrub roses) 320 species and cultivars

Rosa species

Peter Beales Roses
London Road, Attleborough
Norfolk NR17 1AY
110 or more species

Tropaeolum species (not *T. majus*)

G. Buchanan-Dunlop
Broughton Place, Broughton
By Biggon
Lanarkshire ML12 6HJ
15 species, 4 cultivars

FURTHER READING

The *RHS Plant Finder* – updated annually, this gives the sources of 99.9% of plants in commerce.

David & Charles have a first-class series of monographs (*The Gardener's Guides*) written in plain language and dealing with a number of important genera. They have a very full list of other gardening books.

INDEX

Page numbers in *italic type* refer to picture captions.

PHOTOCREDITS